PARTIES AND POLITICAL LIFE IN
THE MEDIEVAL WEST

Europe in the Middle Ages
Selected Studies

Volume 7

General Editor
RICHARD VAUGHAN
University of Hull

NORTH-HOLLAND PUBLISHING COMPANY – AMSTERDAM · NEW YORK · OXFORD

PARTIES AND POLITICAL LIFE IN THE MEDIEVAL WEST

By
JACQUES HEERS

Translated by
David Nicholas

1977

NORTH-HOLLAND PUBLISHING COMPANY – AMSTERDAM · NEW YORK · OXFORD

Library of Congress Catalog Card Number: 76-27374
North-Holland ISBN: 0 7204 0539 4

Published by:
North-Holland Publishing Company – Amsterdam/New York/Oxford

Distributors for the U.S.A. and Canada:
Elsevier North-Holland, Inc.
52 Vanderbilt Avenue, New York, N.Y. 10017

Library of Congress Cataloging in Publication Data
Heers, Jacques.
  Parties and political life in the medieval West.

  (Europe in the Middle Ages; 7)
  Bibliography: p.
  Includes index.
  1. Political parties--Italy--History. 2. Political
parties--Europe--History. I. Title. II. Series.
JN5651.H44   329'.02'0902   76-27374
ISBN 0-7204-0539-4

Printed in Singapore by Times Printers Sdn. Bhd.

293978

General Editor's preface

This volume of Europe in the Middle Ages is unusual in at least one important respect: the English translation has been made from the author's typescript, so that this is indeed a completely new book by Professor Heers; but published in English. In view of this, a lengthy preface by myself would be out of place, especially in view of the fact that the translator of this book is himself a medievalist, and my work of revision has in consequence been minimal. The English text has been read and approved by the author, who wishes to record his indebtedness to the translator in going beyond the usual functions of translators by adding two pages on party struggles in Holland and a section on the beginnings of the communal era in the Flemish towns (pp. 226–228 and 245–246 below). The index is the work of the translator.

January 1977

Richard Vaughan
General Editor

Contents

Introduction

All historians have been very much aware of the extreme complexity of the events, clashes, conflicts and calms which gave rhythm to or troubled the internal life of the political communities of the medieval West. All certainly deplore the impossibility of presenting anything like a coherent train of events or of reducing them to a relatively simple scheme for purposes of explanation.

As soon as narratives of these events become sufficiently detailed, they give a general impression of astonishing confusion. The chronicles, compiled from day to day by obscure merchants or artisans or by a clerk, canon or abbot, men who were more interested than others in political affairs and who were often intimately involved in all their city's problems, all seem to defy analysis. There are only interminable successions of chronic conflicts, sometimes latent, sometimes violent, taking place before judicial tribunals and even in the street between families, between all types of social groups. To this already very complex and turbulent background of often incomprehensible quarrels must be added external pressures and the armed interventions of sovereigns or of neighbouring or rival towns, even apart from the sudden rage of uncontrolled mobs. Such excitements were quickly pacified and were often ended by force; they were certainly not mere outbreaks of discontent or despair, particularly in the towns of Italy and Germany, but perhaps, too, in all cities of the West.

To establish a simple chronology of the most spectacular of these outbursts would seem to be a terribly tedious and futile exercise. To disentangle the astonishing confusion, the skein of multiple relationships, bound together with flexibility and striking fragility, of alliances between political groups or individuals, between towns or even be-

1

tween sovereign powers would be a monumental enterprise. The analyst moved at the outset by the noblest of motives feels himself in the long run seized by an irresistible desire to abridge and simplify rather than follow a thread which continually escapes him. Every remotely clear presentation of events, ordered, selected, tied to well-defined causes, provoked by a logical chain of events, thus seems to be in some degree an artificial construction.

We already feel ourselves on more solid ground when we study not events but institutions, written or unwritten laws, 'constitutions' which govern or seem to govern political life in different milieus, different types of governments: seigneurial, royal or even monarchical, ecclesiastical and urban institutions at all levels and places. Many direct or indirect sources permit us to do this. Some of these describe the establishment of different political or administrative organs, while others permit us to follow their functioning and to define their spheres of competence. Such sources likewise describe the royal entourage, the various specialized courts of the central princely government, administrative officers at the local level, and even more the very numerous municipal magistrates with different prerogatives. Several generations of scholars have devoted themselves to these studies and have thus made a precious contribution to our knowledge of medieval political machinery and means of governing, and particularly their evolution.[1] For the Italian towns the works and detailed analyses of various specialists and the syntheses of Y. Renouard[2] have permitted us to define the main lines of an evolution from the aristocratic commune of the consuls to the government of the podestà, then to the power of the *popolo*, then to the more or less firmly established hereditary tyrannies of despots of diverse origins. For Italy this relatively simple course may be compared to a picture of the evolution of economic activities and social relations, themselves marked by constant modifications, sometimes by true dramas of adaptation, and by the rise of newcomers toward fortune and power. For certain authors the evolution of institutions would thus reflect that of economies and societies, so that economic development would aid in the comprehension of political life. This hypothesis, which has long been imposed as an established truth, is doubtless not totally inaccurate, and the study of institutions, far from being a formal exercise, narrowly relegated to a special area, should be tied closely to that of other aspects of public life. Still, the history of political institutions *per se* encounters many hindrances and remains a very imperfect means which always leaves the reader stranded after introducing him to many interesting points.

First, in matters of detail, numerous institutions and persons holding administrative or judicial positions or, better stated, charged with political responsibilities, still escape our knowledge. Thus, for example, knowledge of a particular 'feudal' (or rather 'vassalic') law does not necessarily entail that of the means of government within the framework of the seigneurie or the castellany. Only a few studies, and these usually confined to the very great fiefs only, allow us to see the essence of political lordship throughout the Middle Ages, to distinguish this political lordship precisely from the possession of territory and the economic administration of lands and to define clearly the realities and limits of power over persons.[3] For no 'medieval' period do all administrative organs of royal or princely governments present themselves clearly and without ambiguity to us. Often only the great officials are known, while the very complex internal organization of the households poses as yet unresolved problems. Names and functions are only very blurred outlines, varying constantly between periods and between princely courts.[4]

Even within the framework of the Italian cities, which have been studied with indefatigable care and which have such abundant narrative and administrative sources, the systems and portraits put forward are obviously only mental constructs. This is easily explicable for various reasons well known to specialists, but often neglected by those who have the virtually insurmountable task of drawing lessons and establishing ideal lines of development. First, there is the difficulty that each urban milieu presents a particular case, almost always different from the neighbouring one. Peculiar circumstances are present which can direct, slow or advance the evolution of any particular town: the weight of the past, more or less real external pressures, economic potential and thus greater or lesser capacity to resist, and particularly the nature of social structures. Hence there are significant chronological variations, already noted by Y. Renouard, in the appearance of new types of government. Moreover, these innovations often deceive, so that the historian is too willing to believe in a succession of 'revolutions': quick and radical changes of political régimes when new institutions are imposed and others disappear. This is an intellectual viewpoint completely at variance with the political customs of medieval times. New organs of government were not then generally substituted for old, but rather joined them, even if in the long run two or three forms of government or systems of representation, or administrative or judicial institutions, were maintained concurrently and vied for a power which to us seems very ill defined. This confusion of powers and responsibilities undoubtedly disconcerts, but it is nonetheless very characteristic of medieval political life in European countries.

Of fundamental importance is the fact that the description of institutions obviously does not allow us to grasp the realities of political life from the social point of view. Organs and functions are only abstract names behind which we must be able to place the names of men located exactly in their familial, topographic, economic, and social environments. This, with exceptions so rare as to be all the more valuable, still remains to be done. If, as for example for France, we know well enough the officers of the central administration, the members of the councils, and many members of the Parlement or the *Cour des Comptes*, provincial officers remain rather more obscure.[5] The same is true, surprisingly enough, for municipal magistrates. Thus, the entire study of the 'communal' movement in the kingdom of France has consisted essentially of recitals of events: conflicts, revolts, agreements and establishment of charters. The individuals escape us.

We speak constantly of 'commune' without knowing what portion of urban society the commune represents. The method of recruitment of political officers, whether by cooptation, sometimes nomination by the prince, or perhaps even election, is often ill defined. The rhythm of renewal, the more or less affirmed permanence of responsibilities and functions among the same families or the same groups, the framework or the bases for appointments or elections, all of this is unknown. Even more, the names of the persons are only very rarely available. Even a simple chronological list of mayors, *jurés* and *échevins* would give precious new information for each city. The social environment might thus be defined more easily. We are very far from that. Thus, for example, for the French communes the unanimously held idea is that recruitment was exclusively urban. The members of the commune were bourgeois living in the city. Yet several perfectly explicit documents contradict this generally received thesis. In the 1380s the deliberations of the magistrates, the municipal accounts, and the reports of judicial officers of the town of Mantes refer to *communiers* of Mantes inhabiting villages several leagues from the city.[6] A list of persons in the commune of Provins from about the same time cites

1,741 residents in the city and 960 in eight villages of the environs. If 900 men of this commune were working in various textile trades and 450 in the assorted 'mechanical' guilds, more than 500 cultivated their fields and vineyards. Another interesting point which contradicts *a priori* ideas is that the commune of Provins included 350 women.[7]

For Italy we certainly know the names of the tyrants, the men of the great and powerful families, who took the initiative in important and dramatic political activity, but a systematic study of the composition of the various councils of citizens and the different colleges of magistrates has yet to be made for all the cities. We know the names of magistracies but not those of the men. In this way political life remains an abstraction, cut off from social realities. This is also true of the men of the opposing faction. Every revolt was called 'popular', and this fact drains all precise research of its interest in advance. The real identity of the rebels, how they were incorporated into the city environment in the various social categories, their degrees of wealth, their professions and personal and political ties would be information indispensable to any real analysis of the conflicts. Until very recently, we have constantly spoken of the *Ciompi* of the Florentine revolt of 1378 without knowing them at all. They have been identified superficially, slanderously, and totally erroneously with the poor textile workers, particularly weavers, and in any case as poor persons without property, the oppressed. This approach, which is still found, is nonetheless imprecise.[8]

We should all the more distrust words which no longer mean political or administrative organs, but have come to designate political or social entities which are ill-defined groups. The political vocabulary of the medieval period deserves systematic study in all Western countries so that the use of various words by chroniclers, moralists, and in institutional or administrative documents, may be defined more accurately. These studies will doubtless necessitate systematic analyses and extensive tabulations, but also must demonstrate a particularly attentive reading of the texts and a very subtle sense of analysis. Even for Italy the most ordinary words, those which seem to us to be used most frequently, often remain real mysteries. Their meanings evolve over a period of time; they vary also between regions and sometimes differ according to the background or values of the chronicler. They cannot be comprehended without constant reference to a more or less distant past.

Thus, to evoke socio-economic distinctions first of all, let us consider the words 'trades' and especially 'tradesmen'. For us the tradesmen would obviously be guildsmen, persons of little property and low social standing. Yet at that time the master tradesmen were almost always wealthy. By appropriate analyses of social milieus, various authors have shown that the coming of the tradesmen to political power left the city government with its predominantly aristocratic character. It is not even certain that the 'political revolution' of the 1290s, which marked the exclusion of the 'magnates' from power and the victory of their opponents, entailed serious changes of governmental personnel. E. Christiani has shown that at Pisa the draconian ordinances against the 'magnates' had no spectacular practical effects and that most of the prominent families of the old aristocracy continued in power without interruption.[9]

In a more strictly political domain, we feel the necessity of rigorously defining such key words as 'republic', 'communes', and especially 'people'. The temptation would be strong, too strong, even irresistible in a certain ideological context, to apply their present meaning to these terms without qualification. Our textbooks speak of Italian 'merchant republics' and thereby assimilate them to the modern or contemporary period. Adorned with all virtues, these republican states were *ipso facto* democratic according to this view. The commune would then be a sort of government perfectly representative of the whole urban population, and the 'people' would represent the lowest levels of these groups. In any case, the 'people' would certainly be opposed totally to the nobility and the aristocracy. We know well now, even if the textbooks and popularizations do not say it, that these ideas are inaccurate. The Italian *popolo* in the social meaning of the word was, on the contrary, a form of aristocracy whose members were sometimes richer than 'magnates'. In the political meaning, *popolo* is a very complex idea, capable of change and hard to define.[10] All involuntary or voluntary parallels with the modern period inevitably lead to errors.

The organs which official documents say existed, the councils, colleges, or individual magistracies, the multifarious governments such as the commune or the *popolo*, are only frameworks of uncertain and variable content. Actually, political activity undergoes the constant influence of more or less well-organized or even secret pressure and action groups which dominate the city, imposing upon it choices, divisions, and rotations which provoke rivalries and conflicts of all sorts. The explanation of the seemingly incomprehensible quarrels frequently resides here. The eternal struggle to seize power is organized from these groups, leagues and alliances which were sometimes ephemeral and which sometimes never even assumed a stable form. The historian who consults only official documents will see only fully established organs, stable districts where elections are held: the quarter, the parish, the guild association. But to give life to this framework we must consider the actual groups acting from within and striving with all their might. Hence the great families,[11] their clans and federations, are even more central as political societies than the parties. On the other hand, in the numerous times of trouble, institutions and regular frameworks break down. Mass movements impose their authority, the law of warfare, the trials of force, the orders and the transient powers of men who are acclaimed enthusiastically but without any mandate or investiture with authority save that of the action groups. It would thus be very useful if we could determine, albeit imperfectly, the role of these societies and parties in the growth of opposition movements and in the organization of popular revolts and street fights:[12] slogans, demarcation by a whole arsenal of external symbols, recruitment of the combatants. Civil war, which troubles and bloodies the life of the cities and sometimes of entire realms throughout the Middle Ages, cannot otherwise be explained. It is a phenomenon which obviously finds its origin and powers outside the regularly existing institutional structure.

These political action groups generally escape the standard procedures of historical investigation; whether spontaneous creations, bound by tacit ties, or concealed under a false appearance, they seem unknowable. The moment of their establishment and foundation remains obscure. They are born without a contract; no statute was compiled. Their government and even their structure seem very flexible, imbued with constant empiricism, submitted to the play of all sorts of influences and even to internal conflicts. They have no archives of their own. We know them only indirectly, and especially from two types of document: on the one hand the chroniclers who attribute to them all kinds of misdeeds, and on the other the acts of repression committed against them by the established government. The very limited and specialized character of this documentation certainly does not facilitate research; many features thus remain obscure and numerous questions unanswered.

Political societies functioning within the framework of the towns hold our attention more easily when they are concealed under other aspects, for example confraternities which claim that they are merely religious, charitable societies of mutual assistance, but whose members are active in every aspect of public and private life. Such a devotional confraternity, placing itself under the patronage of a saint or the Virgin, cares for the sick, prays for the dead, assists its members who fall into poverty, but also protects them against brigands and trouble-makers, then eventually against judicial abuses, and finally against their neighbours. Thus, Peace Brotherhoods appear in every troubled and dangerous period, born of a spontaneous defensive reaction, particularly in central and southern France. Limited first to a narrow geographical area, but often extended later to an entire diocese, these fraternities later maintained, by taxes levied on all and thanks to an armed force, the security and even the government of entire pro-vinces.[13] We know, moreover, the political role played in the towns of Languedoc during the earliest French occupation, just after the Albigensian Crusade, by religious confraternities which were often either powerful means of action in the hands of the prince or the Church or were active forces of opposition. From 1211 Bishop Fulk founded a confraternity at Toulouse to fight heresy. Its vocation, however, was political and military, and troops of the association fought at the siege of Lavaur. But another fraternity was formed simultaneously at Toulouse on the count's side. Somewhat later, in 1328, a confraternity named after St Louis and placed under royal patronage was also in opposition to the episcopal power. This Con-fraternity of St Louis, first established at Albi, was also organized in Saint-Afrique, while at Rhodes a Confraternity of Notre-Dame of the same nature united 700 brothers in 1454, including numerous nobles.[14] Thus, the associations here were a bastion of princely power against the Church.

In the French Midi the confraternities ended by acquiring genuine political experience and gradually assumed the government of village or city, even in the greatest towns, such as Montauban and Marseille. They were thus involved in the origin of the commune or at least of a more or less autonomous government. Very often the house of the confraternity, for example that of Saint-Esprit, became the city hall.

Moreover, the religious fraternities sometimes became focal points of dispute, then of political agitation. They afforded refuge to the discontented, the isolated, those excluded from power. They were more or less secret political societies and were considered dangerous. At Florence between 1420 and 1425 the authorities watched very closely and even persecuted the fraternities and congregations whose mysterious meetings were held in places given false names. Their initiation ritual, it was said, recalled that of peripheral associations of poor persons. These brotherhoods were dissolved at least twice, their registers confiscated, their meeting places destroyed and their goods distributed to the people.[15] The royal inquisitors in Languedoc thought that many religious brotherhoods there were supporting and even organizing acts of opposition to the French occupation. At Toulouse the Carmel brotherhood, numbering 5,000 persons from both nobility and bourgeoisie, held one secret meeting annually to elect a governor to whom all owed obedience. The organization was prohibited by the treaty of Paris of 1259. These active fraternities were subsequently dissolved by the civil or ecclesiastical authorities: in 1267 by Alphonse of Poitiers, in 1270 by the seneschal of Carcassonne, who ordered the overly lenient viscount of Narbonne to have their meetings stopped, and much later, in 1368, by the Council of Lavaur.[16]

In England the royal councillors investigating the origins of the Peasants' Revolt of 1381 considered the religious guilds, so numerous throughout the country, to be genuinely seditious secret societies. Hence in 1388 Richard II directed all masters and wardens of the confraternities to answer an extremely detailed questionnaire about their guilds, including date and circumstances of foundation, form of government, festivals and assemblies, liberties, customs, and properties. All replied by insisting that their activities were religious or charitable in nature. They declared that there was nothing dangerous about their meetings and especially that their members took no oath of any kind.[17]

Over and above these confraternities, on which historical research seems relatively easy, other political associations were created in the towns of the West and particularly of Italy during the communal period. As with the religious brotherhoods, some of them originated in a defensive reaction, in ties of neighbourhood and military alliances. They were essentially armed groups holding fortified places. The chroniclers often mention mutually hostile tower and gate societies in northern and central Italy. The former are merely family clans or unions of clans, more or less structured and stable, and their role underscores nicely the importance of the prominent aristocratic family in government, in the conflicts, and even in the revolts inside the city. The existence of the gate societies is well known to us. Traditionally they are considered 'popular' companies charged with defending the walls and the most exposed quarters of the city. If their activity and internal organization (recruitment, elections, meetings, and forms of government) escape us almost totally, we can well imagine their weight in the political and military life of their city. Indeed, these societies often contributed to the topographical division of their city into a number of quarters equal to the number of gates and gave their names to these quarters. Over a long period, while the commune was recruiting mercenary companies for foreign wars, the militias of these gate societies secured internal peace.

The authors of chronicles or private journals frequently speak of 'parties'. All narrative sources for troubled times leave the impression of worlds always marked by savage rivalries between political groups relentlessly pursuing power. The parties seem ever present, eager to reopen quarrels, to pursue explosive vendettas. They begin all discords and constantly disturb the peace. They are undoubtedly the most influential and vigorous of the political action groups. But we must admit that the motives of such actions are very complex. Reduction of these rivalries to a simple conflict of two political or religious ideologies, of two foreign powers, or even of two social categories or divergent economic interests, is obviously an excessive oversimplification, a very incomplete view of affairs. The schema long regarded as classic and still often propounded in our own time for the Italian cities has a simple opposition of imperial and papal partisans, but this cannot withstand even a superficial examination. The goal of research on these political groups is to try to paint a more subtle and complex picture.

The internal situation of the parties, moreover, is no better known than that of other groups, and it is difficult to ascertain, even very approximately, the composition of such unstable, even mysterious societies. The party was not a formal institution and evidently had no statutes except for rare cases which in themselves show a kind of sclerosis. We are thus dealing with uncertain and incomplete historical research, necessarily limited to chronological and geographical areas where the documentation seems least meagre and most diverse. These spontaneous political societies, which were no more than pressure or influence groups, generally appear most vividly when a higher political authority which might obtrude upon and often

destroy them was lacking. Hence the sovereign acts through his agents
in his principality or realm, for example in the countryside and even in
the towns of France and England. Even in self-governing cities,
virtually outside princely authority, the central government can function so that party action may be difficult or impossible. Everything
depends on power relationships within the town. The era of parties
thus corresponds to the period of the construction and maturing of
municipal institutions and governments. Sometimes it can be very
short, when a greater power of so-called 'popular' form imposes itself
rapidly, but it can also be quite lengthy, lasting even beyond the
medieval period.

This deficiency of princely or municipal authority furthers the
action of social groups of all types: clans, confraternities, guilds or
hanses, societies and associations, and even more parties, which would
never have been tolerated at other times. In the medieval West, this
pattern can be observed in many situations. Two types of circumstance
nonetheless catch our attention most forcefully: for the towns, the
periods when governments were still not firmly established, when
institutions had not been rigidly imposed; and for the kingdoms, when
the sovereign, weakened or absent, could not maintain unity and when
factions or parties formed around rival princes competed and then
clashed for the conquest of central authority.

Notes to the Introduction*

[1]For France, compare particularly the classic work undertaken under the direction of
F. Lot and R. Fawtier, *Histoire des institutions françaises au Moyen Age*, 3 vols. to date
(Paris, 1957–1962). For the entire West and including much more variegated viewpoints,
see B. Guenée, *L'Occident aux XIVe et XVe siècles. Les états* (Paris, 1971). These two
works include excellent bibliographies.
[2]Renouard[46]. Also useful are L. Simeoni, *Le Signorie* (Florence, 1950); C.G. Mor,
L'età feudale (Milan, 1952); and, in particular, Brucker[18].
[3]For example, M. Garaud, *Les châtelains de Poitou et l'avènement du régime feodal,
XIe et XIIe siècles* (Poitiers, 1957), and C. Van de Kieft, *Etude sur le chartrier et la
seigneurie du prieuré de la Chapelle-Aude (XIe–XIIIe siècle)* (Amsterdam, 1960).
[4]L. Douet d'Arcq, *Comptes de l'Hôtel des rois de France aux XIVe et XVe siècles*
(Paris, 1865); O. Cartellieri, *The court of Burgundy* (London, 1929); A. Lecoy de la

* Numbers in square brackets refer to the Bibliography.

Marche, *Le roi René, sa vie, son administration, ses travaux artistiques et littéraires d'apres les documents inédits des archives de France et d'Italie,* 2 vols. (Paris, 1875); F. Piponnier, *Costume et vie sociale: la cour d'Anjou (XIVe–XVe siècle)* (Paris, 1970); A. Champollion-Figeac, *Louis et Charles d'Orléans* (Paris, 1844); Comte de Tougoêt-Tréauna, *Les comptes de l'Hôtel du duc de Berry. 1370–1413* (Bourges, 1890); F. Lehoux, *Jean de France duc de Berry* (Paris, 1966); A. Leguai, *Le Bourbonnais pendant la guerre de Cent ans* (Moulins, 1969).

[5]But see the magisterial study of B. Guenée, *Tribunaux et gens de justice dans le bailliage de Senlis à la fin du Moyen Age (vers 1380–vers 1550)* (Paris, 1963).

[6]C. Poisson-Bourlet, *La justice du Maire-Prevôt à Mantes-la-Jolie à la fin du XIVe siècle.* Mémoire (University of Paris X, 1972).

[7]F. Bourquelot, Un scrutin du XIVe siècle, *Mémoires de la Société des Antiquaires de France,* XXI, 1852.

[8]On this subject, see the observations and the conclusions drawn by Brucker[19] from careful research in the sources which give names of those involved.

[9]Cristiani[21]. On this point see also Salvemini[49].

[10]On the various meanings of the word *popolo,* see pp. 208–214.

[11]On the role of the clans in the political life of the Italian cities, see Heers[31, pp. 105–124, 231–237].

[12]Brucker[19].

[13]Such was the case for the famous *Hermandades* of Castile, among which the *Hermandad vieja de Toledo* was destined to have a brilliant political future. See L. Suarez Fernandez, Evolution historica de la hermandades Castillanas, *Cuadernos de la historia de Espana* (Buenos Aires, 1951), and J. Puyol y Alonso, *Las hermandades de Castilla y Leon* (Madrid, 1913).

[14]On this general question, see A. Gouron, *La règlementation des métiers en Languedoc au Moyen Age* (Geneva, 1958).

[15]Gutkind[28, p. 75], without indicating exact source.

[16]Gouron, *Réglementation.*

[17]H.F. Westlake, *The parish gilds of medieval England* (London, 1919).

PART I
POLITICAL FACTIONS IN
MEDIEVAL ITALY, 1100–1400

CHAPTER ONE

Medieval Italy: the primary study

The continual struggle between several, or rather two, political factions seems a constant feature of public life in the cities of the West during the communal period. The influence and activity of the parties is evident proof of this. No author speaks of the troubles of his city without mentioning parties and usually considering them responsible. We are not dealing with isolated episodes, accidents or exceptions, but rather with a fundamental course of action undoubtedly related to certain characteristic features of the civilization of cities. Hence we must link this study to all aspects of urban life during the establishment of the earliest forms of municipal government.

These party struggles were certainly not equally significant everywhere; they appear most often and most seriously in Italy. The existence of these political factions has been recognized and portrayed in popularizations or works of synthesis only for Tuscany and to some extent Lombardy. This has generally been done in the standard form of describing the clash between the Guelfs, presented as papal partisans, and the Ghibellines, portrayed as adherents of the emperor. This primacy of Italy is not accidental. It can be explained by different original conditions, by social structures within the towns, and by the interplay of foreign pressures and interventions.

Socio-political structures in the Italian cities

The real character of the urban societies and the amazing variety and complexity of the environments in Italy have long been misunderstood.

Most historians have held to simplistic, traditional models, inspired by rigid ideological convictions. This image was strengthened in the nineteenth century, when everyone was glorifying the virtues of the 'bourgeoisie' of the communes and the republics, which were dressed up in democratic colours. At this time too the theories of Marx on class struggle and of Engels on a supposed urban revolution against the 'feudal' world began to triumph without discrimination, nuance, or genuine historical examination. Despite the ravages of time and in spite of all the scholarly works which lead inexorably to different conclusions, these ideas are still found among many authors. For them the medieval town was the world of renewal, of revolt against old forms, in a word, of liberty. Compared to rural societies still dominated by the 'feudalism' of the lords, it constituted an original, totally different environment. For these authors the separation of town and countryside in all respects is an act of faith. The antagonism between 'feudal' and 'bourgeois' aristocracy is accepted as incontestable. The commune was a government of bourgeois, all more or less equal or at least having the same social origin, pursuing like professional activities, having kindred life styles and ambitions. They were, in short, merchants. This government is admitted into the pantheon of democratic forms: periodic rotation of magistrates and officers, free elections, wide social base of recruitment. The people, peace, and law ruled everywhere. In an anarchic 'feudal' world, the prey of social injustice and violence, the urban commune was a kind of haven, a political Eden. When troubles broke out, they were accidents coming from outside, provoked by men persisting in the old traditions. All of this is erroneous. These are but opinions, simplistic and puerile, to be dismissed as *a priori*, useless ideas. In fact, a quite different point of departure imposes itself, without which no research can progress: even in the communal period the Italian town was a world perfectly conforming to and in complete harmony with all the neighbouring social milieus, totally integrated into a much larger whole. It was the antithesis of a ghetto.

Three important points merit discussion here. First, a seigneurial aristocracy resided in the city. This is an important but too often misunderstood fact. The same type of seigneurial aristocracy dominated both towns and countryside. The masters of the 'merchant' cities in virtually all regions were great lords, nobles owning lands within the walls or in the suburbs, but who also held fiefs and domains in the countryside or in the mountains. They had castles (*rocche*) to guard the valleys and roads, together with powerful fortresses in the city, palaces surmounted by high towers. They held seigneurial rights over men and land and over the means of production and exchange in the town, the harbour, and on distant routes.[1] The instruments of economic expansion – woods, forges and mills – were in their hands.

We have realized since the work of R.S. Lopez on the origins of Genoese capitalism[2] that the lords were first the initiators and the principal agents, then later the rich beneficiaries of the awakening and of the mercantile expansion in their Italian towns. Commercial enterprise was then merged with the armed expedition, with hunting Moslem pirates and the continuing war in the Mediterranean. The leading warriors naturally took charge. The commodities of international trade were often only shares of booty. The first Italian colonization in the Holy Land, in the twelfth century, was primarily a seigneurial undertaking, as for example for the Genoese Embriaci family, masters of Giblet.[3] Under such circumstances, this aristocracy, though it certainly practised mercantile activity,[4] was not composed of 'merchants', let alone of 'bourgeois', as has been and still is claimed by many authors. All these wealthy people had an eminently noble style of life. They were captains with fortresses and armies who ruled their men, subjects and clients. They maintained ties and negotiated all sorts of alliances with the greatest of lords, masters of vast territories. This noble aristocracy, all-powerful in the first period of the communal era, fought for several centuries to preserve its power over the city. It often succeeded in replenishing itself and in becoming enriched with new elements within the very framework of its own institutions.

Secondly, governmental forms were unstable and were devised by constant empiricism or indeed eclecticism. At first, the powers of the Italian communes were limited and fragile. They were not well-regulated organisms, constructed on firm foundations, appealing to a wide citizen participation and capable of controlling everything in the city. The Italian commune remained an aristocratic, noble affair throughout the medieval period.[5] In the beginning and for a long time thereafter, all the councils and colleges were staffed not by elections with a wide popular base, but by subtle interplay in which cooptation and nomination by intermediate bodies is most frequently found. These groups, which were also very powerful economically, were comprised especially of great families or groups of families acting jointly. These clans were very influential whatever the means by which the city magistrates were chosen. They alone held real power. They always placed their own men in command posts and their protégés, clients or subordinates in executive or administrative positions.

Moreover, the government of the commune was merely the result of agreements among family powers, in all a sort of very fragile compromise. Its beginning is very difficult to grasp, but all evidence suggests that the commune was not born of a 'revolution' or an 'enfranchisement', but rather of a slow evolution involving complex negotiations of all sorts. This new political 'society' of the commune often regrouped primary 'societies'. Thus at Genoa, whose annals are relatively precise about this earliest period of municipal life, the government was born of the union of six, seven, and later eight *compagne*. This term suggests a merchant company, and these companies do seem to have been formed in the exact image of a commercial association by an agreement in good and proper form which respected the interests of each individual.[6]

The earliest magistrates, the consuls, did little governing in any town of northern and central Italy. Their principal functions were commercial and judicial: they settled litigations, resolved conflicts and imposed arbitration. At Genoa between 1100 and 1130 they bore the title *consules de comuni et de placitis*.[7] The two functions were separated in 1130: *in novo consulatu unius anni fuerunt consules tres de comuni et xiii de placitis*.[8] Only in 1164 did the definitive form appear: *consules in re publica*.[9] These consuls were above all judges; "they judged and held pleas", says the annalist Caffaro, "if a person from one *compagna* impleaded someone from another".[10] The municipal magistracy thus only intervened when conflict occurred between men belonging to two different political 'societies'. Conflicts were certainly resolved within each *compagna* without recourse to the commune, undoubtedly by the aristocrats, the most powerful heads of families. Subsequently these *compagne* remained the solid and unchanging territorial bases of all political, economic and social life in the city of Genoa throughout the Middle Ages.

Consular government thus seems superimposed on the life of the city. Its activity was limited to establishing a kind of division or alternation of power among the great families. The town built no communal palace, and the meetings of the consuls and councils were held by turns in the great family palaces of each noble quarter.[11] The authority of this municipal government in no way impaired the previously existing structures or fundamental customs. It left the field free for every ambition, for the furious pursuit of power, usurpations, quarrels and violent conflicts. The period of the aristocratic commune of the consuls was a time of factional strife. The installation of a podestà, a development occurring at widely varying times in different cities, was at first exceptional, but later became an annual affair.[12] His presence certainly made the consuls' power more effective, but it changed nothing in the socio-political structures or even in the forms of the real government of men.

Thirdly, violent conflicts can only be explained by recalling the presence of a large poor population, frequently maltreated and very often unemployed. These persons, often called collectively *popolo minuto* by the Italian chroniclers, were essentially composed of more or less recent immigrants from the countryside who had been attracted by better jobs:[13] garden work and the suburban vineyards, the woollen textile industry and the building yards. These men were evidently poorly integrated into the urban world. They had left their birthplace and family. Kept apart from collective social activities, they often lived outside the walls. They were very vulnerable sources of instability, suffering greatly from every disturbance of the economic or monetary equilibrium and especially from poor textile sales and unemployment crises.[14] Poor wages, a peculiar social situation from which there seemed no escape, and their rural origin all meant that these urban proletariats were often despised and feared by the local citizens. The journeymen blacksmiths and carpenters at Pisa between 1220 and 1250 worked in the winter in the iron mines of the island of Elba and in the forests of the maritime Maremma; they lived in the city only during the summer, while the rich families fled the intense heat for their country houses.[15]

A large number of wanderers, vagabonds and beggars of all kinds was added to this unstable, even migratory working population. Few sources speak precisely of these men on the fringes of society, constantly repulsed and watched, and no author tried to enumerate them. Yet the deliberations of the city fathers show the citizens' qualms well. The many charitable institutions, the gifts to paupers, the hospitals and the hostels, and the almoners' offices also show the influence of this fringe population on the life of the city.

The serious inequity of situations and fortunes and the existence of a very large poor and unstable population must be taken into account in any analysis of street movements and battles. It would obviously be very interesting to ascertain who could reach and direct these men, to see whether some of them fell regularly or accidentally into one or another clientele of powerful men.

External pressures

Every historian has emphasized the absence of a centralizing authority or even of a simple political hegemony in medieval Italy. No kingdom or principality imposed its law even on a limited region. Imperial power was weakening from the early eleventh century, and the few great political seigneuries, such as that of Princess Matilda (1046–1115), disintegrated later in interminable dynastic quarrels. Italy remained a field largely open to ambitions, a densely populated country, active and rich, able to excite the greedy. Neighbouring sovereigns sought at the very least alliances which could provide important financial support for them, if not complete control. Our textbooks inform us that these struggles and interventions usually concerned popes and emperors, but the conflicts cannot be summarized in this simple picture. On the contrary, there were very complex confrontations involving numerous interests. Above all, the chronological framework transcends that of the short 'classical' period between 1240 and 1270 of confrontation between Guelfs and Ghibellines at Florence.

Actually, the struggles of papacy and Empire go back to the earliest period of papal temporal power. The first movement occurred between 900 and 1050 when the emperors, firmly established at Pavia and Ravenna, tried, usually in vain, to intervene in the administration of Rome and to turn the régime of the *Adelspapsttum* to their benefit,[16] especially under Otto III, who wanted to make Rome truly *sedes imperii*. Another period of very serious conflict was obviously that of the Investiture Controversy, particularly under Popes Gregory VII and Urban II. Even after the Concordat of Worms these religious quarrels often assumed the appearance of great political conflicts. A century later came the notorious struggle between Innocent IV and Frederick II, which has remained the more famous because it corresponded to the moment when the parties seemed to be taking more coherent form and adopted the names Guelf and Ghibelline in many towns. This quarrel broke out again in the time of Manfred and Conradin, this time for possession of the kingdom of Naples.

We must emphasize that in these violent struggles which marked the active periods of the quarrel of papacy and Empire, the issue cannot be reduced to the simple confrontation of two champions. The marvellously complex play of alliances is involved. Each of the antagonists tried to secure the alliance of the cities of the Italian peninsula, which were in their turn already being divided by economic rivalries on land or sea, territorial struggles for the possession of a nearby *contado* or distant overseas lands, such as the strife between Pisa and Genoa for Sardinia and Corsica.

The quarrel of papacy and Empire was certainly not the only one which influenced the destiny of the Italian communes. Other ambitions were asserted later, after the Avignon papacy and its ugly consequences and after the imperial renunciation under the fifteenth-century Habsburgs. First there were struggles between city-states: towns which had extended their districts immeasurably, annexing nearby rival towns, undertaking a policy of conquest with large armies, commanding a vast diplomatic network and forming leagues and seeking alliances everywhere. This happened with Florence, which found an access to the sea by seizing Pisa; Milan, which held the port of Genoa for several years and installed a governor there; and Venice, which extended its *terra ferma* into the mountains. Neighbouring princes intervened quite frequently in Italy, in some cases to annex provinces, in others to establish one or more allied principalities there, in still others to exercise a kind of political hegemony. In the fifteenth century, these interventions show real intentions to conquer. Thus from the side of France, the king himself accepted the lordship of Genoa and installed a very active governor there, Marshal Boucicault (1399), who founded the famous *Casa di San Giorgio*.[17] The house of Anjou under King René claimed the Neapolitan inheritance of Queen Jeanne II. He entitled himself 'king of Sicily' and tried several times to recover his lost provinces. Hoping for the support of Genoa, where his son John of Calabria 'ruled' until 1460, he succeeded in occupying the 'kingdom of Naples' between 1438 and 1442.[18] More dangerous interventions were conducted by the king of Aragon, Alfonso V the Magnanimous (1396–1458). Master of Aragon, Catalonia, Roussillon, the Spanish provinces of the Levant and the Balearic Islands, he also held Sardinia and Sicily and thus extended his empire to the major shores and the strategic islands of the Tyrrhenian Sea.[19] This maritime empire greatly influenced the fate of Italy when King Alfonso undertook the conquest of the kingdom of Naples and sought allies among the towns of the peninsula. Defeated at first in 1435 by a Genoese fleet near the island of Ponza[20] and imprisoned by the duke of Milan, he succeeded later, in 1442, in conquering the entire mainland territory of Naples. He established his court in the town, which became a splendid capital city, active in diplomacy.[21] Until his death in 1458 he tried to extend his influence and impose his hegemony on all of Italy by leagues, alliances, and military activity. The disputed heritage of Naples was thus the origin of serious conflicts in which each town had to take sides, a division which recalls that which had once opposed the allies of the pope to those of the emperor. Although the political chessboard was now considerably simplified, for the city-states were much less numerous and more powerful than before, the division between two 'parties' had again left its mark on Italian life.

The problem of the sources

The socio-political structures of many less well-known towns of the West outside Italy, few of which have been studied at all, do not seem very different from those of the peninsula. We easily find there a seigneurial aristocracy which owes much of its fortune and political power to land and to rights over men, for example in Germany, the lands of French Languedoc, and perhaps even in Normandy and the Ile-de-France.[22] We also see municipal governments or communes formed which were dominated entirely by this aristocracy. These communes were not stable, lasting, uncontested political organs.[23] The lands and towns, however, were inevitably coveted by rival princes. External pressures, interventions, and the game of alliances brought in its wake diplomatic clienteles which furthered the formation of hostile parties, as at Bordeaux, where the rival great families served the kings of England or France.[24]

Why then emphasize Italy to such an extent? It is possible that the historian has long felt a subconscious preference for the great merchant cities of Tuscany or Lombardy. Urban Italy has a tremendous attraction: power and wealth, true economic primacy, particularly in finance, the remarkable expansion in the Orient during the crusading era and later into distant Asia, the conquest of a great colonial empire and the establishment of distant branch offices, and above all an urban civilization which was particularly brilliant in every field of art and literature.

But this decisive preference and distortion of viewpoint in many popular histories of the Western world is due also to the fact that Italy is the most studied and best known country. The documentation there is much more abundant and precise than elsewhere. Economic wealth was very early accompanied by a quantifying, literate culture which extended to various social levels, not merely to the clergy.[25] The Italian merchant city thus produced very early a remarkable civilization of the written word: account books, compilations of private documents by the notary, and thousands of business letters. The letters, precise, frequent, and regular, seem to have been the basis of all mercantile activity.[26] They tell us about everything: the flow of merchandise in a coldly numerical manner, the varied circumstances which can influence the market and knowledge of which thus seems indispensable to all speculation, the arrival of ships, hard times, harvests, movements of princes and courts, nominations of great officers and prelates, dynastic quarrels, and diplomatic and military activity. Certain letters remind us of ambassadors' reports. They are little chronicles in themselves, and we find considerable information in them on different aspects of town life.

Particularly from the trecento, the merchant, who was unusually well informed about contemporary affairs, needed to collect his information in the form of annals or chronicles. These writings generally formed a continuous narrative enriched by personal reflections and even analyses. The merchant author is incontestably one of the most original figures of medieval urban society.[27] These great merchants dominated political life and were very prominent in the various city councils. Thus, the registers of deliberations of the city fathers seem to have been kept more rigorously and precisely in Italy than elsewhere.[28]

Moreover, the interest which all regions showed in Italy from this time on, together with the memory of ancient Rome and the prestige of the Church, explains an abundant pseudo-historical literature. Party men and clergy tried to analyse, certainly superficially and not without polemical intentions, the machinery and motives of political activity in the major cities. The historian encounters a substantial and very diverse documentation in this historical or pseudo-historical form alone. The choice of material is not always easy, for these narratives necessarily bear the mark of a definite involvement. Every Italian author is obviously a partisan, in every moment of his life a captive of his interests, his emotions and friendships, and his alliances. He himself is a party man. This passion, this hatred can even inspire poetic outbursts, such as the songs of exile of Dante Alighieri. When such commitment appears with more discretion, it is shown by its preferences, omissions, choice of words, and by biased judgements. When the author, a merchant, can look back to judge an era long past, he can certainly free himself from these hatreds and avoid inflammatory language, but he remains a partisan. He then belongs to another generation characterized by other political customs, imbued with an ideal of peace and equilibrium which condemns the rule of parties and leaders. Thus, especially at Florence, the authors of the trecento viewed the troublemakers of the past with a jaundiced eye. Giovanni Villani, who is still our best, most precise, and most curious guide,[29] tells us his preferences. A member of a wealthy merchant family who were associates of the Peruzzi and the Bonacorsi, Giovanni (1280–1348) was prior and paymaster of the commune of the *popolo*. He had directed the fortification works of his city and was certainly capable of giving a statistical statement of the wealth of Florence. He knew figures for grain consumption and calculated prudently from them the number of inhabitants. He also knew how to estimate the incomes of merchants and captains of industry. His documentation seems trustworthy and his interpretations excellent on all these points.[30] Nonetheless, in the straightforward narrative of political events and especially in his analysis of origins and causes, his hostility to the magnates, the nobles, and the parties, and his admiration of the rich merchant masters of the *popolo*, who he says were deeply concerned for the common good and peace, appear flagrantly.

Such inaccuracies are still more serious with non-Italian authors. In addition to bias, the desire to denigrate and discredit one's opponents and to glorify their own prince, German authors sometimes show a very serious misunderstanding of Italian social milieus, customs and traditions. Hence even in their choice of words to describe an institution, social group or custom, we find obvious barbarisms, born of a simple comparison with the realities of their own country or more often rooted in an idealized, abstract and simplistic construction – the work, in short, of intellectuals. These errors are particularly noticeable in the entire pseudo-historical production of the imperialist writers who claimed to be analysing Roman political life and party government at the time of the *Adelspapsttum* in the tenth century. P. Toubert has recently made a telling critique of the biases and inadequacies of these

'German' chroniclers, such as Liutprand of Cremona, Flodoard, Thangmar, and even Gerbert of Aurillac:

All these authors have in common their ignorance of the Roman environment and a latent or overt hostility to traditions which they misunderstood or which had little interest for them. All have an obvious propensity to feast upon platitudes which were to endure until modern historiography .... No less annoying to the historian is their tendency to schematize political behaviour. While all local documentation lets us feel the force of complex vertical 'solidarities' and bonds of clientage, these foreign sources usually portray Roman political life as the mathematical resultant of abstract forces or social groups of an illusory homogeneity (such as *tota plebs, omnis populus, ordo senatorius*). We must add that when these foreign writers try to transcend this type of generality, they only have at their disposal a vocabulary totally unsuited for the social analysis which they wish to attempt.[31]

These observations, which come at the conclusion of a precise study of milieus and political practices, correctly emphasize the danger of using imprecise, abstruse, or anachronistic words. Indeed, no analysis of social groups can begin without a preliminary definition of the different meanings of words, a study of the political vocabulary of the time.

CHAPTER TWO

The concept of party in the vocabulary of medieval Italian towns

An examination of the idea of party provides an example of how words enable us to approach, even sometimes to grasp, a very complex, fluid and unstable notion. The extremely diverse expressions in use show well the place of the party *vis à vis* other political action groups. They also crystallize the collective reactions of the period, or at least those of its authors. This leads us to point out certain distortions or excessive generalizations.

Most nouns used during the communal period have either changed their meaning over the centuries or have completely disappeared. The historian has only kept a very few rare expressions which give an inadequate, oversimplified picture of the concept 'party'. Actually, our modern historical vocabulary is limited to two rigid sets of terms. On the one hand, all political groups are called 'parties' in all secondary works; on the other, nearly all modern authors, at least in popularizations or works of synthesis, speak only of Guelfs and Ghibellines and additionally, for the later period and for Tuscany only, of Whites and Blacks.

This facile oversimplification is regrettable. A statistic of the terms used in historical narratives would doubtless show that the 'party' words, Guelfs and Ghibellines, were exceptional, and in any case only made up a small proportion of a highly variegated and changing vocabulary. These expressions only became fixed gradually, slowly and in a partial and uncertain manner. This political vocabulary, which we habitually believe is so precise, depends on regions or towns, foreign borrowings and fashions, times or even circumstances, and finally on

27

the author of the narrative himself, who thus voices his judgements and preferences. This abundance and variety of words is already a valuable hint of the complex, variable and uncertain nature of the political group and its origins, characteristics, and evolution.

Terminological uncertainties thus manifest themselves in two distinct areas: in defining the group itself, and in giving descriptive names to groups to designate and distinguish them from one another.

Uncertainties in the evolution of the word 'party'

The political party appears on the fringes of institutions recognized by the city. Its activity often seems parallel to that of the government, if not esoteric and more or less secret. Its origins are naturally obscure, sometimes spontaneous, and its organization remained totally flexible for a considerable time. There were no written acts of foundation. All this accounts for the many uncertainties and hesitations in naming these newly arrived groups. No special, specific word was used from the beginning, and the chroniclers show their uncertainties by employing words recalling older but different institutions, most often by reference to the mercantile activities of the city. This occurs when the organization of the political group seems to them more solid, better structured than at first. In other cases, for truly inchoate groups, the authors resign themselves to using words having a very general meaning or extremely vague formulas.

We begin by considering associations with structures. In the early years of the communal period, such organizations were always exceptional in the political sphere. The word generally used in this case was *societas*, which definitely suggests an association of commercial character. *Societas* was very often applied by chroniclers of the duecento to northern Italy, when the first political groups of this type appeared and were active. A detailed study of Cremona, Brescia, and particularly Piacenza enables us to specify the different meanings of the word and to outline the evolution of its use.[32] Our study is based essentially on the *Annales Placentini Guelfi*, composed in the first half of the thirteenth century, and the *Annales Placentini Gibellini*, written by Mutius de Modetia (died 1313), who seems very well informed about contemporary affairs. He was captain of the 'people' at Piacenza in 1283.[33] These two chronicles borrow substantially from works no longer extant.

Societas was used in the duecento to mean basically any association created by a specific agreement, primarily in business but also in politics. The parallel is obvious in any case. At Piacenza in 1218 the knights and the 'people' arrived after long negotiations at an agreement which established a *societas*.[34] Similarly, two hostile parties at Piacenza settled their differences in 1266 "according to the peace and the 'society' made between them at the time of the general council".[35]

These associations, durably established as *societates*, were unions of knights, merchants of the 'people', or both. The transfer from the exact commercial meaning to a more general sense of political alliance seems evident in all cases. This evolution and double usage recalls the case of the word *compagna*, particularly at Genoa: first a company founded for business ventures, then a political association, and finally a topographical division of the city and the electoral district for choosing the magistrates and members of the councils.[36]

The groups called *societates* in northern Italy seem relatively well structured. The *Annales Placentini Guelfi* show that from 1187 the three rectors of the city imposed a podestà as supreme judge and took an oath from "the men of the councils of Piacenza and the consuls of the offices and the societies".[37] In this same town, political societies seem to have been particularly active in finance and commerce. They ended by merging into a single institution which grouped the masters of the guilds and of commerce: in 1276 a letter from the emperor was read to all important figures of the city, including the "captain of the society of merchants and bankers of Piacenza".[38] These associations, which were societies of businessmen and thus 'popular',[39] occupied a very important position at that time in every city of northern Italy. For example, at Vercelli, a somewhat peripheral city to be sure and with only a modest commercial life, we find among several others the *Società di San Eusebio*, founded in 1169 primarily by merchants, notaries and judges, and the *Società di Santo Stefano*, founded only in 1209, which grouped the rich inhabitants of the suburb, but of which several nobles functioned as consuls.[40] These 'societies' of the 'people' had thus developed and then remained powerful particularly in the new quarters, the old suburbs, near the wall and gates which they guarded.[41]

But we know that 'tower societies' of nobles or knights possessing one or more seigneurial keeps in the city opposed these popular societies, which were often called 'gate societies'.[42] At Piacenza the chroniclers quite freely use the word *societas* to mean a single extended family, surrounded by relatives and dependants, as for example the Lupi of Cremona. In 1193 the forces of Piacenza inflicted a severe defeat upon the Cremonese and imprisoned "150 knights of the Society of the Lupi",[43] while in 1271 the exiles from Piacenza, once more conquerors of their opponents and already enriched by a splendid booty, were routed from their camp by a surprise charge of the Lupi.[44] According to this author, who was perhaps indulging a complacent admiration and some exaggeration, these political societies of the nobles sometimes had an important military potential. In 1250 the podestà of Cremona, threatened by the Capelleti clan or faction, received support from their opponents and "created a society of 2,000 Barbarasi".[45]

The two chroniclers of Piacenza sometimes use *societas* for all or most of the nobles and knights, the members of the great families. When the 'popular party' of Piacenza seized a fortress in the countryside in 1220, the consuls of the 'society of knights' took reprisals.[46] In 1266 the papal legates instigated in the same city the foundation of a *societas consortii*, which included all the chief partisans of the Church.[47] This association was not limited to a single more or less well-defined social group, but included both knights and men of other origins (*boni et communales homines*), provided that they belonged to a powerful family (*consorzio*). The meaning is thus more general and approaches that of the modern word 'party'. Finally, the same chroniclers call the Lombard League, an urban anti-imperial association dating from 1167, the *societas lombardia*.[48]

We thus see the varied degree of success and the frequent political applications of a word which originated in the merchant's vocabulary. But these applications seem limited to northern Italy at a relatively early period and to comparatively well structured political groups which were organized under the guidance of responsible persons in imitation of merchant companies.

Turning to unstructured groups, we find that early authors are even more reluctant to give names to spontaneously formed associations which do not resemble merchant societies in any respect, but which on the contrary were preserved or renewed by oral agreements and uncertain alliances. The vocabulary used in Italy for these associations was for many years quite variable, and the uncertainties accentuate the complexity and in some degree the novelty of the phenomenon.

The word 'party' was by no means generally used in Tuscany, and several writers sought other expressions. Often the memory of a clan which constituted the nucleus and the origin of the party seemed an obvious choice. Giovanni Sercambi, a Lucchese writing later, between 1410 and 1420, constantly uses the expression *e' figlioli* ("and their children") in reference to the conflicts of the thirteenth and fourteenth centuries in his town: thus in 1203 "the rebel knights of Lucca who were at Montecattino with their foreign friends, Guido Borgo Borgognoni and his children".[49]

Giovanni Villani, writing around 1340, also speaks constantly of civil wars between political groups, but uses the word 'party' neither for Florence and Tuscany nor for Lombardy and Genoa, and neither for an early nor a more recent period. He deliberately says "those of the house of" (*quegli della casa degli*) on several occasions. Thus, for example, with reference to the condemnation of the Ubaldini in 1345, he writes: "all persons of the house of the Ubaldini were tried and found guilty".[50] But above all, and almost systematically, he constantly uses the word *setta* (sect), accompanied by the name of a person or family, for example for the conflicts at Bologna in 1321[51] or those at Pisa in the following year.[52] It is hard to analyse this usage and to ascertain the author's intentions, for a pejorative nuance seems certain. The usage is regular in any case and almost exclusive. It seems to demonstrate quite well the writer's ignorance of the word 'party'.

On the other hand, Giovanni Sercambi speaks of various persons or families *colla loro setta*,[53] but also writes freely of *brigate*.[54] This rarely used word meant bands of young people, often nobles or their retainers, who paraded in the city streets, often armed, all wearing multicoloured livery.[55] The author's choice of this word demonstrates a significant association: the political faction, when it appears in the city, evokes thoughts of armed, cheering bands outfitted for games and festivals. Military combats and holidays were thus the two chief occasions when the party might arise spontaneously and take arms.

Somewhat surprisingly, the word 'party' evidently appears earliest among chroniclers outside Tuscany, but hesitantly and late even so. A statistical study of its use by the chroniclers of Piacenza leads to the following conclusions.[56] In the *Annales Placentini Guelfi*, finished around 1235, the word was used exactly 126 times in roughly forty pages of text. We count 548 utilizations in some 180 pages in the *Annales Placentini Gibellini*, written about half a century later. Thus, the more recent text mentions the term more prominently and somewhat more frequently. Yet in the earlier chronicle, we find only ten cases, or eight per cent of the total, where the meaning is precise, specific, and limited exclusively to politics. In all other cases the party was not a political party but rather a segment of some social group or indeed a particular geographical or topographical region of the city. By contrast, fifty years later in the *Annales Gibellini*, 300 utilizations of the word 'party', or fifty-five per cent of the total, have a precisely affirmed political meaning. The concept had thus become more exact. This development seems the result of a double evolution in the Lombard authors. There was first the transition from the military to the political meaning. The party quite often began as an armed band, a formation of allies on a war footing. The term could be applied to knights, to infantrymen, and to clients of a great family or a powerful lord. We thus find numerous references of the type "with all his people" or "and all their people with them".[57] But the word was also applied quite deliberately to an entire city or nation. The author of the *Annales Guelfi* describes the battle of 1213 where the armies of Cremona and Milan fought and says that the Cremonese took prisoner "about three hundred knights of Milan and their party".[58] The same chronicler also uses more definite expressions such as "party of the Milanese", "party of the men of Pavia", "party of the men of Piacenza and Brescia", or even "men of Cremona and all those of their party".[59]

Secondly, there is a transition from the legal to the political meaning. The parties were originally adversaries during a trial, judgement or arbitration. This use of the word seems quite frequent in the early years of the thirteenth century. Thenceforth the meaning emphasized a league or alliance. A judgement was rendered at Piacenza in August 1260 "between the parties", who were the citizens of Cremona, the exiles from Piacenza, and the marquis Oberto Pallavicino on one side and the citizens of Piacenza on the other.[60] The evolution was more marked still in another judgement of the same year, which stated "that all who are citizens of Piacenza ... who are outside Piacenza in whatever capacity, for the party or on behalf of the marquis Oberto Pallavicino and Obertino de Andito, shall be freed from banishment".[61] This double military and juridical origin of the word 'party', while certainly not surprising, still gives us an important insight: the word recalls alliances born during wartime and in legal actions, two circumstances where bonds of collective solidarities would obviously and necessarily be forged.

Uncertainties in the choice of party names

We find the same uncertainties in describing, christening or giving names or surnames to the parties in all texts of this period. Of course the historian writing a synthesis or popularization rarely worries about details and subtleties. His interpretation, resolutely based on foreign politics and the idea of total uniformity of circumstances and institutions for the entire peninsula, generally leads him to speak only of Guelfs and Ghibellines. But this is unhelpful. A careful study of these party names reveals on the contrary a very slow and uneven evolution of important changes and restorations of old traditions, and striking differences among towns and, above all, the simultaneous use of several different names for one and the same group.

Moreover, the examination of these evolutions and differences provides very interesting clues for the historian of collective mentalities and reactions. Until now we have been able to establish the formation of the word 'party' only through the narratives of the chroniclers, who were often clerics. This is an intellectual phenomenon which concerns essentially the written language. Yet the names given to these parties derive from a popular spontaneity, a collective and oral phenomenon which better reflects general mentalities; here we can reach the reactions of the mob. Our reservations are undoubtedly numerous. Much was not retained by tradition and was totally forgotten. These extremely varied names reflect well the many preoccupations of the moment. They show how political alliances were perceived and explained. They sometimes place in bold relief the primitive nuclei to which the party owed its origin.

Naturally, surnames or sobriquets reflect political attitudes. Often coloured with popular humour or irony, they of course only appear in a very narrow local framework, reflecting some particular social or political situation as it struck the man on the street. They are often only mere banterings without great significance, and their meanings sometimes remain impenetrable, too tied perhaps to an unknown event or a very special circumstance. Thus, for example, we find that the *Zamberlani* and the *Strumieri*, words whose meaning escapes us, divided the towns of Friuli among themselves in the fifteenth century.[62]

Other names recall a striking political event. At Pisa in the trecento the two parties were not Guelfs and Ghibellines nor Blacks and Whites, but Raspanti and Bergolini. Villani gives the origin of these two names.

The party of the count della Roccha was master of the government and all offices of the city, "and they are called the sect of the Raspanti" (from *raspare*, to scrape or scratch). The others, who were excluded from power, had nothing, "and they are contemptuously called the Bergolini" (dupes, deprived).[63] It is worth noting that the chronicler says "they are called" (*gli chiamavanno*), indicating a collective if not a popular movement. The two names stuck. Villani uses them constantly, as does Giovanni Sercambi later: "and thus was formed the party of the Bergolini at Pisa". But the usage was not yet exclusive, for he also writes that "the Bergolini pillaged and burned the houses of the della Roccha".[64] Here is a hesitation between the surname and the expression "those of the house", which indicates well how poorly established the name then was. Still, the official agreement signed between the opposing parties in 1355 took account of thirty Raspanti and thirty Bergolini who were consulted and assembled to nominate a new list of magistrates.[65]

At Orvieto all opponents of the pope had to leave the city as exiles in 1338, but some remained or returned after a short absence and continued to agitate in an active opposition. Their leaders, called the *Malcorini* (oathbreakers, faithless) from that time, found themselves at the head of a political faction which had quite definite characteristics for the man on the street, while the others, who accepted exile passively, were derisively called the *Muffatti* or *Beffatti* (the mocked).[66] At Florence in 1295 the two great parties of rival families, the Cerchi and the Donati, had not yet assumed the names of Whites and Blacks; the contestants rather assembled under the names of the two powerful families, but during several weeks the Donati, who were "people of good birth and warriors, but not of great wealth", were ironically called the *Malefani*".[67]

Other surnames show a firmer political choice, an attachment to a program, a sort of profession of faith. The partisans of the council of the commune at Verona between 1215 and 1240 included eighty members commonly called the *Quattroventi*[68], while the chroniclers used the expression "the count's people"[69](*illi de comite*) to designate their opponents, partisans of Count Ezzelino da Romano.[69] The situation *vis à vis* the established power evidently led the exiles to form a true party on their lands or in friendly cities.[70] Contemporaries, especially in Lombardy, called it "the external party" of such or such a town. The *Annales Placentini Gibellini* speak in 1271 of the political mobilization of a settlement near the city, saying "and nearly all the people of Montano obeyed the count and the external party of Piacenza".[71]

Moreover, it would be profitable to examine the systematic use by the north Italian authors of the expressions "party of the knights" and "party of the people", which doubtless delineate a more lively rivalry there than in the other cities. Only a social analysis of the parties and especially of the social composition of the 'people' could establish a better definition of an opposition which was much more complex than is apparent on first glance.[72] Yet these two party names, which I think reflect different political styles rather than well-defined economic and social connections, were very commonly used in these urban milieus of Lombardy.

As to political programs and finally political slogans, two examples, also from northern Italy, come to mind. At Bologna, shortly after 1321, those who opposed the government of the heirs and clients of the rich merchant Romeo Pepoli were called *Maltravensi* (those who fight evil).[73] In Venetia, at Bassano, Vicenza and in several other less important towns, those who revolted against the protégés and dependants of lord Ezzelino da Romano took the name "party of the free" (*pars liberorum*) in 1229.[74]

The aspect best known and most often discussed, albeit from a distant perspective, of the quarrels between political parties is that of foreign alliances. This is the obvious origin of the interest attached to the names Guelf and Ghibelline and of the desire to apply these two words to all towns and periods, a simplification not supported by the sources of the age. We must note, on the contrary, that the names Guelf and Ghibelline were applied only relatively late, and that they were not invariably used alone, without a search for new names or a return to old traditions. The two terms tended to disappear toward the end of the Middle Ages.

Three important points of this history of party nomenclature undoubtedly merit emphasis. First, the constant or sporadic opposition between the allies of the emperor and the pope's friends was obviously made manifest much earlier than the declared and spectacular antagonism between Guelfs and Ghibellines in the city of Florence around 1240. This was true, for example, in Rome at the time of the *Adelspapsttum* between 950 and 1040, when the two opposing parties simply assumed their leaders' names.[75] Likewise in northern Italy and especially at Milan, during and just after the Investiture Contest, there was a confrontation between the Romans and the Patarines or *Ambrogiani*, who were so called because they were faithful to the Milanese clergy and their patron saint, Ambrose.[76]

Secondly, the names Guelf and Ghibelline are not found throughout Italy even in the thirteenth century. The Lombard chroniclers preferred to speak, for example at Padua and Venice, of *pars ecclesie* and *pars imperii*, parties of the Church and of the emperor. At Piacenza the first mention of Guelfs and Ghibellines in the *Annales Gibellini* occurs only in 1247. This reference concerned Florence; these names had not occurred in this source until that time, and afterward the expressions *pars ecclesie* and *pars imperii* were still the most often used.[77] The tradition forged at Florence did not spread easily outside Tuscany.

Thirdly, this evolution of the political vocabulary in favour of Guelfs and Ghibellines seems irregular even where it occurred. The new names did not always excite permanent enthusiasm. Two parties were certainly vying in continual struggles at Genoa, but the terms reflecting a papal–imperial duel only appear very late. Between 1160 and 1170 these parties bore the names of their leaders, Castello and Avvocati. The town only chose between the two potentates with difficulty, and the party names were always those of the great families of the moment even as late as 1230. New names, the *Rampini* and the *Mascherati*, appeared only toward 1244–1250. Their origin is unknown and seems inexplicable. The former favoured the pope and the latter the emperor, but the names do not reflect this in any way. Later, finally, the Genoese chronicle speaks of Guelfs and Ghibellines.[78]

The evolution seems even more complex in the region of Frignano, located in the Lombard Apennines near Modena. A federation grouping some forty-eight *pievi*, themselves formed from several hamlets, constituted a solid "community of the Valley". This very complex structure did not prevent an active political life, and every text which is even remotely precise – agreements, pacts and contracts – speaks clearly of the division of the 'Valley' between opposing parties, generally two. Here more than elsewhere the study of party nomenclature illustrates the many aspects and complexity of the choice of name. The sources note two great families, the *Corvoli* and the *Gualandelli*, in the eleventh century and until around 1220. A little later there were surnames: the parties of *Montecuccolo* (bird, cuckoo) and of *Montegarullo* (gossiper, chatterer). In 1280 party names again become family names: *Roiti, Ubertelli, Scotti, da Varola.* The Guelfs and Ghibellines appear in the following year, but the *Montecucculo* and the *Montegarullo* returned in 1337. A list of the communes of Frignano in 1488 cites the *parte mediata* and the *parte immediata*, names whose origin does not seem very clear.[79] These last two examples show that if foreign politics ended by imposing a certain choice of party names, this only happened slowly and hesitantly, not definitively. Strictly political names compete here with other more traditional terms which were undoubtedly better understood by contemporaries.

As we have noted several times, family names occupied an important position in all these complex choices. We should bear in mind the frequent use by the Lombard and Tuscan chroniclers of such expressions as "the sons of", "those of", "those of the house of", or "those of his party",[80] which indicate that for the authors and undoubtedly for their contemporaries, only the family name could designate the nature of the political faction satisfactorily. The authors of the two main chronicles of Piacenza frequently mention parties throughout northern Italy having no other name than that of their chief warrior, especially around the 1240s: Ezzelino da Romano, of course, but also Alberto da Fontana and Oberto Pallavicino.[81] Somewhat later at Piacenza and other northern towns, the political group emphatically assumed a family name, calling itself simply by a plural form of that name: *pars tizonorum* (family of the Tizoni, of Giacomo Tizono) at Vercelli in 1265, *pars Robertorum et illorum de Fogiano* (party of the Roberti and those of Fogiano) at Parma from 1246, *pars Lanzeveziorum* at Alexandria in 1276, *pars Fallabrinorum* at Pavia during an expedition against the town of Ivrea in 1269, and *pars Vicanorum* at Como in that same year. In all we have more than twenty different examples during a few years, all taken from the *Annales Placentini Gibellini.*[82] This is even true on the level of a tiny settlement in the Apennines, Pontremoli, where the *Oddoberti* and *Aurighi* families similarly vied for power.[83]

Other better known examples illustrate this very frequently found custom of calling the party by the name of the most active or powerful clan. The Ghibelline party of Bologna was often called *parte Lambertazza*, after the great Lambertazzi family. Vying with them were the Geremei, and a document of 1287 takes account of the "party and association of the Geremei of the city of Bologna".[84] At Piacenza the traditional terms were for a long time *pars Marchiani* (of the marquis of Este) and *pars Eccelini* (of Ezzelino da Romano).[85] Finally, at Orvieto in the thirteenth century two powerful parties disputed which bore the names of the two great families of Monaldeschi and Filippeschi.[86]

Finally, spontaneous collective reactions retained extremely varied and often ephemeral names, which accentuate some striking external characteristic, to indicate political factions. Thus, we find them called first by their residences and localities within the city. Even if the parties only very rarely corresponded to compact territorial blocs,[87] their names nonetheless can occasionally indicate a very concentrated settlement. This was undoubtedly the case at Brescia, where the *Annales Brixienses* speak of a *pars superior* (upper town) and a *pars inferior* (lower town) in 1213, while the *Annales Cremonenses* also mention two hostile parties in that city in 1209, each led by a different podestà: "the inhabitants of the old city" were juxtaposed to "those of the new city", and to the latter were added "those of the great parish of Saint-Pantaleon", who were thus already organized into a little political society, a considerable complication of the simple topographical division.[88]

The man on the street was particularly interested in banners and insignia to rally around in battles. At Bologna the partisans of Romeo Pepoli, master of a great fortune and protector of a large clientele, or rather of a band of mischiefmakers, were thus called the *Scacchesi* between 1310 and 1326 in reference to this powerful man's escutcheon, which had the form of a chequerboard.[89] At Orvieto in 1338 the two rival branches of the Monaldeschi family bore the name of their mascots as portrayed on their banners, the *Cervara* and the *Vipera* (the stag and the snake).[90] What was originally a family quarrel in Tuscany arrayed the Guelfs against one another shortly before 1300, first at Pistoia and then in every other town, and the new parties were then named after the colours around which they rallied, the White and the Black. Finally, at Parma in 1305, the popular mind noted the division between the Church party, which had ruled without break since 1266–1268, and a new faction formed on the occasion of a marriage alliance with the Ghibellines: the *pars antiqua* and the *pars nova*.[91]

We thus see that the great variety of names and nicknames of accidental nature, and their often ephemeral character, indicate clearly that the party, while certainly a political group, actually had a much more complex nature than this term might suggest. To understand the recruitment of members, their way of life and the power of these political factions, we need to explore every aspect of social life, all possibilities and occasions of conflict.

CHAPTER THREE

Political rivalries

The very name 'party' implies political activity. We have found that the word originally had a military and legal connotation which showed the importance of alliances and solidarities,[92] groups which to a greater or lesser degree were organized for political combat. These parties formed cadres and were instruments of power and means of action for certain leaders.

In any case, they were engaged in a total struggle to conquer power. This was an absolutely essential characteristic of political life in the first centuries of Italian municipal autonomy. Party activity was not circumscribed within a complex system involving division of responsibilities and power. The purpose of the party's activity was not to win a limited number of seats in the magistracy or a given share in the councils, either by the electoral process or by agreements made in competition with several other similar groups. Rather, the party wanted to seize and keep all power and exclude other political forces completely. Rivalry was thus absolute and victory unforgiving. This explains why with rare exceptions (during brief periods when alliances were still inchoate) we find only two parties vying mercilessly: one headed the government and held the entire town at its mercy, while the other was excluded, forced into opposition and frequently driven into exile, teeming with hatred and plotting revenge. No compromise nor form of collaboration was possible between the two.

This savage competition was demonstrated in two ways. On the one hand, princes from outside both the city and the region competed to

41

reduce them to obedience; and on the other, the citizens and their leaders fought internecine combats to monopolize all authority and seize all offices for their relatives and friends. These two contests caused continuous disruption, and the political life of each district, marked by this double conflict and astonishing vicissitudes of fortune, seems strangely complex to us. The ambitions of all, of foreign princes and nobles of the city alike, were often interrelated. But which was most influential?

External rivalries

Every historian has emphasized this aspect and has described the cities of Tuscany and Lombardy as constantly involved in the conflict between popes and emperors. This viewpoint has a dual merit: it ties the political history of these towns directly to the great issues of Western history and reduces the internal rivalries to a relatively simple scheme which can be explained quickly.

A divided land with no political unity, Italy seemed a constant bone of contention between the two principal powers of Christendom, particularly between 1000 and 1300. Actually, these three centuries of often violent rivalries were particularly marked by the assertion and progress of papal power and even more by the affirmation of the total autonomy or independence of the great merchant cities of central and northern Italy.

The stakes were high, of course. Much of the peninsula was definitely part of the Empire. The emperor tried to maintain his authority there and to govern by any means at his disposal. He was helped by a large army which often imposed his rule by force. He could also invoke the unity of the Empire and call to mind the remarkable experiences of imperial administration in southern Italy at least twice in the past, in the time of the Ottonians and later under the Hohenstaufen Henry VI and Frederick II, who actually governed from Palermo.[93] The example provided by the kingdom of southern Italy might inspire several ventures, at least in Lombardy.

The imperial coronations in Lombardy and at Rome were occasions for intervention south of the Alps and in the affairs of Christendom itself in equal measure. The activity of the emperors at Rome, the installation of popes who were either imperial friends or protégés under the Ottonians, and during the Investiture Controversy of the eleventh century even the support of German antipopes, all show well the emperors' desire to impose a firm tutelage upon the Church. Activity in Italy in any case allowed them to limit the pope's territorial ambitions and pretensions to rule a strong state involving a sort of papal hegemony in central Italy.[94] This disagreement extended to the realm of ideas, as ideological weapons did battle for the two adversaries and their pretensions to world domination.

Yet neither pope nor emperor could form in Italy a great state directly subject to himself. Imperial authority crumbled in the face of the rise of town liberties. The patrimony of St Peter remained very modest and was expanded only very slowly. Thus, there was no open warfare between two well-defined territorial states, but a rather a more diffuse and confused struggle over spheres of influence. This involved a constant search for allies throughout Italy, even beyond the borders of the papal and imperial lands. Cities could offer noteworthy strategic advantages to their allies. They were fortifications which could bar the road to the enemy and protect the frontiers and lines of communication. They could also lend their militias and above all provide indispensable economic assistance: financial aid and corn, both of which were assured by the great merchant companies of Tuscany.[95] For all these reasons, the popes and emperors forced the cities sooner or later to choose between themselves.

The citizens never made this choice unanimously. The various great families obviously viewed the interests of the city differently, for their attitude was naturally guided by consideration of their own advantage. Thus, the envoys of the pope or the emperor easily won allies. They could support and exacerbate conflicts, bringing about the formation of a party favouring their suzerain even in a town where the majority was opposed to him. Party quarrels were superimposed upon more ancient rivalries. But the intervention of a powerful prince, who had plenty of money or large armies, suddenly gave them another significance, a more dramatic turn.

First, each town thus found itself divided between the two powerful parties of Church and Empire, at least in the thirteenth century. This was the origin and moving force behind the constant, irreconcilable civil wars, which were punctuated by the alternation of glorious victories and banishment. At Florence, for example, Guelfs and

Ghibellines battled mercilessly from 1210 on. The Guelfs, who were resolutely hostile to the emperor Frederick II, mobilized their forces against Frederick of Antioch, his natural son, who was imposed on the town as podestà in February 1246. Defeated in bloody street fighting in the winter of 1248–1249, the Guelfs were hounded from their homes and exiled. They returned in triumph and routed the Ghibellines two years later, but several indecisive conflicts and vicissitudes of fortune nonetheless led to a new Guelf defeat in 1260 and the destruction of several hundred of their homes. They finally returned to their city as conquerors on Christmas night 1267, drove the Ghibellines into a distant exile at Forlì and organized their government with a firm hand.[96]

This party activity then provoked a veritable political partition of all of Italy. Each side joined one sovereign or the other. The choice was certainly not imposed clearly and definitively. Each side experienced frequent revolutions and found itself periodically in different camps. The alignment frequently varied by virtue of very unstable relationships, balances of power, and unexpected accidents. A single appearance of the emperor south of the Alps or even the arrival of some German reinforcements could throw everything into question.

Yet despite these vicissitudes, certain traditions were established, and each town came to be considered fundamentally of one party or the other. A kind of 'theoretical' political map of Italy was formed, reflecting at least the most frequent if not the invariable choices. Our investigation shows too that this division underscored the primordial importance for each region of traditional conflicts between rival towns or more often between the very great and rich city as conqueror and the other neighbouring towns as prey. In Tuscany, Siena, Lucca, and Pisa, all three considered Ghibelline, were generally ranged against Guelf Florence. In Emilia, Modena, which joined the imperial party, received the help of distant Rimini when confronted by Guelf Bologna. In Lombardy, Milan, which was generally faithful to the Church, had to fight against the allied Ghibelline forces of Monza, Pavia, and Cremona. Mantua, Ferrara, and Padua formed a Guelf bloc in the lower Po plain against generally imperial Verona. The ambitions and interests of individual towns are clearly seen here.

All of Italy north of Rome thus took sides. Internal quarrels seemed to be cast in the mould of the papal–imperial conflict in the mountain communities of the Lombard Apennines[97] and distant Friuli[98] as well as in the great centres. Evoking movements of popular opinion after the victory of Charles of Anjou and the pope over Manfred in 1266, the author of the *Annales Placentini Gibellini* wrote: "King Manfred's death caused great joy and gaiety among the Italians, or to be precise among the clergy and those who announced their allegiance to the Church party."[99]

Armed interventions by foreign powers thus assumed considerable significance. The German expeditions in Italy, often brought on by the imperial coronation ceremony at Rome, so greatly influenced the relationship of the opposing forces that they were undoubtedly decisive moments in the history of the entire peninsula. This had occurred, for example, as early as the reign of the legendary Frederick Barbarossa. The emperor first crossed the Alps in October 1154. He immediately imposed a peace upon the towns of Milan, Lodi, Como, and Pavia and had himself crowned at Rome. He summoned an imperial diet there, at which Milan was placed under the ban. Frederick conceded to its rival city Cremona the right to coin money. His second expedition, at the head of an immense army which made a great impression on contemporaries, took him first to Verona, where Milan was again condemned. The city surrendered on 8 September 1158 and obtained clemency in return for an oath of fidelity and a payment of 9,000 gold marks. Milan revolted against the emperor's deputies the following year: besieged and starved out, it surrendered a second time in February 1162. The consuls of the city had to come to Lodi to abase themselves, deliver 400 hostages, accept crushing taxes, and see the insignia of the city torn from its *carroccio* (battle wagon). The town was then razed to the ground. The remaining inhabitants fled into the suburbs, and the emperor ordered a palace to be constructed at Monza with stones taken from the ruins of Milan. Frederick made a third and final descent into Italy in 1174, but this marked the end of the German victories and culminated in the defeat of his army by the Lombard League at Legnano on 29 May 1176.

These imperial expeditions, from Charlemagne to Henry VII of Luxembourg, who was crowned at Rome in 1312, were thus always in the forefront of the military and political situation of Italy. They syncopated life, bringing aid and assistance to one party and new hope to the exiles who were anxious to reconquer their town and were eager for revenge. In moments of despair they seemed a last resort, the only power capable of changing a situation which had become intolerable. This is still shown in a surprising way at a very late date. In 1261 the

Guelfs of Florence had been driven from their city into the surrounding countryside, where they were constantly pursued by the Ghibellines and Manfred's armies. They sent several emissaries to Germany to the young Conradin to persuade him to come to Italy to claim his rightful inheritance.[100] These armed invasions provoked feverish defensive reactions by the other party, including the construction of a new wall to defend the suburbs.[101]

Compared to these imperial expeditions, the interventions of the pope remained very unobtrusive for quite some time. Rome acted more through its allies and leagues. The web of alliances entailed diplomatic activity. The search for loyalties and their relationship was a constant concern for the papal and imperial adversaries, even if their forms of activity were of a very different scope. Certainly the papacy led crusades against its adversaries whenever possible. In 1256 Verona was still under the yoke of the tyrant Ezzelino da Romano, who was supported by several great families. The pope then intervened and sent a legate, Filippo, archbishop of Ravenna, who led an army, composed largely of Venetians, which recaptured Verona in June 1256.[102] This was a prelude to the vigorous crusades launched by Alexander IV in 1266 and 1268 in support of Charles of Anjou, who was fighting Manfred and later Conradin of Hohenstaufen for control of southern Italy.[103] This new practice of the crusade on Italian soil, not against infidels or heretics, but against the imperial party, constituted a serious aggravation of the conflict, as the considered desire of the pontiff became to seize Italy from the German party at whatever cost and to drive the emperor from the peninsula. Such armed interventions as German expeditions and papal crusades thus periodically fostered party warfare. If they radically altered the balance of power, such actions by an aggressive faction easily gained the victory when opposed by a counter-party operating without reinforcements.

Imperial vicars and podestàs were also important in party warfare. Otto IV of Brunswick entered Brescia in April 1210, imposed his peace, and nominated Thomas of Turin as podestà.[104] The desire to impose a hierarchy of leaders and faithful followers as imperial officers and a solid administrative organization upon every town, not only those which had fought and then submitted, but also upon those allied with the emperor in northern and central Italy, undoubtedly inspired the policy of Frederick II. This form of action varied tremendously according to area and circumstances, but it originated in the early accomplishments of Frederick Barbarossa and the first Hohen-staufen.[105] It always shows the desire to provide an institutional framework within which the forces of the imperial party might operate during times of waning German influence and while the emperor and his army were absent.[106]

Frederick II tried first of all to install a friendly podestà, appointed by himself, at the head of each commune, as his already legendary grandfather had done. The podestà, a municipal magistrate closely involved with the life of the city, was endowed with judicial powers and was leader of the only armed force. Placed above all other officers as a judge, he could easily influence municipal policy, favour the imperial party, and guarantee the alliance. Since this official already existed in many cities, the emperor had only to appoint a loyal person and support him for some years thereafter. But this crass form of imperial intervention miscarried on several occasions. At Florence the podestà Guglielmo Vento, who came from a Genoese family with Ghibelline leanings, had to withdraw before the Guelf champion, the Milanese Rubaconte di Mandello, who was so popular that the citizens gave his name to the next bridge built upstream across the Arno. Ten years later, in February 1246, Frederick II imposed his natural son Frederick of Antioch as podestà, but the latter could only assume his position after terrible winter battles in a town half demolished by a formidable army. Likewise the imperial envoy, the archbishop of Magdeburg, had the Cremonese Gerardo de Dovaris designated podestà at Piacenza. This choice immediately provoked a rising by all the knights "who swore that they would not consider this Gerardo podestà or rector, that they would not make any oath to him, and that they would not deal with his emissary". These knights then supported as podestà Giacomo de Burgo, who was also from Cremona, and who in the end was generally accepted.[107]

Elsewhere, especially in northern Italy, in the city suburbs and the countryside, the emperor installed a genuine territorial administration in the form of enormous districts which in certain respects resembled the 'marches' of the *regnum*. Most of these well-defined territorial vicariates were instituted in 1239 and 1240. On 1 May 1239 Frederick II created a vicariate of Venetia, whose capital he established at Padua, and another called *Papie inferius*, which centred on Cremona. Their powers far transcended the sphere of authority of the town. The choice of novel titles shows clearly the emperor's desire to subordinate the political order of the city to a much more extensive and perhaps more stable organization. Ezzelino da Romano was called "vicar and lord of the cities of Padua, Vicenza, Verona, and also of Trent, Feltre, and Brescia".[108] These appointments were at first for a term of years, but soon came to be held for life.

Finally we find a third type of imperial institution and activity: the organization of permanent armed forces as units of command and castle guards. These responsibilities were entrusted to powerful nobles who were sometimes already imperial vicars. In 1237 the same Ezzelino da Romano in his capacity as leader of the Ghibellines of Verona was twice called *capitaneus* or *capitaneus et consiliarius partis imperii*. He was to command all the supporters of the emperor in the towns of his district, thus relying on armed force to administer a vast territory. Ezzelino rendered a judgement in the same year "by virtue of the imperial authority with which we are invested in this region". He could appoint podestàs. In 1238, by virtue of this imperial investiture and evidently by direct order of the emperor, he ejected Simone de Chieti, podestà of Verona, and installed Aldobrandino Cacciaconte as head of the Ghibelline party. Ezzelino also tried to violate municipal traditions by appointing one podestà for two towns, Padua and Vicenza. This policy was effective for a time, but it was dangerous nonetheless and fraught with important implications. The establishment of vast vicariates could prepare the territorial basis of future 'seigneuries', and these multiple offices and superior powers entrusted to great nobles increased their power and prestige. When the imperial presence weakened, Ezzelino da Romano tried to govern alone and assert his own rule. One Buoso de Dovara, appointed "podestà, lord, and rector of the castle of Soncino" for a two-year term in 1248 and simultaneously podestà of the castle of San Giorgio of Uceis (Orzinuovi), retained these functions for life by proclamation of the citizens of Soncino in 1255. On a much larger scale, at Cremona and Piacenza, the marquis Oberto Pallavicino, already appointed "captain of our triumphant army" by Frederick II in 1250, received the title "by the grace of God podestà, captain general, and vicar of all Lombardy . . . in the name of the lord Conrad" in 1251, after the great emperor had died. He sought the traditional investiture by the communes and installed his relatives in several cities, particularly Brescia, but even at Milan.[109]

These imperial innovations and interventions in themselves thus furthered a new form of territorial and political organization in northern Italy. In any event they aided the establishment of the authority of powerful lords who were increasingly emancipated from any kind of subjection or allegiance to a higher authority. When the general council of the Ghibellines of Lombardy met at Soncino in 1318 and named Cangrande della Scala "captain general of the Ghibelline party to make war against all their opponents", neither the emperor nor his emissaries were mentioned.[110]

The Lombard leagues merit particular attention. The popes obviously used one means of action in the papal states and another in dealing with the outside world.[111] Their intervention beyond their own borders was naturally much less direct, relying more on the cities, which were organized into communes, and on their bishops. The essential purpose of papal policy was to maintain close alliances and to form and support leagues of the Church party, of which the first Lombard League of 1167–1183 affords the most spectacular example.[112]

The success of Pope Alexander III, in Lombardy of all places, where imperial influence had been very strong, was undoubtedly due to the reaction of the towns to the destruction of Milan in 1162 and to Frederick Barbarossa's demands. Verona, Vicenza, and Padua formed a first alliance against him beginning in 1164. In 1167, after Milan had been rebuilt, a union was formed which centred on Cremona, which until then had sided with the imperial party. In the same year the fusion of these two groups, led by Verona and Cremona, resulted in the establishment of the Lombard League. The League at first included sixteen towns whose consuls took an oath, which was renewed in 1170. It included as many as thirty-six cities at one time, naturally sustained several defections, and was weakened by many conflicting interests. But the League still created a common council and named two consuls. It founded the new town of Alexandria to bar the route of German invaders toward Rome, and in 1176 it inflicted a crushing defeat on the imperial army at Legnano. Representatives of twenty-four cities sealed the truce of Venice the following year.

On the surface, the first Lombard League thus appears to be a remarkable triumph of the Church party. But the role and influence of the pope himself are hard to trace. The peace of 1183, concluded with the emperor outside Italy at Constance, was arranged against the wishes of Rome by the communes, which were disappointed by the pope's attitude and already annoyed by his ambitions. Actually, this league is more indicative of the movement for autonomy among the cities of the north than of close fidelity to the papacy.[113] This situation becomes much clearer subsequently. Good examples are the second Lombard League, which was formed against Frederick II in 1226 and was annihilated at Cortenuovo in 1237, and especially the famous Guelf League, created in the time of Charles of Anjou, maintained and reinforced by Pope Urban IV, and prolonged with many vicissitudes for a century until 1376. The pope acted only as an ally in these bonds and leagues, in which the autonomy and then the genuine independence of the great merchant cities of northern and central Italy was asserted so strikingly.

Thus, we may question whether these papal–imperial rivalries had a truly decisive effect on the fate of the cities. Neither the military interventions, German expeditions or papal crusades, which may have been crude but often had no long lasting result, nor the ambitions of the imperial administration, nor the diplomatic activities of the popes seem to have had a deep, permanent, and regular effect on the fundamental political life of the cities. In any case the quest for alliances and the favours granted to the friendly party would instead have furthered the autonomy of both the great lords and the cities and thus reinforced every sort of particularism.

We can make several assertions regarding the significance of these external actions and their limitations. First, hostilities broke out late and were continued by a limited force. The entire political life of Italy was not always conditioned by the papal–imperial conflict. On the contrary, the quarrel does not appear at all central to the ordinary preoccupations of the great maritime cities, which for a long time were the richest and most powerful towns and the only ones which were active in international affairs. Thus, Venice nearly always remained outside this conflict, for parties using the name of pope or emperor were exceptional there. The choice of the town in 1177 as the site for the conclusion of the truce between the Lombard League and Frederick Barbarossa shows its reputation as a neutral. Pisa and Genoa lacked this political originality or 'border character', and they could invoke no allegiance toward the Byzantine Empire. Yet they had entered the party struggles only very late and even then tentatively. On this point, the detailed study of V. Vitale for Genoa offers valuable elements and decisive conclusions.[114] While the ecclesiastical and imperial parties strongly asserted themselves in neighbouring Lombardy, the Genoese factions, which were already quite active in that city, did not claim any foreign alliance. The two Genoese party heads in 1167 belonged to the Castello and Avvocati families, which were to be in the same Guelf association later, while the della Volta, who were closely tied to the Castello, were Ghibellines. All agreed around 1200 to attack the Riviera settlements, which were protected by the emperor, and simultaneously to assault Alexandria and Tortosa, both of which were in the Lombard League. Thus, at a very late date the desire for territorial expansion outweighed all other considerations. Only in 1232, when Frederick II at the diet of Ravenna forbade the installation in the Italian cities of any podestà originating from member cities of the Lombard League, did Genoa, which had already chosen a Milanese and whose merchant convoys had been confiscated while crossing imperial territories, find itself obliged to make a choice; and this caused considerable trouble.[115] From this time on, everything was arranged around this conflict by a phenomenon of crystallization and simplification which was common enough. But these papal and imperial parties were only superimposed upon older parties of a totally different type. In any case, a chronological gap of over a century separates the towns of Lombardy and the great Ligurian city beyond the Apennines.

Secondly, an ideology was conspicuously absent. During the Investiture Controversy, between 1060 and 1100, then later during the conflict between Frederick II and Innocent IV, the emperor and the pope gained support from strong doctrinal currents, ideological arguments which were maintained and reinforced by their partisans or clerks in their entourage. But did this ideology penetrate the party politics of the Italian cities? The perspicacious analysis of M. Pacaut offers a decisive response here and clearly demonstrates the originality of the political theories which were current in the cities of northern Italy which were papal allies at the height of the conflict surrounding the first Lombard League.[116] Guelfism was in no sense an absolute loyalty to papal pretentions. On the contrary, an examination of the two oaths taken by the consuls of the cities in 1167 and 1170, the two sets of rules established for the negotiation of truces, and a selection from the *Annales* of Romuald, archbishop of Salerno, for 1167, show that the members of the League always considered the emperor the supreme sovereign of the Lombards. But they also unanimously affirmed the maintenance of Italian liberties. They refused all forms of incorporation and insisted on the importance of local autonomy and diversity. The fidelity of the citizens to the League was only demanded "according to the customs of each city". There was no question of submission to the papacy, and the connection with papal policy was more apparent than real. Subsequently, in the thirteenth century, M. Pacaut sees both the moderate Guelfs and Ghibellines espousing this same policy, while the active Ghibellines, who were extremely committed before the emperor disappeared as a viable political force, called for the total unification of Italy, and the Guelf extremists urged on the contrary the complete independence of the cities.

This lack of ideology is verified too by examining the behaviour or actual practice of the leaders of the parties which had declared themselves in principle for emperor or pope. The adherence of the great Genoese families to one faction or the other between 1230 and 1240 was determined much less by theoretical convictions than by circumstances, particular interests, accidents of all kinds which only a perfect knowledge of the local situation would allow us to ascertain. If the Spinola were later in the imperial party, this was because their territorial expansion beyond the Val Folceverra, on the other side of the Apennines, was resisted by the marquis of Gavi, and the Spinola nobles found it advisable to join the Ghibellines to obtain imperial assistance. The same is true of the Fieschi and the Doria, who were also very active in the Appenines.[117]

Throughout these interminable conflicts, this absence of ideological commitment explains tentative attachments, changing attitudes, and frequent sudden modulations everywhere. All alliances, either of pope or emperor, remained marked by uncertainty at Verona in the time of Frederick II. Between 1236 and 1238 the marquis of Este, Azzo VIII, who had been on the papal side until then, sought imperial favours and fought in Frederick II's camp beside his enemy, Ezzelino da Romano, at the battle of Cortenuovo against the Lombard League; but the Este again became allies of the Church soon after.[118]

At a still later period, this attitude sometimes only represents a label, and the jurist Bartolus of Sassoferrato (1314–1357) stated in a treatise entitled *Concerning Guelfs and Ghibellines* that in his time the two parties no longer had anything to do with the emperor. Parties in different cities having the same name might have nothing at all in common. The same man might be considered here a Guelf, there a Ghibelline.[119]

The importance of local politics was established more firmly in party quarrels as the cities gained autonomy and power. But this supremacy of local interests had already been decisively demonstrated at the height of pontifical and imperial power. This was true very early, at Rome in the time of the Ottonians and the *renovacio imperii.* On this subject, P. Toubert flatly denies the existence of imperial or papal parties at Rome between 960 and 1040.[120] He shows the weakness of imperial interventions in Roman life. Rome "had never been the goal of a vital political ambition". Otto I made only brief stops at Rome; he avoided the patrimony of St Peter and convened diets or imperial synods outside the papal city. His coronation in 962 and that of Otto II in 967 were occasions of violent outbursts of xenophobia which show the deep linguistic and cultural gulf between the two peoples. The Romans always refused to recognize Pope Leo VIII (died 965), who had been nominated as their pope by the emperor. Certainly the ambitions of Otto III seem totally different: witness the construction of a new palace on the Palatine, the creation of an imperial court with aulic titles, and the installation of Gerbert of Aurillac as Pope Sylvester II in 999. But this program disappeared after 1002, when these two sovereign allies died, and it was only "a short and inconsequential episode". Italy was then only a *Nebenland* for German historians. The emperor's occasional presence in Rome at this time, particularly for his coronation, "certainly allowed the formation of strange but ephemeral alliances" and "unstable convergences of interests", but not the maintenance of a solidly united party. "Interrupted momentarily by the inopportune appearance of the emperor, the course of local politics resumed all the more vigorously for having briefly looked the other way." "In this complicated game which the aristocratic clans so enjoyed, the Romans always got the better of the royal killjoys."

Matters had certainly evolved considerably over the centuries. Subsequent emperors, particularly the two Fredericks, were more active in Lombardy. But we must wonder whether this last conclusion of P. Toubert, who emphasizes the primordial importance of local interests, cannot be applied to all milieus for all periods when parties called imperial and ecclesiastical confronted each other. J.K. Hyde shows clearly that all thirteenth-century chronicles of the vicinity of Padua draw the same lesson from the events and the dissolution of alliances: the quarrels between pope and emperor were scarcely considered, and adherence to these two causes was always subordinated to the imperatives of local politics. These authors even regarded

Frederick II as the dupe of Ezzelino da Romano, who had used the Empire to conquer and hold Padua and even the entire march of Verona against the Este.[121]

Thus, the emphasis which historians have constantly placed on the duel between empire and papacy is undoubtedly the product of a very personal and even erroneous viewpoint. These foreign interventions and alliances were certainly important. They were active and sometimes decisive forces, but they do not explain everything. The very early affirmation of particularism is an essential element which we must not forget. Political parties seem above all to be instruments for the conquest of local power.

Internal rivalries.   Parties and power within the city

This struggle for power within the city seems to be by far the strongest force behind and the most certain reason for the existence of the parties. It unceasingly dominated all political life in the towns and even in the countryside of central and northern Italy. It explains clearly the permanence of these parties and their violent and sometimes bloody clashes, even at times when pope and emperor had just concluded a lasting peace, and later also when their influence in Italy seemed very weak and their hold crumbling. It also explains the fluidity and instability of these political pressure and action groups, the constant alteration of leaders and prominent members, the complexity of recruitment of membership, and our difficulty in defining their composition and structures adequately.

The parties corresponded, then, to a true system of government which, as we have seen, reflected a precise goal: to seize the offices and magistracies and to monopolize power in all its forms and in all areas. It was power or exile for each party, total victory or at least the temporary loss of all influence and even of all their property in the town for the leaders. This explains the superfluity of more than two parties. There can be no division among those who rule, and there is total union in a single bloc of all who are excluded and hope for a sensational revenge. The party régime was maintained for centuries, although it was attacked by determined adversaries who wanted to impose totally different forms of government which would rely on a more regular and flexible division of preferments, responsibilities, and profits. It disappeared at very different times in different cities and regions, and not without serious convulsions, numerous reversions to old ways, and resurgences when everything again was submitted to the parties. Political customs in certain regions were not completely emancipated from these traditions until the very end of the fifteenth century, and even later the party régime, then called the 'colours', still dominated every choice and action and became a genuine institution.

We must first investigate the nature of party rule in the city. From the very first years of the communal period, when a certain administrative autonomy had been attained, the town had constantly witnessed several powerful family groups confronting one another, but they had then coalesced very rapidly into two parties which fought violently and with no possibility of compromise.

The testimony of contemporary authors must be noted carefully. Modern historians have particularly or even exclusively emphasized the external conflicts between papacy and empire. This explanation has the advantage of presenting a very simple, easily accessible model whose elements, defined by important works, are well known. This uncomplicated scheme also satisfies their and their readers' principal interests in diplomatic and military history, in ideas and ideologies, in the origins of Italian nationalism, indeed even those of a certain sort of European consciousness. The almost total disregard of social and political structures within the Italian cities and their astonishing complexity would discourage the best of intentions and might explain this choice. But contemporary authors were not so deceived. All understood very well and constantly emphasized that the chief goal of these conflicts was political rivalry for the government of the city. We have first the theorists, jurists and authors of political treatises, who were not content merely to observe and describe but tried to explain events and phenomena. Certain of them even present in their own fashion a philosophy or a system of political ethics. Bartolus of Sassoferrato (1314–1357), whom we have already seen deny the importance of the dichotomy of papacy versus empire in his treatise *Concerning Guelfs and Ghibellines,* insists on defining parties in terms of obtaining and holding offices.[122] Giovanni Villani mentions several times what he and many others call the *gara degli uffici* when he investigates the origins of the quarrels between Whites and Blacks and especially when he tries to explain their permanence. Marchione

Stefani, a Florentine author writing around 1385, says clearly that every faction or party has for a long time had only one cause: this *gara* (competition) to monopolize offices. At Florence, he says, the parties were not established in the time of Frederick II, when the names Guelf and Ghibelline became prominent, but rather earlier, under Frederick Barbarossa, when the Uberti with their clan and allies vied with the other great families to dominate the consulship. The murder of a leader, Buondelmonte, only accentuated an internal division which had already been quite marked.[123] D. Herlihy notes that the chroniclers at Pistoia always emphasize the race for municipal offices, this *gara degli uffici*: such, for example, was Dino Compagni, who noted that in the 1350s "the town, governed unjustly, fell into a new peril, for the body of citizens began to split as they sought offices".[124]

In the narratives themselves, the most ingenuous writer always notes the importance of this competition by his vocabulary and choice of expressions, but draws no lessons from the situation. The Genoese chroniclers, Caffaro and his continuators, show clearly that throughout the twelfth century in their town the parties were thinking only of this competition and not at all of pope and emperor. Only family rivalries, grudges and vendettas, and even more the desire to dominate others, mattered there: "all the nobles wanted to be consuls".[125] The expressions of Giovanni Villani are more meaningful. He saw the parties and sects of Florence dividing along lines of one group governing and the other not, at all times in the history of his city and especially when the quarrel between the Whites and the Blacks was at its height. The expression 'those who govern' (*quelli che reggeano*) recurs constantly in his chronicle. Thus, for the single year 1324, in speaking of different social milieus, he says that "certain leaders of the great and of the people who governed the city of Florence had fallen out"; "and thus, for those of the ruling clique as for those who did not govern"; "one of the sects and parties of the people, those who did not govern the city"; and finally "one of those people who have not ruled".[126] These expressions moreover are more precise, showing still more the extent and exclusiveness of power for the early period of the struggle of Whites against Blacks and the appearance of these new parties between 1300 and 1304. "For fear of losing their position, those of the White party who controlled the city government . . ."; or again, "the pope caused to appear twelve of the greatest leaders of the Guelf and Black party, who managed the government of Florence".[127]

Actual practice confirms the chroniclers' general statements. An analysis of the situation at Florence at the turn of the fourteenth century shows clearly the absolute, intransigent character of the struggle. The party in power attempted to preserve it totally, refusing any division, trying by all means to forbid its adversaries any access to offices, even a participation deprived of responsibility. The Guelfs had held the town firmly for a long time, and the installation of a college of priors in 1292 in no way weakened their power, which rested on other bases. The most active Ghibellines were thus in exile. But the Guelfs were suffering internal divisions even in 1292. The two factions formed new parties which somewhat later assumed the names of Whites and Blacks. These two parties alternated in power: Whites in 1292–1295, Blacks in 1296–1299, Whites again in 1299, but then a sort of precarious compromise was reached when the priors managed to drive the principal leaders of both parties from the city. Villani discusses these difficult and particularly troubled years at length. His testimony describes very well the attitude of each party when it was in power. The Guelfs were all unhappy at the beginning of the quarrel.

Because of the aforementioned innovations and of the two sects of the Black and White parties, men feared that because of these sects and the quarrel between them the Ghibelline party would return to Florence, for it had already shown that intention, and many gentlemen from their side had begun to obtain offices for themselves under the pretext of good government.

To avoid this promotion of their traditional foes into office, the Guelfs had to unite. Hence the parties appealed to the pope.

Shortly thereafter, the rivalry of Whites and Blacks came to outweigh all other matters, and the papal legate, Cardinal Matthew of Acquasparta, a Franciscan friar, could not maintain harmony. The Whites, who were then the stronger side, refused to compromise and allied with the exiled Ghibellines[128] against the Church, which had given its business to the banking houses of the Blacks. Thus, two factions were reconstituted, and this remained the customary political régime for two centuries. Total rivalry did not allow the existence of three factions.

This monopoly of offices by one party was the rule in all the cities and the countryside of northern and central Italy, but it could come about by diverse means, as is shown by the serious political crisis of 1313–1315 at Orvieto. The Guelfs, who had been temporarily exiled, returned to their city in 1313 with the aid of armed contingents from Perugia. Two successive constitutions were then imposed, but each involved a total monopoly of offices by the victorious party. First, the seven consuls of the guilds then in office were replaced by the Five, who were magistrates for a term of one month. In the beginning all the Five were Guelfs, and at the end of each term the Five chose a *balia* of eight members who named the next Five, thus establishing genuine cooptation. Actually, the composition of the college had been fixed for fourteen months of the twenty-eight of its existence, and it appears certain that all the great Guelf families were represented among the Five during this time.

This first government foundered over a quarrel with the papacy, and when the revolt against the papal vicar failed disastrously, the *popolo* and the consuls of the guilds were re-established on 14 December 1315. But there were cries of "Long live the Guelf *popolo*" in the town. Actually, this *popolo guelfe* supervized the similarly Guelf Five, and the party held all power securely in its hands. It was necessary to belong to the *parte guelfa* to hold even the lowest office. All its members or adherents enjoyed important fiscal advantages. The Ghibellines who were allowed to live in the town had to pay double the amount charged the Guelfs for each category of taxpayer in a forced loan of 1320. The Guelf commune sold confiscated Ghibelline property and used the money for its own expenses and to buy grain to distribute to the poor.[129]

In the foothill villages of Venetia, far from Orvieto, this political monopoly was organized just as stringently and was virtually put into institutional form. The parties there were identified as alliances of several exceptionally prominent families. Three family groups at Feltre, two at Agordo and four at Belluno reserved for themselves the unilateral right to exercise administrative responsibilities or to entrust them to 'friends'. At Belluno there was also the imposition of the *rotuli*, rolls upon which the members of the principal house of each family party were inscribed with the leaders of friendly families. Each might sell his office to another member of the kindred or faction.[130]

This *gara degli uffici* held the attention particularly of the Tuscan chroniclers. In every town, one party acquired power and excluded the other completely from the conduct of public business. When the Raspanti seized power at Pisa in the 1340s and maintained it until the revolution of December 1347, "the other sect did not govern and held no office of the commune".[131] Around 1330, Siena lived under a kind of constitution drawn up toward 1300 which imposed a harsh régime on the city under the aegis of a single party, the Guelfs. A significant number of rubrics (355–411) of this general statute speak of societies and companies created to maintain order, and of the organization of the militia. Each man holding an office in one of these companies had to swear that he was Guelf. The commune moreover raised a corps of 5,000 peasants in 1302 who were to be "faithful and friendly to the holy Roman Church and to the peace of the commune of Siena".[132]

At Florence, a city more turbulent than others and one which often lent tone to political affairs, the intransigence of the Guelfs in power was shown strikingly on at least two occasions. When a group of French knights brought reinforcements on Christmas night, 1267, and the exiled Guelfs returned to power as masters, "the intransigent domination of a single party" appeared at once. The Ghibellines were excluded from all offices. The Guelfs governed through six captains (one for each division of the city), all of them nobles; a secret council (the *credenzia*) of fourteen Guelf nobles; a great council of sixty members; and a series of officers, the most important of whom had been chosen from persons who had denounced the Ghibellines and continued to inform on them to their own party. Six priors administered the confiscated property.[133]

The Guelfs were still ruling Florence in 1346, but the news of the election of Charles IV of Luxembourg as emperor disquieted them. They feared that the Ghibellines would return. The men in power accused others in the party of insufficient vigilance. The contents of the purses, in which the names of those were placed who might be drawn by lot to occupy offices, had not been unmixed, for some Ghibelline names had been inserted against the Guelfs' will. Certain persons also said that for the purpose of infiltrating these bags the Ghibellines had concealed their true identity by posing as artisans eligible to hold office. Hence a brutal reaction and reinforcement of the exclusions occurred. No Ghibelline who was the son of a rebel, who had rebelled since 1300, or who had lived on the land of rebels might hold an office. If he were chosen, he or his electors were to pay a fine of 1,000 florins, on pain of his life. No one might hold office if he were not "considered a true Guelf and a friend of the party of holy Church". The fine was 500 florins for the offender and 1,000 florins for the judge who failed to convict him. Proof of membership in the party could be given by the oath of six witnesses approved by the council of the guilds or by the priors. Several artisans were indicted and convicted because of this crude exclusiveness, and, Villani continues, "other citizens refused to hold offices for fear of being condemned or receiving insulting treatment, and others were summoned in their place".[134]

The same extremely harsh policy was pursued in Arezzo in the same year. The Guelfs thought "that too many Ghibellines were involved in the offices and government of the city . . . and that the Ghibellines should no longer be eligible to be chosen by lot as rectors or officials".[135] This refusal to share power occurred everywhere: the purses for drawings by lot could only contain the names of men in power.

This party régime necessarily met strong resistance. Wherever it existed, it evolved and underwent significant changes in the course of time. All regions of Italy, towns and countryside, sooner or later, permanently or temporarily, and under very different forms, knew personal power, tyranny, or rather, according to the vocabulary of the time, personal lordship.

What were the tyrants' relations with the parties? Was there 'popular' tyranny, outside the party structure? The town lord who succeeded in controlling all the public offices was already a powerful personality who disposed of considerable executive powers. He had fiefs and castles and a large body of followers if not a personal armed force. He was a captain who could rely on alliances with foreign princes or neighbouring tyrants. Within the city itself moreover his tyranny might rest on a very broad social stratum, for beyond his own clientele the master attracted and held the favour of the poor people who were constantly mobilized on his behalf by his prestige and by his various acts of generosity.

Yet these tyrannies "on the ancient model" which were imposed by direct contact with the population, without the assistance of intermediary bodies and thus without the help of great families and parties, had only a precarious and tumultuous existence in the Italian merchant cities. They lasted only briefly and resulted in resounding reverses after a few months. Orvieto witnessed the tyranny of Ermanno Monaldeschi, himself head of a faction and member of a great clan of the city. He came to power in 1334 with the help of his brother, who was a great lord and master of fiefs in the mountains. He also relied on an alliance with Perugia, on several wealthy merchants, and especially on the poor people, who were won over by frequent grain doles. But he fell from power quickly when faced with increasing troubles of all kinds. Tyrants subsequently succeeded one another without interruption for twenty years until 1354. All were equally incapable of resisting their opponents, and party warfare raged worse than ever.[136]

Another rather more spectacular and better known example of total failure was Walter of Brienne, duke of Athens, who was chosen lord of Florence for life in 1342. Giovani Villani describes him as installed "by the favour of great and small alike", but the circumstances of his rise to power show clearly that the assistance of the poorest people was fundamental. It was a real mass movement, with acclamations stirred up through the streets of the city. The duke took power "at the call of the people", and "certain journeymen wool carders, some of the poorest plebeians and some retainers of a few powerful men began to cry 'Long live the duke's régime'". This reference to the poorest of the lower classes and the use of a pejorative term loaded with scorn and reproof (*popolazzo minuto*) seem extremely significant here. As soon as Walter had taken control of the city, "the poor people had great joy". His popularity seems to have been one of the chief sources of his political activity: "whenever the duke rode on horseback through the city, everyone followed him crying out 'Long live the lord duke', and his coat of arms was painted on nearly every house and palace in Florence".[137]

Even the government of the duke of Athens relied constantly on the poor. A few weeks after he had come to power, he took away all the offices from the great men and the companies of the *popolo* and gave them to tripesellers, wine merchants, carders, and all kinds of *artefici minuti*, "giving them the offices of consuls and rectors according to their wish, breaking for them the guild regulations to which they had been subjected so that they could obtain a better wage for their labours".[138] This resolutely 'popular' policy, deliberately demagogic in many ways, and taking no account of traditional institutions and political action groups, provoked a lively opposition in various noble and merchant circles and gave rise to a number of plots. Hence parties uniting the discontented were formed around prominent persons who were frustrated by and hostile to the duke's policies. Giovanni Villani says that there were "three sects and conspiracies"[139] of parties which were preparing a revolution in the city when the duke was overthrown in the summer of 1343.

The party might, however, be the tyrant's mainstay. The tyrannies were personal lordships which could not last without the support of powerful, hierarchical parties which assembled vast clienteles. In this sense, the triumph and preservation of a tyrant seems quite simply the particularly spectacular success of one of the two parties which vied for power in the city. The other party was displaced during the tyrant's sway.

This is a very old tradition, for we find an example of it as early as the government of the noble popes during the *Adelspapsttum* régime at Rome between 960 and 1040. According to the detailed analysis of P. Toubert, the mechanism of power rested there on the ancestral rivalry of the Crescenzi and Tuscolani parties. The Crescenzi completely monopolized power until 1000; their family party imposed a genuine diarchy in the leadership of the city: the pope (a *Familienpapst* for the German historians) and a patrician, a dynast of the Crescenzi *gens*. The office of patrician disappeared later under the Tuscolani. The *palatium* was then monopolized by a group which was much more restrained than the Crescenzi, but this was only an alternative form of the same political régime of personal lordship based on a party of family origin.[140]

The subsequent history of the Italian merchant cities also offers many examples of powerful personalities cornering all authority, ruling as tyrants, and maintained in power with the help of parties which assembled strong clienteles. Of course, these tyrannies demonstrate different characteristics, but whatever the social status of the leader, the political process remained the same. The earliest tyrants were lords of fiefs who based their power essentially on vassalic bonds of fealty and on a party held together by acts of homage, the ties of man to man. This projection of 'feudal' political customs into the city moreover shows the close ties which bound rural and urban societies. The bishop Arderico ruled Lodi in the twelfth century. To attract a large following, he alienated the most important part of the episcopal patrimony in fief to vassals, many of them his relatives. Thus, we see "the growth of a party of vavasours and captains" in the city.[141] A similar case occurred a century later at Bassano, where the successive tyrannies of the da Romano took root without interruption. Certainly these lords retained ordinary municipal institutions, particularly the council of forty members and the chief city magistrates, the two *marici* and the two *giurati*. They did, however, shamelessly rig the elections. Between 1220 and

1260 we find sixty men of the *masnada* of the da Romano among the occupants of these two essential magistracies, as well as certain notaries. Actually, the entire commune, particularly under the tyranny of Ezzelino da Romano (about 1230–1260), was dominated by this warrior band, this *masnada* made up of fighters who received fiefs and municipal offices simultaneously from their lord and who guaranteed the loans of the commune on their patrimonies and drew attention to their social standing by sumptuous habits.[142]

These relations between tyrant and party were altered later, just as the nature of the political group or party was changing. The members, the faithful followers, were undoubtedly more numerous and were drawn from much more varied social backgrounds. They were no longer bound to the lord by vassalic homage, but by acts of fidelity, allegiances of a more 'political' but also less certain character. Such was the case, for example, at Pisa, which in 1340 witnessed a sort of double tyranny in the government of two personalities, Messer Dino and the count della Rocca. These leaders introduced into the city faithful followers from their district, a force whose support allowed them to govern and who, "together with other partisans of the people", formed a party or sect called the *Raspanti.* Their opponents, the *Bergolini,* drove them out on the night of 24 December 1340 with cries of "Long live the *popolo* and liberty", but this new party in power merely installed a second *signoria,* "and Andreà Gambacorti and his followers became its lords".[143]

The city tyrants were sometimes rich businessmen who had come to power after a calculated and patient conquest of all political institutions. Even more than the original 'feudal' lords, they based their power on a political party of faithful adherents who had been bought by money and the promise of benefits. At Bologna around 1300 one Romeo Pepoli was "a great and powerful citizen and nearly lord of the town, with all his following. He called himself the richest man in Italy, but had acquired nearly all his money by usury. He had more than 20,000 florins of annual income apart from his personal property." He attracted the urban poor by his acts of generosity, protected criminals who became his clients, and constantly used corrupt practices to surround himself with a large party. Driven out in 1321, he fled to the marquis of Este, to his relatives at Ferrara, then to Avignon. His lands were confiscated and his houses destroyed, but his heirs returned later. Taddeo Pepoli became lord of Bologna in 1336–1337, and after him his sons, who had coins called *pepolesche* struck, governed in the same way through their party.[144]

A similar development occurred somewhat later at Florence, when the power of the Medici (or, more exactly, that of the elder Cosimo against the Albizzi and the Strozzi) was established from 1430 onwards. Cosimo relied on his brothers and his intimates who formed *una cerchia di seguaci* (a circle of followers) around him. These men, led by Puccio Pucci, a man of modest birth who had been given an office in 1429, were thus called the Puccini. Their influence seemed quite modest at first, but when Cosimo, after being driven briefly from the city, returned from exile in November 1434, he no longer governed through Pucci alone, but also by means of a party which, apart from the Puccini, included from this time great families and their leaders (Agnolo Acciaiuoli, Neri Cappani). The lesser offices were then systematically bestowed upon men of low station, a practice which allowed them fine opportunities for social advancement and kept them faithful to the party.[145] In establishing and maintaining the personal lordships of both noble and merchant tyrants in every town, the rule and power of the parties were thus certainly involved. They were an indispensable political power and were rewarded by the offices which were the major stakes in all competition.

The constant wars, which caused damage, loss of life, and destruction of houses, weakened many great families. Above all, they troubled the peace of the town in a manner dangerous for the conduct of business, and provoked a lively disaffection and feelings of rebellion among those who remained excluded. Hence risks were constantly taken to see other types of government established than that of the parties, perhaps more stable régimes in which responsibilities would be divided more evenly. These fears of letting power escape them, pressures of all sorts, and the influence of the peace movements explain why the leaders of the two parties sometimes sought agreements which, while reserving the offices for their respective clienteles, would avoid violent clashes.

These agreements were frequently limited to a few offices. Often too they were only temporary and established a precarious peace, such as at Bologna in 1265[146] and at Pisa in 1355, where thirty Raspanti and thirty Bergolini were entrusted with the task of compiling a new list of the Ancients, but this group was to be exiled four months later.[147] Division of offices was proposed at Florence in 1300 by the papal legate and in 1324 the leaders agreed that the names of magistrates should be drawn by lot every six months "by mixing the names of the sect who had governed the city from the time of Count Battifole until now with some of those who had not governed".[148] A very exact division was made which thus left the two parties their individuality. Florence moreover had to intervene several times in neighbouring towns to impose a solution of this kind, such as at Pistoia, which was seriously rent by factional warfare. In 1373, 1376, and 1393 the Florentine magistrates decided to institute a revision of the arrangements for drawing lots for offices at Pistoia. Thenceforth two separate purses would be provided, one for the *compagna di San Paolo* (Panciatichi party) and another for the *compagna di San Giovanni* (Cancellieri party). The names of the new officers of the commune would be taken from each of these in turn.[149] These equitable measures certainly show some desire for peace, but also a wish to preserve the party régime. They were only in force briefly; the conflicts soon began anew, and other political formulas finally carried the day.[150]

Yet one city, Genoa, maintained the party régime throughout the medieval period, undoubtedly as a result of the permanence of divided authority which became a genuine institutional custom. Quattrocento Genoa still lived under the regular régime of parties, called Whites and Blacks after their colours. Drawing by lot was equally divided between purses which contained only names of the same colour. This was true for all levels of administrative and political functions as well as for offices reserved for 'nobles' or *popolani*. Among the *popolani* some places were reserved for both merchants and artisans. The Council of the Ancients, composed of eight members who rotated every four months, included two Black and two White nobles and one merchant and one artisan from each party. This division was established on all levels, for the podestàs, consuls, officers of tolls and weights, and the judges who administered the Riviera villages which were under Genoese authority. The procedures established in the distant colonies in the East differed only slightly from those of the homeland and demonstrate even more forcefully the desire to respect the principle of equal distribution of offices. There the isolation and the small number of positions, together with the absence of colleges and councils, made a true annual division of offices difficult. Hence the rule was alternation: all officers were Blacks one year and Whites the next. Only the administration of the *Casa di San Giorgio*, a very special type of institution which administered taxes and superintended commerce, escaped this party régime. But the *Casa* was not a political institution, and the party leaders were not interested in it.[151]

The situation at Genoa was certainly exceptional, perhaps unique and archaic. It could only take root where no other form of political life had been established. But it remains true that in all other cities and regions of Italy, forms of government which were hostile to the parties only materialized later and were victorious only after some checks and reversions to the traditional patterns of conflict. The race for power seems all-important and must be considered the chief motive force of all the parties.

CHAPTER FOUR

Economic rivalries and pressures

Many historians who are aware of the importance of conflicts of interest in acquiring markets are naturally tempted to see the origin of the parties in economic rivalries or even in the clash of two social categories or 'classes'. This is particularly true of the adherents of certain models or familiar patterns who make a dogma of historical materialism. This explanation was able to achieve credibility or at least merit close attention during a period when the economic side of events came to be emphasized deliberately, in particular between 1930 and 1960. Historians of this time saw all conflicts as an opposition between clearly defined social groups which were engaged in mortal combat. The validity of such explanations which concentrate on economic rivalries between individuals or companies, or indeed on a class struggle, varies with the individual work, but neither viewpoint, particularly that of class conflict, can be accepted without extensive analysis of social divisions and thereby of the composition of the parties.

Economic rivalries and weapons

The conflict between the great merchant societies or companies in Lombardy and later in Tuscany certainly left a significant imprint upon the entire social and political life of the cities. The problems of the companies, their bankruptcies and collapses, and the triumph of newly successful associations show how precarious their situation was, conditioned by constant change, together with the sometimes striking instability of their institutions and personnel. Several Italian authors, nobably Armando Sapori, have made especially thorough studies, and Yves Renouard has left us a remarkable description of these rivalries between Tuscan towns, between Florentine companies, and even between 'generations' of companies which attracted different clienteles and often emphasized divergent styles, but which were united by the same desire to prevail.[152]

The commercial rivalries obviously engendered alliances, as each side sought clienteles and external support. The opposing blocs might thus to some extent constitute the framework of the parties. The intervention of the pope, whose orders and clientele were a source of considerable wealth for the bankers, could guide one's choice of party and disturb a political equilibrium. The papacy had used this weapon liberally from the 1260s. Urban IV exerted terrific pressure with a striking constancy from 1261 on the leaders of the Ghibelline league to change sides. He was a native of Champagne who was keenly aware of the financial problems and weaknesses of the Tuscan merchant companies. At that time, after the triumph of the imperial party at Florence, the league included some ten towns, among them Siena, Pisa, and Florence. In January 1263 Urban excommunicated the Sienese bankers, his usual clients, and freed the clergy from the obligation to pay their debts to these companies. Buonsignori and Salimbene soon submitted to the pope. A serious crisis a year later, the threat of spectacular business failures, led 110 merchant and banking families, including the powerful Tolomei, to leave Siena, take refuge at Chiusi or Radicofani, and swear allegiance to the pope.

At the same time, the pope similarly threatened the assets of the Florentines who had loaned considerable sums to the bishops of France, Italy, and England. On 12 August 1263 the envoy of the great Scali company came to Orvieto to swear obedience to His Holiness. He promised to combat Manfred, impound all accounts of the pontiff's political opponents, and inform the pope of other companies' affairs. Urban IV aggravated this pressure and had all property in transit across his lands seized. This forced the Florentine merchants to ally with Roman businessmen to escape the guards. In this way the pope within two years received the submission of 146 associates of various

Florentine business companies. They in turn collected huge sums in 1265 by transfer from the Champagne fairs to Lombardy and Rome to finance the expedition of Charles of Anjou.

The voluntary exile of the bankers who left Siena and Florence seriously weakened the Ghibelline party in those cities, and the popes' action increased the power of the Guelf exiles, thus paving the way for their return as masters of Florence on Christmas night, 1267. The triumph of the Guelf party can be explained only as the consequence of papal economic and financial pressures.

Economic rivalries to secure papal business also played a considerable role in the later establishment and composition of the White and Black parties at Florence. Papal patronage was limited in 1294 to the Buonsignori of Siena, the Riccardi of Lucca,[153] and the Mozzi of Florence. But the Spini took this business away from the Mozzi and assumed leadership of the Black party of Florence with their allies, the Donati, the Pazzi, and the Medici. Then, with the Mozzi ousted and the Cerchi excluded as rivals of the Spini, the Scali came to dominate the Whites, and Vieri de' Cerchi, the head of their company, became party leader. The division of families between the two new factions thus closely reflected the economic rivalry among the great companies, which only ceased to play a political role under particularly trying circumstances in 1307, when the French pope Clement V stopped using bankers to collect tithes and transfer funds.[154]

Rich against poor?

Did parties and their conflicts originate in a division of rich against poor? The contrary is suggested by the fact that the so-called 'social' disturbances were often led by the powerful. The celebrated Ciompi revolt, which some still consider a manifestation of social conflict, class hatred, and a seizure of power by the workers, actually seems to have been provoked in large measure by the activity of the magnates, exiled members of the greatest families who were hostile to the party in power, which was called the 'peace' party. They were supported by vast clienteles in the city and the *contado*. Even if we consider only the active rebels, the Ciompi were not miserable, exploited proletarians, but rather guild masters who were often prosperous employers of labourers. This was demonstrated very convincingly several years ago by G. A. Brucker.[155]

More recently, W.M. Bowsky has furnished an equally original and precise analysis of a so-called 'social' revolt at Siena in 1311.[156] Contemporary chroniclers spoke of a conflict led by the butchers and blacksmiths, guilds which were already prosperous. But two groups were particularly hostile to the régime of the Nine at Siena. The rich banking clan of the Tolomei was excluded from the Nine, but remained very powerful in the other city magistracies and held many castles in the *contado*. Their participation in the revolt is demonstrated clearly by the fact that the Nine destroyed all their property in the city after the uprising was quelled. The judges and notaries, who were aristocrats of a type different from the Tolomei, participated even more actively. Once order was restored, the officers of the commune tried to minimize the extent of the disturbance. Thus, they spoke only of the butchers and certain notaries and not at all of the involvement of the Tolomei and the other magnates, who were their principal enemies.

Giovanni Villani provides very colourful and exact descriptions of two noteworthy examples of popular revolts incited and directed by the magnates in this same period of 'social' turmoil. The powerful men of Florence, who were hostile to the new régime of the duke of Athens in 1343, hoped to provoke mass movements and direct the poor people against him:

The Adimari, Medici, and Donati were the most conspicuous. On Saturday, St Anne's Day, 1343, when the ninth hour had sounded and the workers had left the shops, certain ruffians and men of little substance assembled by prearrangement in the forefront and cried "To arms, to arms." Thus all citizens went for their weapons, whether they fought on foot or horseback.[157]

On a second occasion, soon after the fall of the duke of Athens, "in the heavily charged atmosphere of the city there appeared an insane knight of the people, Messer Andreà degli Strozzi", a man of a very prominent family. He mounted his horse and incited the rabble, the journeymen wool carders and "likewise several thousand equally bent on rapine". He promised to make them all rich and to give them grain and power within the city ("and to make them lords"). He led them across town shouting "Long live the poor. Down with taxes and the rich". The mob reached the town hall, "saying that they wished to install messer Andreà and make him lord of the city". Thus, a 'popular' uprising was made to serve a tyrant's personal ambition. It was an absolutely mad and hopeless enterprise. After all the shouting and a few rocks thrown at the windows of the town hall, the mob was easily dispersed.[158] The street disturbances and mob violence were not clear signs of a 'class' conflict or even of a rivalry between social groups. The initiative in most such escapades came from political operatives, aristocratic party leaders.

The interpretation based on implicit economic determinism is also weakened when we realize that the 'lesser people', the urban proletariat formed of the poor, participated only rarely and in a very limited way in political life at Florence. G.A. Brucker has demonstrated that a striking degree of horizontal mobility occurred among the urban poor. In analysing two Florentine tax registers of 1378 and 1379, he noted that in one proletarian district of the quarter of Santa Croce, forty-five per cent of the poor inscribed on the lists (which excluded beggars and all kinds of wanderers on the peripheries of society) were no longer there after a year. Their political activity seems negligible, for they established no association or action group. They did not attend the local assemblies; that to choose a new parish priest attracted only twenty-five parishioners, among them seven prosperous artisans. The quorum for assemblies of city districts was a mere twenty persons.[159]

A similar situation is found at Padua, where the collateral relatives, the clients of the great families, were only admitted to the town council at a late date and even then did not participate in the sessions. The membership of the Great Council was raised to one hundred in 1449, but a pronouncement of 1504 vigorously condemned absenteeism and denounced persons of modest social rank who, "bringing scant honour to their office, go to the squares and streets, walk in the gardens, and talk among themselves instead of coming to the council".[160]

Studies based on other evidence confirm these tendencies and lead inexorably to the same conclusion: political life in the merchant cities of Italy was dominated by aristocrats throughout the medieval period. Whether directly or through their clients, they monopolized all administrative and political offices. By provoking street fights or revolts in which the 'lesser people' were encouraged to participate, they were responsible for every agitation and conflict. The disagreements between parties were the business of the aristocracy. In no way did the weak, the poor, or even the journeymen of the trades form a political party.

Nobili and *popolani*

The collision of two aristocracies of differing origin in a merciless quarrel to maintain power or acquire the major offices is another theoretical construction which has enticed all historians of the Italian towns. Several authors have shown conclusively that the first urban aristocracy was led by and composed primarily of noble families, although this contradicts standard viewpoints about the supposed 'urban revolution' of the eleventh century. But a second postulate has quickly replaced the first: the concurrent rise of a new aristocracy of commerce, enriched exclusively by trade. In this view, the conflict between 'nobles' and 'merchants' dominated and troubled all aspects of city life, in some cases as early as the 1150s. Viewing this conflict as a true class struggle within the aristocracy seems essential to the historical concept of many and is still often accepted as a self-evident truth. Institutional evolution, the coming of government by guilds and hence by implication by the 'people', and the condemnations of certain aristocrats, such as occurred at Florence with the Ordinances of Justice of 1293, were the obvious reflections of this essential division. But was the dichotomy really so clearly marked? Who were the nobles and the new merchants? To what extent did two opposing political parties reflect this antagonism?

Lombard and Tuscan chroniclers alike, in describing street combats or analysing political rivalries within the city, use the words *nobili, magnati, signori,* and *grandi* for one side and *popolani, popolo, uomini* or *maestri degli arti,* or even *mercanti* for the other. With these words, they indicate the social station of men and even parties. A fight might thus be summarized as a conflict between two factions thus designated. Hence Villani clearly presents the hostilities which bloodied Pisa in May 1322 as a fight between the great, led by the Lanfranchi, the Sismondi, and the rural lords, and the *popolo.*[161] Such an exposition is very unusual with the Tuscan authors, but appears more often with the Lombards. Here the words *pars militum* and *pars populi* appear only on a few occasions when the lines of battle were particularly well drawn and the party rested on a relatively solid base, as for example in 1257, when "the marquis Pallavicino, acting in accordance with the will of the citizens of Piacenza, by treaty with the *popolani* and their party ordered the castle of . . . destroyed".[162] The vocabulary of the sources constantly emphasizes this division of the city and the confrontation of two parties, those of the knights and of the *popolo*. To aid Milan in 1217, Piacenza sent armed reinforcements: "the knights and the people of the gates of St Bridget, Milan, and Garivertus".[163] A stereotyped form was used to describe a difficult situation which had generated troubles: "in that year there was great dissension between the knights and the people (*popolo*)".[164] This was done in reference to Piacenza itself and also for other towns; the author mentions *milites* and *paraticos* at Brescia in 1196.[165] The annals of Piacenza furnish many other examples of violent and bloody conflicts between these two factions.

We shall cite only three particularly significant examples. On the occasion of an ordinary brawl during a game at Piacenza in 1190, "a certain knight iniquitously did battle with a man on foot". The inhabitants of the town took sides between the antagonists, and "a great tumult arose between the people and the knights". The battles soon became homicidal. The knights withdrew to their castles outside the city, and this situation continued for seven months, "from February to the octave of St Michael".[166]

At Brescia, a 'popular' society of San Faustino was founded in 1200, and this development soon provoked a violent conflict with the knights, who found external allies at Cremona, Mantua, and Bergamo. The rivalry of armed factions thus became involved in foreign politics between 1201 and 1208.[167] Fortunes varied, but here too it was basically an internal quarrel in which neither pope nor emperor intervened.

Finally, the *popolares* and their societies revolted against the government of the knights at Piacenza in 1250. "Some twenty or thirty consuls of the societies of the people of Piacenza" met in the Church of San Pietro in Foro. The occasion of conflict this time was a crisis in the grain supply: certain knights and their allies outside the city were accused of diverting to Perugia the grain intended to revictual their own city.[168] We thus find confirmation in the sources of a confrontation between social groups called 'knights' and 'people', particularly in Lombardy.[169] But this in no way implies that these so neatly defined groups inevitably imposed a rigid division within their city.

A further warning against the tendency to see a social class struggle involved in the Italian party conflicts is given by the fact that many sources show knights, great men, and persons called *popolani*, "of the people", all in the same party and accordingly allied for a common course of action. The chroniclers often note the variety and complexity of the social base of membership in the two factions. Absolutely convincing proof is afforded by the testimony of an artisan noted by J. K. Hyde.[170] During an ordinary trial at Treviso in 1314, a tailor named Manfredino answered the question "What is a party?" by saying that a party existed "when some *popolani* and other persons ally with one magnate and others with another".

It is really quite easy to find such alliances in the chroniclers' narratives. Rolandino states that in the thirteenth century "a constant schism existed in the government of Verona, for not only the knights, but also the *popolani* and the merchants were divided into two parties".[171] V. Vitale, who has studied in detail the division of families between factions at Genoa, emphatically rejects the idea of a social cleavage as the basis of the *Rampini* and *Mascherati* parties between 1240 and 1260. He maintains that there was no question of a class conflict, different degrees of wealth, nor even a confrontation between old noble lines (the *visconti*) and new ones (the *consolari*), or between nobles based inside and outside the city.[172]

When the Ghibelline party, the *Lambertazzi*, was driven from Bologna in 1274, the houses of the leaders and officers of the faction were confiscated or destroyed. The commune and the victorious party made an exact record of this, and one of the registers compiled on the occasion bore the title *Magne domus nobilium et popularium*. People of widely divergent backgrounds were exiled that year,[173] such as Guido Guinicelli, three Accursiuses, and several other famous masters, who left Bologna University to seek asylum at Padua. The pope thought briefly of transferring the *studium* of Bologna to Padua after they had been joined there by their students. The Ghibelline exiles also included L. Fabruzzo, a poet renowned in his own city,[174] and the priest Azzo with many of his students, most of them foreigners.

This is rather late, and one might have expected the new aristocracy to be quite clearly established and individualized by this time. Yet contemporary Tuscan chroniclers also show how ordinary such alliances were in their cities. Luca Dominici said that "nearly all families of Pistoia, gentlemen and *popolani* alike, were divided".[175] Giovanni Villani gives particularly remarkable analyses of this state of affairs. His best example is his description of the division of families between the new White and Black parties in 1300. This list demonstrates perfectly the diversity of their recruitment. Hence among the leaders of the Whites, the Cerchi, were "all the Mozzi, whose wealth and social standing made them very powerful at that time", and "nearly all the great and powerful house of the Cavalcanti". These were nobles whose fame was of long standing and whose power was well established. But he notes that the Whites also included "all the Falconieri, who were a powerful *popolo* clan", and even "alongside them many other *popolo* families, lesser artisans as well as all the great Ghibelline *popolani*".[176] More ephemeral and unstable alliances evidently had a similar structure. One Coscetto del Colle, a party leader who was "*popolano*, a man of great valour and courage", came to power at Florence in 1322. He was defeated and driven from the town, then was taken by surprise while trying to flee to Pisa. After he was apprehended, officials of the city appeared in the countryside "trying to find members of the sect of Coscetto del Colle so that they could massacre them". Villani then mentions several nobles and *popolani* who were "members of the sect of the aforesaid Coscetto but who kept out of politics".[177] Alliances within the parties of nobles and *popolano* leaders thus seem to have been quite ordinary, and were certainly more common than parties consisting of only one of these two groups. *Nobili* and *popolani* seem to have fought each other as classes only on special and relatively rare occasions.

Social definitions indeed seem absolutely impossible in this context. We must question whether the leaders of the knights or magnates and men of the *popolo* really came from clearly differentiated social milieus. The answer is by no means clear.[178] In all Italian towns those called *popolani* belonged or seemed to belong to an aristocracy of relatively recent origin.[179] Their economic and political fortune may have gone back only to the early days of the commune. In this sense, the social cleavage was sometimes based on more than a mere intellectual abstraction. But if we study these groups when they obtained power, around 1200 in Lombardy and half a century later in Tuscany, we find no fundamental distinctions between *nobili* and *popolani*. All were merchant bankers, industrial entrepreneurs, and investors in all sorts of commerce, often at the head of great companies. All too were very wealthy and had the same life style, including a plush town house and similar dress. Finally, all possessed considerable land, great seigneurial domains, castles or manor houses whose fortification dominated an entire village. We find no clear opposition between classes nor collision between groups, each of them motivated by a particular ethos.

The *popolani* included plutocrats with clienteles in all the cities. These were often very powerful aristocrats, sometimes even knights who hoped that their behaviour or marriage alliances might link them with the titled nobles of more ancient lineage. Villani notes this quite clearly in speaking of the measures taken against the magnates at Florence in 1290: "several *popolano* families and houses were more worthy to be placed among the great than most of those already in that exalted station".[180] G.A. Brucker has remarked trenchantly that immense fortunes were amassed by artisans at Florence, while the Martelli, Gaddi, and Vespucci, all of which were powerful families in the city in the 1370s, were descended from petty artisans.[181] The *popolano* Romeo Pepoli, a Bolognese usurer and banker, party leader, and master of the arts of power, depended on the support of a numerous clientele of the poor. Villani says that "his departure terribly upset the Guelf party at Bologna".[182] This man, a powerful lord of the *popolo*, actually found asylum quite expeditiously with the marquis of Este and his family and allies at nearby Ferrara after he had been exiled in 1321 with the Beccadelli and other nobles.[183]

Piacenza also had several great *popolano* families. Including both established wealthy and *nouveaux riches*, they all had elements of noble status and lived as warriors and knights. The all-powerful Scotti family affords the best example.[184] They appeared in the 1250s and soon built up a remarkable financial and political fortune. They were merchants, of course, and accordingly belonged to the *popolo* party and quite often were its leaders. They were captains of the people of Piacenza on several occasions, and in 1321 bought the castle of Grango from the commune for £3,000 of Piacenza.[185] Another example from this city is Guillelmo de Andito, who came from a knightly noble family which included Albertino de Andito, who was called 'count' throughout his life. Guillelmo assumed the leadership of the 'party of the people' and became podestà or rector of the people in 1234 and 1235.[186] Membership in the *popolo* or even in its political party when that existed was thus not the obvious sign of a definite social station or even an indication of a particular family origin.

It is also extremely difficult for us to determine precisely the social circumstances of the great magnates. Contemporary writers, whether chroniclers, legislators, or judicial or police officers could not define exactly the peculiar quality which made one a magnate, although the word was used constantly. The Florentine Ordinances of Justice of

1293 claimed to make the magnates ineligible for all important public offices. Exceptional measures decreed their political incapacity, imposed a heavier penal code upon them than upon others, and forced them to deposit a substantial annual bond. The ordinances also established a militia, the "thousand footsoldiers of justice", to take reprisals against the property of magnates who committed crimes against *popolani*.[187] This action seems resolute and determined, but the picture becomes less simple when we examine the course of events and their consequences.

First, the most active campaigner against the magnates was a prior, Giovanni della Bella, who was related to the upper nobility of the city and was a merchant associated with the Pazzi. Thanks to these Ordinances, which he seems to have inspired directly, and the support of the *popolo*, he exercised a veritable dictatorship for two years until he fled to Paris in 1295. A tyrant of noble origin was thus acting decisively to seize power for himself.

Secondly, the leaders of the *popolo* who controlled the city found it impossible to define 'magnate' satisfactorily. A first distinction had been made from 1286 which defined as magnates all whose family had included a knight during the past twenty years. This in effect attached the status to a single external sign of minimal importance,[188] and the magnates thus defined proved inconveniently numerous. Thus, in 1293 the responsible officials decided that "all shall be considered magnates who are reputed as such", which shows a total inability to define precisely this uncertain and fluctuating social quality. The practical consequences of this move were truly singular for the magnates. The members of 147 families were classified as magnates. Seventy-four of these were obviously seigneurial lines from the *contado*, while seventy-three were from the city. Of the latter group, forty families were specifically 'nobles', while thirty-three came from the business world. The complexity of the group declared 'magnates', together with the distinction often recognized between nobles and magnates (for not all magnates were considered noble) are quite important and reflect nicely the very blurred line between social groups.[189]

Further proof is afforded by a much later example. In 1343, at the very moment when Giovanni Villani was composing his chronicle, the leaders of the *popolo* undertook a reform which moderated the Ordinances of 1293. They allowed the least wealthy and powerful magnates, those who did not seem dangerous, to become *popolani*:

"certain magnate families owning less than others and without evil intentions may be considered members of the *popolo*". Villani provides a precise analysis of these families. Some five hundred men were withdrawn from the ranks of the magnates. They included both small groups without collateral relatives or clienteles ("and other families nearly extinct") and individuals who had been reduced to very modest material circumstances ("and most prominently other families of the *contado* who had been reduced to nothing or to working the land").[190] The latter, who had been considered until then to be great men or magnates, had even lost their quality of lords, nobles, prestigious proprietors.

The dichotomy between great men or magnates or even knights on the one hand and men of the *popolo* on the other is not always evident: indeed it seems less usual than alliance within the party of persons of similar background. Nor can this dichotomy be interpreted as a conflict between two well-defined social groups. The labels were often used, but it is very difficult to ascertain their precise meanings.

CHAPTER FIVE

Neighbourhood bonds

Urban society in medieval Italy thus was not delineated exactly into two social categories or well-defined classes which opposed each other in constant conflict or in a bitter class struggle which would suffice to explain the formation of two rival parties. Economic rivalries of a more personal or familial, or indeed often accidental, character influenced the political choices of each family, group of families, or merchant company. They can furnish partial explanations for the action taken at a given moment. But the social categories were not the moulds within which all political life was shaped. The extremely powerful bonds of the neighbourhood, which often had a great influence on city life, seem to have been equally important.

Was the town divided into two irreconcilable blocs?

May we consider a separation of the Italian merchant city into two large topographical units which were resolutely hostile to each other as the origin of the parties and the prime mover of their activity? Electoral or administrative circumscriptions called thirds, quarters, or sixths were frequently human and social realities and 'solidarities'. But did these neighbourhood 'solidarities' unite into more compact blocs which corresponded to the two parties? Did each party have a particular topographical base of recruitment, or did it draw its active forces from different parts of the city?

The dichotomy of two areas, which occurs very frequently in the towns of western Europe, reflects an essential phase of urban expansion between 1100 and 1300. In Germany, for instance, the old city (*Altstadt*) was often juxtaposed to the large new settlement (*Neustadt*) which slowly developed around the market square. The cathedral and the episcopal quarter were often located outside the *Neustadt*.[191] In Languedoc and the entire French Midi, for example at Toulouse, Narbonne, and Lyon, *cité* and *bourg* similarly stood against each other in different politico-religious associations and even in bloody revolts.[192] Even if the social standing of the inhabitants did not vary greatly and if the aristocracies which dominated *cité* and *bourg* had many points in common, the two blocs seemed solid, firmly delineated bases for all political competition.

This situation was quite exceptional in Italy. In Tuscany and Lombardy, the only highly urbanized regions of the peninsula, town life was not characterized by sudden developments in which a 'new town' could rudely oppose the old quarter. The continuity of urban civilization since Roman times, the maintenance of old walls, and the permanence of the major arteries of communication all characterize the towns of Italy from the early years of the commune until the twelfth century. Urban expansion thus remained diffuse, proceeding continuously in several directions, as demonstrated by the construction of new walls. The suburbs in Italy were inchoate and always very diverse, having several nuclei of settlement which differed markedly. The scene was complex, a haze rather than a sharply defined dualism.

Even though certain large quarters naturally assumed a particular colour and at times even displayed a lively political individuality, exceptions to this general rule are very rare. The River Arno obviously held a primordial position for Pisa and Florence and was enough to produce marked differences between the quarters located on opposite banks. The Roman towns and later the first medieval walls in both cases were on the northern or right bank. Important suburbs developed later on the south in a large bloc. At Pisa, expansion beyond the ancient Roman city in the form of *borghi* was accomplished in two substantial but compact topographical units.[193] The great business quarter of Fuoriporta developed upstream east of the old Roman wall, while that called Ponte grew up west of it and included as well the entire episcopal district and the *Campo Santo* on the north. The great Chinsica quarter (the name is of oriental origin, probably Arab) developed on the south bank as the home of the businessmen who engaged in long distance trade. These four blocs formed the administrative basis of the city and were extended under different names into the *contado* to form special rural districts.

Yet at Pisa the peculiar character of the Chinsica quarter within the city was emphasized by two developments. First, when the forthcoming visit of Frederick Barbarossa was announced in 1155, a new wall was begun for the entire town. But construction only commenced south of the Arno in 1162 and proceeded slowly, plagued by many delays. It was continued intermittently until the 1260s.[194] The southern settlement was thus deliberately left outside the new protective wall. Secondly, the new bridge was built at a late date and involved exceptional effort. Only an old wooden bridge, doubtless on the site of the ancient Roman structure, crossed the Arno, which was about one hundred metres wide at that point. Not until 1182 did a *consorteria*, a group of families on the north bank (particularly the Duodi and the Gaetani), propose that a new stone bridge be built. Although Pisa had already been an important sea power for a century at that time and had acquired a considerable fortune through trade, the suggestion was resisted by the *Chinsica* families, who wanted to preserve the particular identity of their quarter. The town as a whole nonetheless imposed a compromise, and the bridge was finally built, but very late.[195] The rivalry between the quarters of the two banks continued to be expressed over the centuries by a sporting festival and mock fight which was staged each year on 15 August, when the residents of north and south vied to capture the bridge in the *Gioco del Ponte*.[196]

The most strongly marked neighbourhood particularism at Florence was likewise that of the quarter south of the river, called Oltrarno. When Giovanni Villani described the troubles of 1330 through 1345, he constantly stressed the solidarity during the fighting of the families of Oltrarno, entrenched in the fortified palaces and towers within their quarter. Everyone noted this particularism and isolation. When the Florentine government tried to limit hostilities between the newly formed Black and White parties in Pistoia in 1294, an antagonism especially strong in the all-powerful Cancellieri family, it decided to exile the principal leaders to Florence. There they established themselves on opposite banks of the river: "the Black party settled in Oltrarno with the Frescobaldi, the Whites with the *Cerchi* in the *Garbo* [on the right bank]". But the two sides were inadequately isolated from each other, and the conflict spread "just as a sick ewe infects the entire flock". The Pistoian exiles soon dragged the entire city of Florence into their conflict.[197]

The solidarity of the people on the opposite side of the river was shown emphatically in defensive measures undertaken by Florence in difficult times. During the last days of the tyranny of the duke of Athens in 1343, when the town was in an uproar and the citizens were threatened by mounting violence, "the men of the quarter of Oltrarno, great and *popolani* alike, took an oath of mutual assistance, sealed with a kiss on the mouth, and blocked the exits from the bridges with the firm intention of defending themselves even if the whole town on the other side of the river were lost".[198] The entire Oltrarno in effect constituted a fortified redoubt, protected by the river, whose access could easily be controlled or forbidden by defending the bridges. Villani emphasizes the primordial role of these bridges across the Arno in the political life of Florence and their military and strategic importance. He speaks at great length of their condition and of the reconstruction of the Ponte Vecchio. The troubles which occurred shortly after the duke of Athens departed show their defensive importance very nicely. The great families of Oltrarno, the Bardi, Rossi, and Frescobaldi, "who held power on all the bridges", began by fortifying their palaces, which were beside the river at the foot of the bridges ("the palaces of the great men of Oltrarno ... were strengthened, and they took control of the exits from the bridges"). Armed bands could not cross the Ponte Vecchio

because the power of the Bardi and the Rossi was so great and the barricades so strong, and this part of the town was so well armed, as were the palaces of the sons of Messer Vieri de' Bardi and the houses of the Manuelli at the head of the Ponte Vecchio that the people could neither have access nor cross there .... It was worse on the side of the Rubaconte bridge by virtue of the power of the Bardi palace of San Gregorio.[199]

We are obviously dealing with a very strong separatism, a marked desire for isolation, but Oltrarno was even more than this: on several dramatic occasions it was a defensive redoubt, but not a permanent base of political activity. The Oltrarno quarter can never be identified with one of the two political parties of Florence.[200]

Two Lombard towns also seem to present a political division resting upon well-defined topographical blocs, at least at certain times. We have noted that the two parties of Cremona in 1209 and 1210 referred to the old town as *pars superior* (upper town) and to the new settlement located down the hill as *pars inferior*. Each chose a different podestà, and the two factions had several conflicts before the bishop Sichardus intervened. The topographical division was not the entire explanation for the quarrel, however, for the parishoners of San Pantaleone, which was located in the upper city, opted for the party of the new town.[201]

The *Anonymus Ticinensis* mentions that the Pavians fought with wooden lances every Sunday between January and Ash Wednesday to train for military engagements. The entire town thus enjoyed the spectacle of a *bataliola*. The city was divided for purposes of these fights into two parts, the *superior* (north) and the *inferior* (south). Each party comprised several *societates* or *cohortes* which corresponded to the most important parishes. The war games were held in three open areas on the borders of the two *partes*.[202] Such games which became public festivals attest well the sense of separation felt by the two camps, as does the very use of the word *partes*. Such exercises could prepare the framework for other, more violent and seriously intended clashes, and in any case could be the origin of a firm political rivalry.

As we learn more of the social structures of these cities, we may be able to discern other examples of divisions based on topographical circumscriptions. It nonetheless remains obvious that such open confrontations were exceptional, and that they had a decisive influence neither on the origins nor on the recruitment of membership of the urban political parties. This fact, however, in no way denigrates the role of neighbourhood ties in other aspects of political and social relationships.

Meeting places and centres of concentration

Political situations in every city were often articulated under the aegis of strongholds, fortified places of assembly or refuge where men might hold meetings, elections and councils, organize and govern, or even retrench and defend themselves. Aristocratic or popular meeting places often reflect ancestral customs or even recall rural traditions. For example, the adversaries of the governing group at Florence in January 1328, led by Ugolino di Tano degli Ubaldini, "with certain lesser men of Florence" who were led by an *ad hoc* leader, Giovanni del Sega da Carbone, hoped to start fires at four places in the city. These distractions would allow them more easily to assemble their partisans and other Ghibellines at the great Ognissanti meadow, at the town gates,[203] to prepare there a revolt by mass uprisings in the streets. The communal meadow was a place of assembly in the countryside, and indeed was a symbol of the village community.

Such meetings or reconnoitrings of crowds or councils were more frequently held in certain privileged buildings which towered over the urban landscape. At times these symbolized the power of a social group within the city. Foremost among them was the church. Associations of citizens to protect, build, and repair the parish church (*opere*) were frequently the vehicles for meetings which were actually apprenticeships in practical politics. The members of the *opera* acquired the practices and skills of administration and government. They felt a keen sense of solidarity with one another. All political life in Florence from the time of the earliest communal organization was dominated by the two great *opere* of the city. The *opera* of San Giovanni, founded in 1157, and the more popular *opera* of San Miniato, established in 1180 on the edge of the densely populated part of the city, were administered by the *societas mercatorum* of the wealthy businessmen. The military wagon of Florence, the *carrocio*, was maintained in peacetime by the *opera* of San Giovanni, and the poles on which the banners were displayed were kept in that church. The name of the patron saint was the war cry on the battlefield.[204]

The Tuscan party leaders frequently met in a given church and assembled their retainers in the nave or the outer sanctuary. When the Guelfs were again masters of Florence in 1267, they held their meetings, under the presidency of their three captains, in the church of Santa Maria sopra Porta. They deposited their documents as security in the church of the Servi di Santa Maria.[205] The chronicle of Giovanni Sercambi (1347–1424) shows us that in 1203 "the rebel knights of Lucca . . . held a meeting in the church of Montecatini". As late as 1396, when the Lucchese had prevailed over a rebel faction as well as their Pisan enemies and had captured their banners, "they decided to use the banners as altarcloths at Santo Martino".[206]

To move to a totally different region, the *Annales* of Piacenza afford many instances in which episodes of party warfare – meetings, elections, secret conclaves, and reconnoitrings – occurred in one of the churches of the city. During the famous 'popular' revolt against high food prices in 1250, "on 5 July Antolino Saviagata assembled about twenty or thirty consuls of the societies of the *popolo* of Piacenza in the church of San Pietro in Foro. He acted at the instigation of the Scotti, for he was their neighbour, and others". But, continues the author, the consuls of the *popolo* met at the church of Santa Maria del Tempio and convened their council for the following Sunday in the church of San Pietro. The crowds there were so large that they could not remain, and they retired to San Sisto. But in a new twist to an already complex affair, certain of them who could not come inside the church closed the doors ... and he [Antolino], clothed in scarlet and new squirrel's fur, held a great assembly early in the morning on the square of San Pietro. After they had observed this festival day, the council assembled in the largest of the churches and elected by acclamation ....[207]

Thus, all the events and political assemblies which had decided the fate of the city were held within a few days in three churches. Similar instances can be attested for all towns of Italy on many occasions.

The city hall such as the Bargello of Florence was a symbol of order and the centre of the life of the *popolo*. It served as the meeting place for the communal council and even family groups and was the seat of the podestà and the principal judicial and police officers. The eternal desire for security led the officials of the Florentine *popolo* to undertake the construction of a new fortified palace in 1298. It was to be more solitary, isolated and protected from the activity of the great men and the mobs: "and the priors who governed the *popolo* and the entire republic did not think that they would be safe where they had met heretofore, in the house of the Cerchi Whites behind the church of San Broccolo".[208]

Family palaces were extremely important centres of social life throughout Italy. Their covered *loggia* and porticos at the narrow point between their walls made them convenient meeting places. These palaces were very often imposing, impregnable fortresses with their high, crenelated walls, pierced with few windows. Protected by high towers which were veritable stone keeps, they were redoubts anchored in the heart of the city. They sheltered garrisons of armed men, the faithful followers and their clients. These barricaded seigneurial fortresses of the town easily warded off enemy assaults. Battles within the city were frequently resolved into a series of palace sieges; at Florence in 1343, the leaders of several clans defended themselves with numerous men at arms "thanks to the strong barricades, the towers and palaces, and the presence of many men at arms".[209] As the tower dominated all military activity and street combats, so the fortified palace assembled forces and reinforced 'solidarities'. These considerations explain the importance of the tower societies of the aristocrats.

The gate in the town wall was also one of the pre-eminent aspects of military, political, and social life. In every town, the large gates of the exterior wall were remarkable defensive bastions. Flanked by towers, they commanded and blocked access to the city and afforded refuge for the garrison of the adjoining quarter. While some walls had few or no towers, the importance of the gate, the essential fortification, was thereby increased. The town gate also played a social role, sometimes sheltering a church which protected it and watched over the city, such as Santa Maria sopra Porta at Florence. Before the town halls were built, the gates were often meeting places for men of the neighbourhood. As such, they might be the centre of the entire administrative and political life of the quarter or even of the whole city.

At Florence, the first administrative circumscriptions, the *sesti* or sixths, were established in large measure because of the gates: three sixths corresponded to three of the main gates of the right bank (Porta San Pancrazion, Porta Duomo, Porta San Piero), while two others arose from a subdivision of the blocs of neighbouring houses on the right bank but still on the north side of the town, the Porta Santa Maria. The last, Oltrarno, was outside the first wall. The gates were always the principal objectives in the great street battles, when the Ghibellines again drove the Guelfs from the town in 1260, the fighting centred on the Palazzo del Popolo, but the strategic goals were the Porta San Piero on the east and the Porta del Duomo on the north.[210]

In the Lombard towns also the inhabitants assembled near the gates of the wall and made them rallying points during combats, centres of political life where some action might be prepared, or simply positions from which to administer the city. When Frederick Barbarossa was besieging Milan in 1161, "the Milanese chose two men per parish and three per gate to oversee almsgiving".[211] Somewhat later, when the tyranny of the Torriani was overthrown at Piacenza, "the people chose two captains at each gate of the city who were to govern and defend them and prevent pillage".[212]

The fortified palace assumed important political and military roles in all the cities of central and northern Italy for societies or groups led by knights, nobles, or magnates, while the gate fulfilled similar functions for those under the aristocratic chieftains of the *popolo*. They, with the parish church, were the strongholds of all rivalries and for street fights between two hostile factions which were trying to seize power.

Political role of the quarters

These rallying or defensive points may in themselves explain a certain concentration of forces within the city. Neighbourhood ties, which were so strong and influential in forming contemporary social structures, moreover inspired the establishment of several united blocs upon which the parties might base their power. Recruitment of party membership was thus not invariably done on an individual or family basis, but rather by enlisting entire sectors of the city collectively. The neighbourhood associations were quite different from simple electoral or administrative circumscriptions and greatly influenced various aspects of political life. Rivalries between quarters frequently caused serious clashes and a climate of incessant hostility. They might indeed incite new quarrels between parties.

Still, it is clear that the quarters appertaining to one party or the other did not regroup into two large and compact blocs. On the contrary, the portrait of the political 'colours' of the Italian towns appears rather as a mosaic, a collage of tremendous complexity, a multiple confrontation of hostile forces in all principal sectors of the city. Giovanni Villani's analysis of one serious armed conflict shows this clearly. He demonstrates how each *vicinanza* took arms for its own purposes and defended itself against adversaries: "because of the aforementioned war, many towers were erected and fortified anew by the quarter communities, thanks to the common funds of the *vicinanze*. They were called towers of the companies". This suggests a clear desire for collective defense. But Villani also says that these neighbourhoods supported different parties and were generally arrayed against one another: "and nearly every day, or at least on alternate days, the citizens fought among themselves in several parts of the town, from *vicinanza* to *vicinanza* according to the parties . . .".[213]

The regrouping of such quarters, whether of Guelf or Ghibelline or of Black or White leanings, into more compact blocs around the strong points of the city remained exceptional and very restricted. Only a few topographical appellations or external symbols whose meaning is not absolutely certain show such a concentration of forces. This appears especially in towns where one party had held power for a long time, to the point where it was practically an institution. At Florence in 1244, the Ghibelline conquerors ordered the destruction of "thirty-six Guelf fortresses, palaces, and great towers", and particularly a Guelf tower near the church of San Giovanni called *Torre del Guardamorto*, for they had earlier buried their dead and celebrated their marriages in that church on Sunday mornings.[214] The *Palazzo della Parte Guelfa*, in the heart of the city, was a rallying point which engendered a surrounding array of palaces of the great families of the party. Such a concentration was furthered by exiling enemy clans and by expropriating and confiscating, if not destroying their houses.[215] Villani shows the victorious Guelfs in 1267 assembling their party captains in the church of Santa Maria sopra Porta, which "was on the central square of the city, surrounded by many houses of Guelfs".[216] One of the gates of the wall begun in 1173 was called *Porta Guelfa* between 1270 and 1300.[217]

The Ghibellines too imposed their nomenclature on the town plan of Florence, although less obviously than did the Guelfs. After the defeat and exile of the Guelfs in 1260, Manfred's podestà, Guido Novello de' conti Guidi, who was ruling the town for his master, had a new gate called *Porta Ghibellina* made in the wall, through which he could easily enter and depart the city and thus ensure his safety. He also had a wide road begun, the *Via Ghibellina*, to provide easier access to this new exit.[218] His route later gained popularity and became a focal point of social life, assemblies, and festivals. As late as 1321, about a month before the celebration of St John the Baptist, "teams of guildsmen were arrayed in Florence, one of them in the *Via Ghibellina*. There were at least three hundred persons there, all attired in yellow".[219] Villani also mentioned this boulevard a decade later.[220]

Yet most such indications are obviously vague. The nomenclature of the gate and street of the Ghibellines were related to the circumstances of Manfred's rule and do not necessarily imply that this neighbourhood was really the quarter of the party. Only a precise study of the topographical distribution of settlement for the families belonging to each faction in the city will enable us to determine whether a certain regrouping of partisan clans finally imposed its power. This is not an easy undertaking. But a study of the famous Florentine *Liber damnificatorum*, which lists Guelf properties destroyed between 1260 and 1266 and their exact location in the city, shows clearly a tendency to concentrate settlement in one area. Many more palaces and towers which were razed in two of the six districts of the town, Oltrarno and San Pietro Scheraggio, than in the other four. Little Guelf property is found in the aristocratic sixth of the Porta Duomo. Furthermore, the palaces were crowded into blocs of varying extent, but always in quite compact segments within each sixth.[221]

An administrative account at Genoa in 1450 gives the place of habitation of the forty-six clans which were still active and influential in the city.[222] Twenty-one of these had a definite political 'colour'. Most lived in two groups in the town: the Blacks occupied the heart of the old town near the cathedral of San Lorenzo, which dominated the port from the hilltop, while the Whites tended to live in northern quarters very near the harbour. These sectors were also aristocratic, but they were developing and becoming conscious of a corporate existence only in the thirteenth and fourteenth centuries.

Conclusions

Both economic forces and neighbourhood ties may explain the ferocity of party quarrels. To neglect business rivalries and the 'solidarities' of neighbours would be to misunderstand several essential moving forces behind social life and rivalries. But the fact remains that economic and topographical dichotomies were very poorly defined. The principal competition, the game which surpassed all others, was the race for power and offices. Only this inexorable quest explains why the entire political life of the cities crystallized around two factions. Papal or imperial intervention could furnish only occasional succour. Economic rivalries, conflicts between merchant companies, and hostilities between neighbours could only add complexities to the basic issue.

Notes to Part I*

[1]For a specific case, note the example of Pisa. Lupo Gentile [39, vi, pp. 5–19], and Cristiani [21, pp. 126–127]. In general, see Heers [31, pp. 36–37, 141–154, 174–191].

[2]R.S. Lopez, Aux origines du capitalisme génois, *Annales d'histoire économique et sociale* (1937).

[3]E.G. Rey, Les seigneurs de Giblet, *Revue de l'Orient latin* (1895).

[4]A. Sapori, La funzione economica della nobiltà, *Studi di storia economica medievale*, I (Florence, 1940), pp. 577–595.

[5]Doneaud [22]; A. Lattes, La compagna ed il comune di Genova in Genova, *Il comune di Genova, la grande Genova*, 31 ot. 1923; E. Loncao, Le genesi sociali dei comuni italiani, *Revista italiana di sociologia*, 1901; G. Luzzatto, Vicinie et comuni, *Revista italiana di sociologia*, 1909; P. Sella, *La Vicinia come elemento costittutivo del comune* (Milan, 1908); A.R. Scarsella, Il comuni dei consuli, *Storia di Genova dalle origini al tempo nostro*, III

*   Numbers in square brackets refer to the Bibliography.

(Milan, 1942); and for a final but very different example, Soriga, La compagna della Braida di Montevolpe nell'antico suburbio milanese ed il suo statuto (a. 1224), *Archivio storico lombardo* (1904).

[6]See especially F. Gabatto, Le origini signorili del Comune, *Bolletino storico bibliografico subalpino*, (1903); and, Intorno alle vere origini comunali, *Archivio storico italiano*, (1905); F. Niccolai, I consorzi nobiliari ed il comune nell'Alta e Media Italia, *Biblioteca della Rivista di storia del diritto italiano*, XIII (Bologna, 1940); N. Ottokar, Il problema della formazione communale, *Questioni di storia medievali*, ed. E. Rota (Milan, 1946).

[7]*Annali Genovesi di Caffaro* [7, pp. 5, 13, 15].

[8]*Ibid.* [7, p. 25].

[9]*Ibid.* [7, p. 157, *consules in republica*].

[10]*Ibid.* [7, p. 22]. Isti placitabant ut si aliquis de compagnie una faciebat lamentaciones supra aliquam aliarum, veniebat ad consules actoris ad placitandum.

[11]The town hall of Florence was begun in 1250, for Villani notes that, prima non avea palagio di comune in Firenze, anzi stava la signoria ora in parte della citta ora in altra. See Villani [15, VI, ch. 39, p. 264]. The palace at Genoa was begun in 1291 and finished only during the 1350s. Until then, the councils met in the loggias under the porticos of the palaces of the various eminent families. See G. Costamagna, *Cartolari notarli genovesi*, II (Rome, 1961), cited by Poleggi [45, p. 18].

[12]G.P. Bognetti, Appunti sul podestà (Pisa, 1934); E. Sestan, Ricerche intorno ai primi podestà Toscani, *Archivio storico italiano*, (1924); G.B. Picotti, Intorno ai primi podestà Toscani, *Revista storica italiana* (1926).

[13]See, for example, J. Plesner, *L'émigration de la campagne à la ville libre de Florence au XIIIe siècle* (Copenhagen, 1934).

[14]G. Salvioli, Massari e Manenti nell' economia medievale italiana, *Vierteljahrsschrift für Sozial- und Wirtschaftsgeschichte* (1928).

[15]Herlihy [32, p. 129].

[16]On this point, see especially the exposition of Toubert [55, pp. 950–1037].

[17]M. Michaut, *Le livre des faits du Maréchal de Boucicault. 1368–1421*. Nouvelle Collection des Mémoires relatifs à l'Histoire de France, II (Paris, 1854),), pp. 260ff.

[18]E.G. Léonard, *Les Angevins de Naples. 1250–1481* (Paris, 1954).

[19]A. Canellas, El Reino de Aragon en los anos 1410–1458, *IV Congresso de Historia de la Corona de Aragon. Mallorca 1955. Ponencias* (Palma de Mallorca, 1955); V. Salavert y Roca, El problema estratégico del Mediterraneo occidental y la politica aragonese (siglos XIV–XV), *ibid., Actas y Communicaciones*, i (Barcelona, 1959), pp. 201–222.

[20]A. Era, Momenti delle relazioni tra Genova e Barcelona. Intorno al 1435 (Battaglia di Ponza), *ibid.*, pp. 173–192.

[21]P. Piero, Alfonso V d'Aragona e le armi italiane, *ibid.*, pp. 121–126; E. Dupré-Theseider, La politica italiana di Alfonso il Magnanimo, *ibid., Ponensias*.

[22]For several examples, see Heers [31 (Engl trans.) 191].

[23]See especially C. Petit-Dutaillis, *Les communes françaises. Caractères et evolution des origines au XVIIIe siècle* (Paris, 1947).

[24]On Bordeaux, see pp. 231–235.

[25]A. Sapori, La cultura del mercante italiano, *Studi di storia economica medievale*, I (Florence, 1940), pp. 53–93.

[26]For some examples see P. Emiliani-Guidici, Lettere di Messer Consiglio de' Cerchi e

Compagni di Firenze a Giachetto Rinieri e Compagni in Inghilterra. 1290–1291, appendix of *Storia politica dei municipi italiani* (Florence, 1886); P. Ferrato, *Lettere di mercanti toscani scritte nel secolo XIV non mai fin qui stampate* (Venice, 1869); L. Mirot and E. Lazzareschi, Lettere di mercanti Lucchesi da Bruges a Parigi. 1407–1421, *Bollettino storico lucchese* (1929). On the Datini archives, the best known to date, see Mèlis [42, I] and the letters published by R. Brun, Annales avignonnaises de 1382 à 1410, *Mémoires de l'Institut historique de Provence* (1934–1935). Even aside from business letters, all Italian literature of this period is marked by this singular interest for political and social analyses. A.A. Castellan, En torno a las fuentes indirectas: los Testimonions de la Historia social en la Novelistica italiana del siglo XIII al XV, *Anales de historia antigua y medieval* (Buenos Aires, 1967), pp. 7–94.

[27]C. Bec, *Les marchands écrivains. Affaires et humanisme à Florence (1375–1434)* (Paris, 1967).

[28]See, in particular, the remarkable series of the *Diversorum Registri*, continuous from 1447. *Archivio di Stato di Genova. Archivio Secreto.*

[29]Villani [15].

[30]A. Sapori, L'attendibilità di alcune testimonianze cronistiche dell'economia medievale, *Studi di storia economica medievale*, I (Florence, 1940), pp. 25–35.

[31]Toubert [55, pp. 1031–1032].

[32]Judic [37].

[33]*Annales Placentini Guelfi* [4]; *Annales Placentini Gibellini* [3]. Henceforth the abbreviations *A.P.Gu.* and *A.P.Gib.* will be used. All citations from these two texts are found in the thesis of Judic [37].

[34]*A.P.Gu.*, anno 1218, p. 435, line 44, cited by Judic [37, p. 42].

[35]*A.P.Gib.*, anno 1266, p. 519, line 45, cited by Judic [37, p. 55]: juxta pace et societate facta in consilio generale.

[36]See above, notes 6–10.

[37]*A.P.Gu.*, anno 1187, p. 416, line 31, cited by Judic [37, p. 41]: homines conscilii Placentie et consules offitiorum et societatum.

[38]*A.P.Gib.*, anno 1276, p. 563, lines 25–26, cited by Judic [37, p. 42]: capitaneus societatis mercatorum et paraticorum populi Plasencie.

[39]On this meaning of the word 'popular', see below, p. 209.

[40]Fonseca [26, p. 216].

[41]Salvemini [49].

[42]Santini [51].

[43]*A.P.Gu.*, anno 1193, p. 418, line 37, cited by Judic [37, p. 67]: 150 milites de societate Lupanorum Cremone.

[44]*A.P.Gib.*, anno 1271, p. 552, line 19, cited by Judic [37, p. 235].

[45]*A.P.Gib.*, anno 1250, p. 499, line 22, cited by Judic [37, p. 39]: facta societate duorum milium de Barbarasis.

[46]*A.P.Gu.*, anno 1220, p. 437, line 36, cited by Judic [37, p. 41]: hoc audito a societatis militum consulibus et militibus.

[47]*A.P.Gib.*, anno 1266, p. 462, line 62, cited by Judic [37, p. 43].

[48]*A.P.Gib.*, anno. 1174, p. 462, line 37, cited by Judic [37, p. 45]: omnes civitates Lombardie contra imperatorem societatem contraxerunt.

[49]Sercambi [14, I] (Rome, 1892). The author lived from 1347 until 1424; his chronicle

covers the period between 1164 and 1424. He uses such expressions quite frequently. In this instance: le cavalieri ribelli di Luccha chi erano in Montechatini con loro amici forestieri, cioè Guido Borgognoni e filioli (XXVII, p. 12, *anno* 1203).

[50]Villani [15, XII, ch. 36, p. 65, February 1345]: furono condamnati per processo fatto tutti quelli della casa degli Ubaldini.

[51]Villani [15, IX, ch. 132, p. 232]: Romeo de' Pepoli, grande e possente cittadino e quasi signore della terra con tutta sua setta.

[52]Villani [15, IX, ch. 153, p. 244]: della setta del detto Coscetto.

[53]Sercambi [14, CXXXI, pp. 93ff, *anno* 1323].

[54]Sercambi [14, CXXXI, pp. 93ff, *anno* 1323]: le brigate bergoline sopraiunsero.

[55]See for example Villani [15, XII, ch. 104, p. 20].

[56]On all of this, see Judic [37, pp. 8ff].

[57]Judic [37, pp. 12ff].

[58]*A.P.Gu.*, *anno* 1213, p. 427, line 46, cited by Judic [37, p. 12]: ceperunt circa triginta milites Mediolani et sue partis.

[59]Judic [37, pp. 20–21].

[60]*A.P.Gib.*, *anno* 1260, p. 511, line 22.

[61]*Ibid.*, line 13.

[62]Ventura [56, pp. 182, 194].

[63]Villani [15, XII, ch. 120, p. 181, *anno* 1347]: e per dispetto gli chiamavanno i Bergolini.

[64]Sercambi [14, CXXXI, pp. 93ff, *anno* 1323]: e per questo modo si fè la parte de' Bergolini in Pisa; i Bergolini rubboro e arseno le case di quelli della Roccha.

[65]B. Casini, Patrimonio ed Attività del Fondaco del Taglio di Simono di Lotto da Sancasciano e fratelli, *Studi in onore di Amintore Fanfani* (Milan, 1961), II, p. 232.

[66]Waley [59, p. 141].

[67]Villani [15, VIII, ch. 39, p. 42]: gentili uomini e guerrieri, e di non superchia richezza, ma per motto erano chiamati Malefani.

[68]Gaspar (ed.) [8, pp. 154ff].

[69]Rolandino [13, ch. 2, p. 8], cited by Mor [43].

[70]On the situation of the exiles, see below, pp. 185ff.

[71]*A.P.Gib.*, *anno* 1271, p. 551, line 33, cited by Judic [37, p. 234].

[72]On this point, see below, pp. 208–214.

[73]Gozzadini [27], concerning the Pepoli family.

[74]Fasoli [24].

[75]Toubert [55, pp. 998–1035].

[76]Rossini [48, in particular pp. 437ff].

[77]Judic [37, pp. 32–33].

[78]Vitale [58, pp. 525–541].

[79]Santini [50, pp. 107, 198, 207, 214, and appendices 2 and 4].

[80]Gaspar (ed.) [8, pp. 154ff].

[81]Judic [37, pp. 22–23].

[82]Judic [37, pp. 22–24].

[83]Judic [37, p. 31].

[84]On the latter point see Gozzadini [27, p. 56].

[85]Hyde [35, pp. 194ff].

[86]Waley [59, p. xxi].

[87]See below, pp. 79ff.

[88]*Annales Brixienses* [1], p. 818, and *Annales Cremonenses* [2] p. 805, cited by Judic [37, pp. 158–160].

[89]Gozzadini [27, p. 404].

[90]E. Carpentier, *Une ville devant la Peste. Orvieto et la Peste Noire de 1348* (Paris, 1962), p. 37.

[91]Hyde [36, p. 297].

[92]For this term, see J. Dhondt, Les solidarités médiévales. Une société en transition: la Flandre en 1127–1128. *Annales. E.S.C.* XII (1957), pp. 529–560; translated into English by F.L. Cheyette, *Lordship and community in medieval Europe* (New York, 1968), pp. 268–290.

[93]W. Cohn, *Das Zeitalter der Staufen in Sizilien* (Bonn, 1924), translated into Italian by Catania, 1932; A. Willemsen, *Die Bauten der Hohenstaufen in Süditalien* (Cologne, 1968).

[94]On the formation of the papal state, see Toubert [55, pp. 935–1083], and for a later period Waley [60], and Lo stato papale nel tredecesimo secolo, *Revista storica italiana* (1961), pp. 429–472.

[95]Y. Renouard, Une expédition des céréales des Pouilles en Arménie par les Bardi pour le compte de Benoit XII, *Mélanges d'archéologie et d'histoire publiés par l'Ecole Française de Rome*, LIII (1936).

[96]On all of this, for the political events see especially R. Davidsohn, *Geschichte von Florenz* (Berlin, 1901–1925), Ital. transl (Florence, 1956–1960).

[97]Santini [51].

[98]Ventura [56].

[99]*A.P.Gib.* anno 1266, p. 516, line 21, cited by Judic [37, p. 30]: et illis qui dicuntur de parte ecclesie.

[100]Villani [15, VI, ch. 84]. But, the author continues, trovarono Curradino si piccolo garzone, che la madre in nulla guisa acconsentio di lasciarlo partire da se.

[101]A new and larger wall was constructed at Genoa in 1155 when word was received that Frederick Barbarossa's army was approaching.

[102]Hyde [35, p. 207].

[103]E. Jordan, *Les origines de la domination angevine en Italie* (Paris, 1909).

[104]*Annales Brixienses* [1], p. 817, cited by Judic [37, p. 155].

[105]P. Brezzi, Le relazioni fra i comuni Italiani e l'Impero, *Questioni di storia medievali a cura di E. Rota* (Como, 1946); G. Fasoli, Federico Barbarossa e le città italiane, *Convivium*, III (1962), pp. 7–24; H. Appelt, Friedrich Barbarossa und die italienischen Kommunen, *Mitteilungen des Instituts für Österreichische Geschichtsforschung*, LXXII (1964), 311–325; P. Munz, *Frederick Barbarossa: a study in medieval politics* (London, 1969); A. Haverkamp, *Herrschaftsformen der Frühstaufen in Reichsitalien* (Stuttgart, 1970).

[106]G. Fasoli, *Aspetti della politica italiana di Federico II* (Bologna, 1964).

[107]*A.P.Gu.*, anno 1222, p. 438, lines 22–28, cited by Judic [37, p. 169].

[108]Mor [43, pp. 102ff].

[109]Mor [43, pp. 100–101, 114].

[110]Gaspar [8, p. 198], for the year 1320. On this point and on the internal organization of these leagues, see also below, pp. 143–149.

[111]G. Ermini, *La libertà comunale nello Stato della Chiesa da Innocenzo III all' Albornoz. 1198–1367.* 2 vols. (Rome, 1926–1927).

[112]For the political events, see C. Vignati, *Storia diplomatica della lega lombarda*

(Milan, 1867). For an analysis of the circumstances and the personalities, see especially U. Balzani, *Italia, Papato e Impero nel secolo XII* (Milan, 1930); M. Pacaut, *Alexandre III. Recherche sur la conception du pouvoir pontifical dans sa pensée et dans son oeuvre* (Paris, 1956); G. Fasoli, Valori della Lega Lombarda alla vigilia dell' VIII Centenario, *Cultura e Scuola* (1966), pp. 119–130, and Frederico Barbarossa e le città lombarde: la Lega Lombarda, *Vorträge und Forschungen* (1968), pp. 139–180.

[113]G. Fasoli, Le autonomie cittadine nel Medio Evo, *Nuovi questioni di storia medievale* (Milan, 1964), pp. 146–176.

[114]V. Vitale [58]; G. Doneaud [22].

[115]Caffaro, *Annali* [7, II (1901), III, 63]: Et sic tota civitas exterius et interius posita est in maximo turbuia et errore, et quidam favebant partem imperii, et quidam alii volebant confederationem facere cum illa societate Lombardorum que contrarie est et rebellis domino imperatorii.

[116]M. Pacaut, Aux origines du guelfisme: les doctrines de la Ligue Lombarde (1167–1183), *Revue historique* (1963), pp. 73–90.

[117]Vitale [58].

[118]Hyde [35, p. 200].

[119]Hyde [36, pp. 297–299].

[120]Toubert [55, pp. 199ff].

[121]Hyde [35, p. 198].

[122]Cited by Hyde [36, p. 300].

[123]Hyde [36, pp. 300–301].

[124]Compagni [9, del Lungo ed., IX, 2, I, ch. 20, p. 82], cited by Herlihy [33, p. 203].

[125]Vitale [58, p. 530].

[126]Villani [15, IX, ch. 271, pp. 310–312].

[127]Villani [15, VIII, ch. 40, p. 45 and ch. 73, p. 92]: fece il papa citare dodici de' maggiori caporale di parte guelfa e nera che fossono in Firenze, i quali guidavano tutto lo stato della città.

[128]Villani [15, VIII, ch. 40, pp. 44–45].

[129]Waley [59, pp. 93ff].

[130]Ventura [56, pp. 156–157].

[131]Villani [15, IX, ch. 271, pp. 310–312].

[132]Bowsky [17, pp. 229–272].

[133]Renouard [46, II, 338–339].

[134]Villani [15, XII, ch. 79, pp. 127–128]: e altri cittadini rifutarono altri uffici per non essere condamnati nè riceverne vergogna, e in loro luoghi ne furono chiamati altri.

[135]Villani [15, XII, ch. 80, pp. 128–129]: dicendo che troppi ghibellini parea loro che fossano mischiati tra loro negli uffici e nel reggimento della città . . . . et covenne . . . che i ghibellini ch'erano nei sacchi overo borsoli per essere rettori o uficialis ne fossono tratti.

[136]Waley [59, pp. 129ff, 140ff].

[137]Villani [15, XII, ch. 3, p. 8]: e quando il duca cavalcava per la città, andevano gridando 'viva il signore', e quasi in ogni canto e palagio di Firenze, era dipinta l'arma sua . . . .

[138]Villani [15, XII, ch. 13, pp. 16–17]: dando loro consoli e rettori al loro volere dimanbrando loro gli ordini dell'arti a chi erano sottoposti per volere maggior salario di loro lavori.

[139]Villani [15, XII, ch. 16, p. 28].

[140]Toubert [55, pp. 1015ff].
[141]Cited by Rossini [48, p. 458].
[142]Fasoli [24, pp. 7–33].
[143]Villani [15, XII, ch. 120, p. 181].
[144]Villani [15, IX, ch. 132, p. 232]; Gozzadini [27, pp. 404ff].
[145]Gutkind [28, pp. 87ff, 161ff].
[146]Gozzadini [27, pp. 77ff] for the Andalo family.
[147]Casini, Patrimonio (above, n. 65), p. 232, 28 January 1355.
[148]Villani [15, IX, ch. 271, pp. 310–312]: mischiamente della setta ch'avea retto la città del tempo del conte Battifole infino allora e di quella gente che non avea retto.
[140]Herlihy [33, pp. 204–205].
[150]See below, p. 213.
[151]On this subject see Heers [29, pp. 585–589].
[152]A. Sapori, Una compagnia di Calimala ai primi del trecento (Florence, 1932); Y. Renouard, Les hommes d'affaires italiens au Moyen Age, 2nd edn. (Paris, 1968), pp. 152–200 and Le compagne commerciali fiorentine del trecento (dai documenti dell'Archivio Vaticano), Archivio storico italiano, 1938.
[153]Y. Renouard, Compagnies mercantiles lucquoises au service des papes d'Avignon, Bulletino storico lucchese, 1939.
[154]Hence came a series of catastrophic failures before recovery was made on other bases in 1326. See Y. Renouard, Recherches sur les premières compagnies commerciales et bancaires utilisés par les papes d'Avignon avant le Grand Schisme (Paris, 1942).
[155]Brucker [19].
[156]Bowsky [17, pp. 250ff].
[157]Villani [15, XII, ch. 17, p. 31].
[158]Villani [15, XII, ch. 20, p. 43].
[159]G.A. Brucker [20, pp. 155–183].
[160]Ventura [56, pp. 184–186].
[161]Villani [15, IX, ch. 153, p. 244].
[162]A.P.Gib., anno 1255, p. 507, line 53, cited by Judic [37, p. 32].
[163]A.P.Gu., anno 1217, p. 434, lines 21–23, cited by Judic [37, p. 29].
[164]A.P.Gu., anno 1219, p. 437, lines 21–22 and anno 1222, p. 438, line 19, cited by Judic [37, pp. 108–109].
[165]Annales Brixiensis [1], anno 1196, p. 815, cited by Judic [37, p. 112].
[166]A.P.Gu., anno 1090, p. 411, lines 7–16, cited by Judic [37, p. 96].
[167]Annales Brixiensis, anno 1196ff, p. 815ff, cited by Judic [37, pp. 122–124].
[168]A.P.Gib., anno 1250, p. 499, lines 35–53 and p. 500, lines 1–2, cited by Judic [37, pp. 125–128].
[169]I. Ghiron, La Credenza di San Ambrogio o la lotta dei Nobili e del Popolo in Milano (1198–1292), Archivio storico lombardo (1877).
[170]Hyde [36, p. 300].
[171]Rolandino [13, II, 8], cited by Mor [43, p. 82].
[172]Vitale [58].
[173]Gozzadini [27, pp. 328ff].
[174]See Dante, De vulgari eloquentia, ch. 15, cited by Gozzadini [27].
[175]Dominici [ll, I, II, 14], cited by Herlihy [33, p. 200].

[176]Villani [15, VIII, ch. 39, pp. 42–43]: come la città di Firenze si parti e si sconcio per le dette parti bianca e nera.

[177]Villani [15, IX, ch. 153, p. 246].

[178]On this point see the very interesting reflections of G. Masi, La struttura sociale delle fazioni politiche ai tempi di Dante, Il Giornale Dantesco, XXXI (1928), especially pp. 1–8.

[179]See, for example, F. Patetta, Nobili e Popolani in una piccola città dell'Alta Italia (Belluno) (Siena, 1902); F. Gabotto, Popolani e Magnati a Asti nel secolo XIV, Nuova antologia (1905); Schipa, Nobili e Popolani in Napoli nel medioevo, Archivio storico italiano (1925).

[180]Villani [15, XII, ch. 23, p. 51].

[181]Brucker [20, p. 159].

[182]Villani [15, IX, ch. 132, p. 232].

[183]Villani [15, IX, appendix no, 104].

[184]Judic [37, pp. 88–95].

[185]A.P. Gib., anno 1271, p. 552, lines 50–52, cited by Judic [37, p. 93].

[186]On this man and his activities, see Judic [37, pp. 63–64].

[187]On this general subject, see Renouard [46, pp. 367–369]; G. Fasoli, Ricercha sulla legislazione antimagnatizia nei Comuni del' Alta e Media Italia, Revista storica del diritto italiano (1939).

[188]G. Salvemini, La dignita cavalléresca nel Comune di Firenze (Florence, 1896); Salvemini [49]; and Masi [40, p. 7], where the author notes cavalieri del popolo. Compare these views to U.G. Mondolfo, Il 'populus' a Siena nella vita della città e nel governo del Comune fino alla reforma antimagnatizia (Genoa, 1911).

[189]D. Cavalca, Il ceto magnatizio a Firenzo dopo gli Ordinamenti di giustizia, Revista storica di diritto italiano (1967–1968), pp. 85–132.

[190]Villani [15, XII, ch. 23, p. 50].

[191]For Brandenburg and Hildesheim, see especially H. Planitz, Die deutsche Stadt im Mittelalter (Cologne and Graz, 1954). On the particularism of a Neustadt and its reflections in social life, see H. von Gluemer, Das Konstablergelag in der Altstadt Braunschweig und die Gelagsbrüderschaft, Niedersächsisches Jahrbuch für Landesges-chichte (1933), pp. 71–87.

[192]For Toulouse, see Mundy [44], and for the Lyon revolts, Fédou [25].

[193]E. Tolaini, Forma Pisarum (Roma 1962).

[194]Renouard [46, pp. 188–189].

[195]Renouard [46, pp. 188–189]; [32, pp. 97–98]; N. Toscanelli, Il quartiere di Kinsica e i ponti sull'Arno nel Medioevo, Bulletino storico pisano, 1935.

[196]V. Salvestrini, Il gioco del Ponte di Pisa (Pisa, 1933).

[197]Villani [15, VIII, ch. 38, p. 41].

[198]Villani [15, XII, ch. 17, p. 31]: quegli del sesto d'Oltrarno grandi e popolani si giurarono insieme e si bacioron in bocca e sbarrarono i capi di ponti, con intenzione che si tutta l'altra terra di qua dell' acqua si perdesse, di ternersi francamente di là.

[199]Villani [15, XII, ch. 21, pp. 44–46].

[200]The Veronese chroniclers emphasize the importance of the bridges in the social life of their city and are careful to mention whenever a bridge was built or reconstructed, for example the Ponte di Preda, which the anonymous chronicler says was made of wood in 1232. Gaspar [8, p. 146], and P. Gazzola, Ponte Pietra (Florence, 1963).

[201]*Annales Cremonenses* [2], p. 805, cited by Judic [37, p. 159].

[202]*Anonymi Ticinensis* [5], p. 25.

[203]Villani [15, X, ch. 114, pp. 108–109].

[204]Renouard [46, p. 288].

[205]Villani [15, VII, ch. 17, p. 227].

[206]Sercambi [14, XXVII, 12 and CXXXI, 93ff].

[207]*A.P.Gib.*, anno 1250, p. 499, line 35 to p. 502, line 24, cited by Judic [37, pp. 224–232].

[208]Villani [15, anno 1298, VIII, ch. 26, pp. 29–30]: e i priori che reggeano il popolo e tutta la reppublica, non parea loro essere sicuri ove abitavano innanzi, ch'era nella casa de' Cerchi bianchi dietro la chiesa di San Broccolo.

[209]Villani [15, XII, ch. 21, p. 45]: con grandi serragli e guernimento di torri e di palagi alle loro case dal crocicchio del Corso della logia loro alla piazza di San Giovanni s'erano afforzati con molta gente d'arme.

[210]Villani [15, VI, ch. 33, p. 252].

[211]*A.P.Gib.*, anno 1161, p. 461, lines 1–31, cited by Judic [37, p. 165].

[212]*A.P.Gu.*, anno 1277, p. 566, cited by Judic [37, p. 171].

[213]Villani [15, V, ch. 9, p. 196]: che quasi ogni di, e di due di l'uno, si combatteano i cittadini insieme in piu parti della città, da vicinanza a vicinanza com'erano le parti.

[214]Villani [15, VI, ch. 33, p. 255].

[215]On these destructions, see below, pp. 179ff.

[216]Villani [15, VII, ch. 17, pp. 225–228]: e rannarsi a' loro consigli nella chiesa nuova di Santa Maria sopra Porta, per lo piu comune luogo della città, e dove ha piu case Guelfe intorno.

[217]Villani [15, XII, ch. 18, p. 38 and X, ch. 205, pi. 182–183].

[218]Villani [15, VI, ch. 80, p. 303].

[219]Villani [15, X, ch. 216, pp. 192–193].

[220]Villani [15, XII, ch. 18, pp. 38–39].

[221]O. Brattö, *Liber estimatiorum anno MCCLXIX* (Göteburg, 1955).

[222]Archivio di Stato di Genova, MS. 88. These hints cannot be taken with absolute certainty. They indicate only the *compagna*, a relatively large area, and not the smaller *contrada*.

PART II
PARTY RECRUITMENT AND STRUCTURE

In studying the internal activity, social base of membership, and particular organization of the factions, we obviously encounter many difficulties, the foremost of which is the lack of documentation dealing specifically with these subjects. The political groups which we have already found so difficult to define generally had no real structure: neither well-defined institutions nor firmly established leaders or governments. We must seek indirect testimony and collect scattered pieces of information. These fragments may lead us first to try to determine the social composition of the party, the hierarchies and bonds within each faction, and the creation of their structure, their principal body, the sort of nucleus around which less influential or in any case more transient men were congregated.

CHAPTER ONE

Families and clienteles

One or more great families are always found at the heart of the urban political group. This is true of the specifically merchant cities as late as the fourteenth and fifteenth centuries, when aristocratic society was extremely complex and fluctuating. The aristocratic lineages seem to have been the very life force of the parties and were often identified with them by contemporary writers. As we have seen,[1] the names of the factions were identified at some point with those of the two greatest families of the city. Eventually too the party would appear either as a temporary alliance of several clans or as the creation of a single dominant family, which recruited a substantial clientele from various social strata and thus managed to extend its influence over the entire district of the city and the *contado*. Certain aspects of political life reflect the identification of party and family which many chroniclers clearly perceived. Foremost among them were the circumstances in which the interminable quarrels which led to factional wars originated or were caused.

Quarrels and feuds

There were many causes for such hostilities. The first civil wars were often no more than simple conflicts between two families which were subsequently exacerbated by the desire to avenge spilled blood or clan honour. The political factions then espoused these quarrels and vendettas.[2] The clan led by nobles felt a sacred obligation to avenge every homicide, even every wound received by one of its members.

101

Brawls and assassinations thus had dramatic consequences, provoking bloody quarrels which soon spread throughout the city even if the victim were no more than a distant relative.[3]

Villani and other authors explain the origin of the conflict between Whites and Blacks at Pistoia in this way. The city was ruled by the powerful Cancellieri family, one of whose members had amassed an enormous fortune in commerce. Several children, "who because of their wealth all became knights and men of influence and property", were born of his two marriages. The sons were among the first captains of the *popolo*. It seems, however, that from 1236 the clan was being split into two branches by conflicts of interest. Ranieri Cancellieri loaned money to the society of the *pedites*, while his brother Amadore was the banker of the *milites*.[4] All were still Guelfs, but within this vast, overly numerous family, which was being rent by internal strife, "pride and the workings of the devil created an infamous enmity between those born of different wives". In 1286 a tavern squabble between two undoubtedly inebriated cousins led the kinsmen of the antagonists to come to their assistance. There seem to have been no deaths, but several people were wounded or mutilated. Each side called for aid and vengeance, "and from this incident many fights developed at Pistoia, with grave perils and even homicides. But matters did not stop at Pistoia, and soon the city of Florence and all of Italy were contaminated by these parties".

This pattern, which one might say became 'classic' or habitual, even to the point of becoming a literary theme, is frequently found at the origin of bloody quarrels in other cities. Thus Villani, while speaking of the many changes which occurred at Siena in 1322, recalls an ordinary private crime. "Siena was in a state of excitement because members of the house of Salimbeni one night killed two brothers in their homes. The victims were sons of a knight of the house of the Tolomei, their enemies." Only the fear of armed German contingents and of the *condotta* of Lucca led by Castruccio provoked the wise men of the town to take decisive action to avoid the worst, "so that the city of Siena was preserved from battles in the town".[5]

The same desire for vengeance moved the clan whose honour had been besmirched through the disgrace of one of its women. The men wanted to preserve the family's reputation intact and perhaps subconsciously to safeguard the purity of the woman and the clan. Abductions and adulteries thus provoked conflicts which were just as terrible as those resulting from assassinations. All Paduan chroniclers, particularly the famous Rolandino, cite a gloomy story of this sort as the origin of the interminable quarrles between the Romano and Este parties. In 1216 a young girl named Cecilia, daughter of one Manfredo il Ricco, had been betrothed to Gerardo Camposanpiero, but the da Romano then abducted her and hastily married her to one of their number, Ezzelino II. Shortly thereafter, Gerardo seduced the young wife while she was a guest in his palace at Padua. A general war broke out over this incident which pitted first the da Romano against the Camposanpiero and then against their powerful allies, the Este. Each party sought and obtained considerable assistance in the city and throughout the region, from people like the Sambonifacio, counts of Verona who later lived at Mantua, who fought for the Este.[6] This interpretation of the feud is of course simplistic, perhaps mythical, and at the very least was full of poetic licence. It nonetheless encapsulates a state of mind, a collective mentality shared by all. The historian is perhaps on more certain ground with the dramatic, visceral opposition between the Lambertazzi and Geremei parties at Bologna. The chroniclers deliberately explain it as the consequence of the forbidden love of Imolda Lambertazzi and Bonifacio Geremei. Such unhappy liaisons, like that of Romeo and Juliet at Verona, have inspired many Italian and German poets and novelists through the centuries.[7]

Matrimonial alliances had considerable social and financial importance, and the rivalry between opposing families or between collateral branches of the same clan to attract a young lady actually involved a race for the hands of wealthy heiresses. We shall mention only the most famous and bloody of these stories. In 1401 young Datina, a very wealthy heiress of Pistoia, daughter of Stefano Guazzalotti, was ardently wooed by the two rival factions of the Cancellieri and the Panciatichi. These clans were organized into two companies which were solidly entrenched in the city, those of San Giovanni and San Paolo. Ricciardo Panciatichi then tried to have the leader of the opposing party assassinated, but his deputy in charge of recruiting murderers was arrested in Florence and confessed his crime. Ricciardo then fled into the mountains. Barricaded for most of the time in his castle of Sambruca, he repulsed all assaults and only surrendered after two years of bloody fighting, when he knew that he could no longer rely on Milanese troops for help. This race for an inheritance and to marry the girl thus left a ruined countryside and numerous dead in both camps.[8]

Alliances and family concerns had a more pervasive and complex influence on party life. Certain marriages provoked a sudden change, upset the balance between the parties, and led to a redistribution of their forces. When the Guelf leader Obizzo d'Este married the daughter of the Ghibelline chief Alberto della Scala at Parma in 1287, he may have acted out of a genuine desire for peace, but he also hoped to increase the power and prestige of his own house. His action had the contrary effect, for he broke his old alliances and all his Guelf friends abandoned him.[9]

Such marriages, together with financial compensations, were quite often necessary conditions for the establishment of peace between the two parties. The nuptials of the young people created kindred bonds between former enemies and put an end, at least temporarily, to the quarrels. At Piacenza in 1271

Count Obertino de Lando made a treaty with Guillelmo de Fredencio, Montenario Grasso, and several Balbi. According to its terms, the daughter of the lord Guizardo de Andito was to be given in marriage to the son of Guillelmo de Fredencio. Of her dowry of £400 of Piacenza, the 'external' party of the city would pay £300 and Guizardo £100. The Balbi in turn paid £300 of Piacenza to the party to buy war chargers and fortify their castle. Since other relationships had been made between the Andito and Balbi families, the latter with their men became friends of the count and party.[10]

This is a noteworthy example of a marriage which sealed a peace treaty, which in its turn bound two families in the first instance, but actually became an affair of two entire parties and assumed an important position in the larger settlement of a conflict. It involved marriage, to be sure, but also compensation for expenses incurred during the fighting. This explains why breaking promises of marriage might be resented bitterly by the offended party. The pride and honour of the fiancée and thus of the entire family and political group were wounded by what was also the violation of a financial settlement.

Literary and pseudo-historical tradition posits similar circumstances for the origin of the conflict between the two parties at Florence. According to the traditional, half legendary tale, during a banquet in 1216 one of the great men of the city, Buondelmonte dei Buondelmonti, stabbed Oddo Arrighi dei Fifanti. This was simple enough; the two families deliberated, consulted their friends and allies, and decided that Buondelmonte should marry the niece of Oddo Fifanti, an Amadei. But the young man loved another girl, a member of the Donati family, and refused to marry the Fifanti niece who was to be the surety for peace. In their wedding clothes, the Fifanti and Amadei waited vainly for him on the Ponte Vecchio. Such an insult demanded retribution, which was accomplished shortly thereafter on the very site where the offence had been given. As Buondelmonte and his young Donati bride were walking on the Ponte Vecchio on Easter morning, they were accosted by their enemies in the Via Por' Santa Maria. The man was killed on the spot.[11]

The chronicle also emphasizes the gravity of breaking marital engagements at Piacenza: "a ferocious quarrel broke out at that time [1270] between Alberto de Fontana with his family and Giovanni Palastrello with his, because of the ancestral hatred of the two clans". It began with a double affront: Vitale Palestrello had seduced a daughter of Antonio Leccafarina de Fontana and thereafter had killed Antonio's son. But the party leader, Alberto da Fontana, "gave his daughter to one of Giovanni's sons to keep the peace between himself and Giovanni. This arrangement was sworn by the two parties, but Giovanni did not wish to receive the bride".[12] Bloody battles involving the two clans, and indeed entire parties, broke out to avenge this new insult.

These quarrels of purely private origins, which began as simple, personal conflicts, often provoked clashes within overly extended families. Such clans had too many collateral relatives and for all sorts of reasons were already divided into two hostile camps. Internal power struggles were weakening them, producing vendettas at some time in several cities. The theme of enemy brothers or more often cousins, persons bearing the same name but moved by ferocious and irreconcilable hatreds, is one of the most common in contemporary stories and chronicles, studies of manners, and later in the works of the novelists, who were still being inspired by the turbulent history of medieval Italy as late as Stendhal's time.

At Genoa, the all-powerful Streggiaporci clan was deeply divided between 1241 and 1244. One of its leaders, Guglielmo, declared himself the faithful ally of Frederick II, while the other, Amico, assumed the leadership of the Guelf party.[13] At Bologna the wealthy Cazzanemici family, whose very name evokes thoughts of civil war, was divided into the Cazzanemici *dell' orso* or Cazzanemici *grandi* and the Cazzanemici *piccoli*. The former belonged to the Lambertazzi party, while the latter supported the Geremei.[14] Villani furnishes many examples of such internal conflicts both at Florence and other towns when the events (*novità*) came to his attention. The most spectacular episode was that cited above between the Cancellieri cousins of Pistoia. Similarly, the *Annales* of Piacenza describe at length the internecine discords of the great families of the city, beginning with the Andito clan. Frederico de Andito was jealous of his brother Oberto, "who lived in town on a grander scale than did he". He launched a revolt in December 1255 against the commune, which was then ruled by the Andito party, and entrenched himself at nearby Centenario.[15] The next year, most members of the family joined the open enemies of Count Oberto de Andito.[16] As late as 1266 Fiamerigio de Andito, whose clan was always on the imperial side, maintained in the town a company or society of knights (*societas consortii*) whose clearly stated purpose was to support the pope.[17] The *Annales* also note the internal quarrels of the powerful and prominent Fontana clan. Alberto de Fontana supported the Church party between 1260 and 1267, while the other leaders of his family, Guido and Cagno, joined the imperialists. As a result, they were proscribed when the papacy emerged victorious in 1267.[18] Similar divisions racked the Palestrelli and other important clans.

Insults, assassinations or wounds, affronts to blood and honour, and even petty jealousies thus incited deep hatreds between families or between rival branches of the same house. Inimical groups grew into opposed political factions. Clan rancours provoked social fissures and maintained them effectively.

The vendetta was perhaps one of the most characteristic, striking, and significant social realities in all milieus and regions of Italy for many centuries.[19] Relatives might, of course, avoid impending acts of vengeance by delivering the guilty parties to the kinsmen of the victim. The Cancellieri Blacks of Pistoia did this in 1286, but their opponents treated them shabbily by amputating an arm of each culprit to impose a terrible *lex talonis*. This act inflamed the quarrel once again, and passions were never cooled thereafter.[20]

Numerous circumstances sustained an atmosphere of hatred and violence and produced conflicts having many vicissitudes. Attempts to contain the conflict within narrow limits foundered on the exacerbated desire for vengeance and the strongly ingrained idea of the collective and equal responsibility of all members of the clan. There was a constant threat of punishments which might be inflicted on any kinsman of any alleged malefactor. Retaliation might come years later and under any circumstances, often when the victim was disarmed, or even maimed or imprisoned. There was no feeling of personal honour, no code of human rights. The desire to affirm collective solidarity took precedence over all other considerations. Irresponsible persons could give free vent to acts of personal hatred and vengeance and perpetrate with impunity countless cowardly deeds, ruses, and surprise attacks. All of these actions deeply affected the spirits of the time. The vendetta required no personal courage, for it favoured furtive actions. Socially, the entire clan was involved and soon sought to protect itself and reinforce its power by making new alliances in the city, the *contado*, and even in neighbouring cities. An inevitable process of crystalliza-tion, at times leading to the formation of two great blocs, parties, or hostile factions, often developed around a single family quarrel.

Giovanni della Grossa, a Corsican chronicler writing in the 1450s, provides a remarkable example of such a division of an entire region into two factions as the result of a trivial quarrel between rival branches of the same family. He analyses the stages of crystallization very perspicaciously. Discord erupted on Easter Sunday, evidently for some trifling cause, between two brothers of the Pietrallareta family of Nebbio, Giudice and Giovanninello. Both had six daughters, all of whom had made distinguished marriages to leading men of the island. And

since the two adversaries had many partisans who rushed to their assistance, the discord extended to all of Corsica. The parties of Giudice and Giovanello assumed particular names after this division which lasted more than two centuries and resembled the situation of the Guelfs and Ghibellines.[21]

Although part of this story is legendary, the explanation given and the reference to the Florentine parties shows that this scholarly author, a notary and knight in the service of the Genoese governors and the great Corsican nobles, was clearly aware of the importance of family conflicts and of this tragic train of events.

Families within the parties

After the parties had been established, the great families often retained their positions of leadership or at least were part of the group which dominated them. We must therefore devote some attention to the role of the family lineages within the parties. This line of enquiry leads to several conclusions.

First, political life was often determined by a fundamental hostility between two clans which were identified with the parties. The family quarrels often constituted the basic fabric upon which occasional or fortuitous events were embroidered. Legendary occurrences were sometimes spectacular and became deeply rooted in the collective memory. Two instances at Rome, separated by a considerable time, afford good examples of this: the rivalry of the Crescenzi and Tuscolani to control the papacy between 940 and 1050, and that between the Orsini and Colonna which was equally decisive and continued for several centuries. In fifteenth-century Genoa, competition for the office of doge, with its emoluments and profits, was open at first to four powerful aristocratic clans, then became limited to a confrontation of the two great rival houses of Fregosi and Adorni. Public order in trecento Siena was constantly disturbed by the bloody battles between Tolomei and Salimbeni and between the Malavolti and the Piccolomini.

Such intense interfamily hatred might not only excite all sorts of bloody disturbances and revolts, but might be extended as well to all facets of public life. When the clans had acquired enough influence in the town and had surrounded themselves with a substantial clientele, they dominated a veritable political action party whose entire being was directed toward the contest for power and offices with its rival. Public opinion and the authors who recorded instances of this collective mentality considered every factional quarrel or war of their own day to be derived from the conflict of two large groups, each dominated by a powerful family. Of course, this situation is not found everywhere. It might be of short duration in certain towns, yielding to a different division of forces or to parties of more complex structure.

There is no dearth of examples of such lasting identifications of party with family. Daniel Waley has noted that the parties at Orvieto were dominated by a single family. In the fourteenth century, the names of the Monaldeschi and the Philippeschi were superimposed upon or even replaced the designations Guelf and Ghibelline.[22] The earlier names were supplanted by families at Bologna as well, in this case the Lambertazzi and Geremei clans. These two family groups led the only two large parties which were active in military and political affairs. Nothing was done outside these parties. When the "knights and citizens of Bologna" prepared their expedition to the Orient in 1217, they took an oath on Christmas Eve to go on crusade to retake the Holy Land from the infidel. The leaders chosen for the two parties were Bonifacio de' Lambertazzi and Baruffadino de' Geremei. When they attacked Egypt, the Bolognese used the two clan names as their war cries. When the houses and towers of Damietta were given as spoils to the Bolognese, they divided them into two equal parts.[23]

The assimilation of the political party by a clan appears equally clearly in numerous cities of the plain of the River Po between 1250 and 1270. At Alexandria, a town lacking strong ancient traditions, party warfare amounted to the struggle of Lanzanegi and Benzoni. Wars raged at Pavia between the *pars illorum de Laturre* and the Fallabrini, and at Como between these same della Torre (despite the distance between the two towns) and the Vicani. Fighting at Lodi pitted the Overghaghi against the Sumarivi; at Cremona, the Capelleti against the Barabaresi; and finally at Vercelli, the Tizoni against the Avvocati.[24]

Although he uses a vocabulary better adapted to the Tuscan towns than to those of the north and displays an obvious lack of perspective, Giovanni Villani gives a most intriguing description of the stages by which genuine political parties evolved from family quarrels at Venice. The Querini (the *ca' Querini* in Villani's words) fomented a conspiracy in 1310 against the doge and his men, who were called "the ca' Gradanigo and his clients". The two clans were then organized into strong political factions which dominated the entire town, so that "the city was nearly divided between these two parties. Guelfs and Ghibellines used the cover of their names to resume their fighting". The use of the words 'Guelf' and 'Ghibelline' in this context is disconcerting, a gratuitous superimposition totally removed from reality. The new 'parties' at Venice based their power on no ancient rivalry or tradition, and thus were identified with the adherents of the two great clans (*ca'*). Villani concluded by saying that the Querini were defeated and exiled, their leaders executed, and their houses torn down. "This was the first time that houses had ever been destroyed at Venice."[25]

The party may also be made up of a complex alliance of different families. In certain cities or even entire regions, lesser families might affiliate with a party and thus become allies of more powerful clans in order to keep some share of influence. Thus, the party was not necessarily identified with a single family group, but might also consist of a network of alliances of varying degrees of stability between families of diverse social standing. For example, the Ghibelline party at Imola, in the Romagna, solidly united four powerful families (the Tartagni, Vaini, Cadronchi, and Pighini) between 1450 and 1480, while the Guelfs were led by the Mercati, Sassatelli, and Calderini.[26]

No extended family at Florence seems to have attained or kept enough power to take decisive leadership of a party, impose its name and escutcheon upon it, and reduce others to the status of associates. Florentine factions never bore family names. Their structure was thus more complex and ponderous than those of the parties of Pisa, Siena, or Orvieto. But all Florentine aristocratic houses, *nobili* and *popolani* alike, were nonetheless involved in these conflicts. The observant chronicler, wishing to portray opposing forces in the city, could do no better than divide the great families between two factions. His readers were thus made aware of divisions and fortuitous circumstances. Giovanni Villani did this, particularly for the two occasions when the parties dominated Florentine politics with particular force. For 1215 he lists all "houses and nobles who became Guelfs and Ghibellines at Florence" by sixths,[27] and for 1300, in noting "how the city of Florence was divided and rent asunder by the aforementioned White and Black parties", he enumerates several score of names, covering more than two pages of the chronicle.[28]

This precision in noting the party affiliation of each family is also found in descriptions of more ephemeral parties or *ad hoc* political alliances. To portray power relationships when the papal legate, the cardinal of Prato, arrived at Florence in 1303, Villani first describes at length "the sect supporting the cardinal, whose leaders (*caporali*) were the Cavalcanti, the Gherardini, and the Pulci". He then continues with an equally painstaking analysis of their adversaries ("the opponents of the Black party, whose leaders were messer . . .").[29] He displays the same concern for accuracy in 1343 as he enumerates the forces of the three "sects and conspiracies" which plotted the fall of the duke of Athens. Villani furnishes a veritable catalogue for each of them, carefully noting the names of the principal leaders and their clans.[30]

We may thus conclude that the concept of party held by Villani and many of his contemporaries reflects a widespread intellectual attitude: the political party at Florence, whatever its name or circumstances, was merely a collection of families whose names had to be known precisely from the outset to make the cast of characters and the play of forces at all comprehensible.

The great families maintained command over an entire quarter of the town. This was generally a compact area where the clan leaders, their collateral relatives, and their clients lived along a single street, around the square and the church of the patron saint, in the shadow of the great palaces, which were fortified with high towers. This concentration of the property of aristocratic families into solid blocs created veritable collective fortresses anchored in the city, which turned huge, austere, and threatening walls to the outside world. This feature was one of the most characteristic traits of the Italian urban landscape until after the sixteenth century.[31] All cities contain many examples, and the political power of these concentrations, seigneurial and aristocratic, obviously obtruded on local affairs.

G. Gozzadini's recent study of the great families of Bologna shows as well how their properties came to be collected in compact blocs. For example, the Lambertazzi, who led the Guelfs, possessed a *casamente* which they sold to the town in the first decade of the thirteenth century; it was the site of the later palace of the podestà. The Lambertazzi also owned all the buildings around the main town square.[32] The word *casamento*, designating a group of lots and buildings in the city, is found in several chroniclers' writings, particularly in Tuscany, and emphasizes clearly this concentration of properties. Moreover, the same authors generally used the plural forms 'palaces' or 'houses' when speaking of an important family, and often referred explicitly to "the houses of the sons of ...".

Still later at Genoa, between 1440 and 1480, the registers of the *Gabella Possessionum* strongly accentuate an astonishing degree of concentration of family properties. The register of 1463 lists 888 houses for fifty-eight noble clans (*alberghi*). Family properties were grouped so that only forty-two of these buildings were located outside the quarter which the owners' families dominated. As an example, sixty-two of sixty-seven houses owned by the Spinola di Luccolo were in the immediate neighbourhood of their palace.[33]

This cohesion afforded obvious defensive possibilities, which were accentuated by extraordinary and draconian measures taken in case of difficulties or battles to isolate the bloc more securely and protect it from external attacks. Villani constantly mentions the barricades (*serragli*) thrown up across streets in time of disorder to bar access to the quarters of the *grandi* and facilitate armed resistance. The word *serragli* is used six times within a few lines of the chronicle in the annal for 1343.[34] Another very suggestive expression of this chronicler describes clearly the partitioning of the city to protect the various noble quarters: "each end of the street or the quarter (*contrada*) was barricaded in the city at this time [1343]".[35] These defensive strongholds, particularly those held by the chief families of a party, obviously played a primary role during street combats. They were bastions upon which the factions could rely, and centres for assembly and administration of the group in time of peace.

The great families, whether as leaders of a party or as a fundamental element of its structure, certainly formed the framework of the political factions which fought to seize power. They were the moving forces. Naturally, they incited many quarrels and produced new divisions and balances of varying degree of stability, but they brought their own institutions and means of action in their train.

Parties and clients

The major source of power of the great clans which were engaged in the party struggles was sheer force of numbers. Their clienteles of collateral relatives and dependants, and indeed their very presence, demonstrates the originality of certain social structures. The vocabulary used by contemporary authors is significant. Various expressions in general use emphasize the alliance between masters and the clientele within the same family or partisan group. In this instance, their word choice seems surprisingly variegated. First, it might designate bonds of dependence. Villani uses the word *seguaci* or a derivative expression (*con loro seguito*) for all towns: Genoa ("and then the Doria with their followers"),[36] Pisa ("with other followers of the *popolo*"),[37] Venice,[38] and especially Florence, with reference to which he uses some version of this expression on many occasions (for example, "with a considerable train of their followers from the *contado*").[39]

We also encounter the *seguaci* or *sequaces* in the northern cities. The anonymous chronicler of Verona states that in 1272 "Count Lodovico di San Bonifacio, with his entire faction and followers, was driven from the city of Verona".[40] We find the words more frequently in the Guelf and Ghibelline *Annales* of Piacenza: in 1231 to identify the Milanese party (*Mediolanenses et eorum sequaces*);[41] in 1273, when Pleneamo de Fontana, citizen and podestà of Mantua, "with his followers and those of his party", drove out two of his enemies who had taken refuge in the castle;[42] in 1269, when Obertino de Lando "and his followers from outside Piacenza" seized and fortified a nearby castle, then installed a garrison of twenty-one "followers of his party" there;[43] and finally in 1261, when the bishop and clergy succeeded with the help of the Scotti in driving out Alberto de Fontana and his 'followers'.[44]

The word *masnadieri* seems to have had a more exact connotation of retainers, warriors attached to a powerful personality, very often by a vassalic bond in a direct, immediate dependence. The word was used most commonly in the northern regions, where the power of a great lord or count, master of castles and armies, a city tyrant or at least undisputed chieftain of a party was imposed upon all. This man exercised his power through the agency of his devoted faithful, the *masnadieri*. The da Romano of Vicenza and Bassano were surrounded by a strong *masnada* of fighters between 1170 and 1260. They gave their men municipal offices, even installing them in the notaries' bureaus. Entire families, such as the Graula, were considered part of the *masnada*. The word finally came to mean the entire party of the count. After the fruitless revolt of 1229, the lord's opponents then formed the *pars liberorum*, and the towns were thus divided, for purposes of general opinion and the chroniclers' pens, into *liberi* and *homini di masnada*.[45]

Not far from there, in the region of Mantua, party captains also collected numerous clients bound by relationships of fidelity and dependence. The oath sworn to the Gonzaga in 1361 mentions their *subdidi, fautores, sequaces et adherantes*. That taken to Galeazzo Visconti in the following year cites the *vassalli, subditi ... gli aderantie complici, i seguaci delle parti*. G. Soranzo has compiled a comprehensive list of these words, which are just as applicable to allied or subject towns as to political protégés and clients. Aside from those noted above in the two oaths, they include *accomendati, auxiliatores, censuarii, colligati, confederati, conventionati, defensores, feudatarii, receptatores, recomendati*, and *valitores*.[46] Giovanni Villani also uses such words in connection with the fray of May 1300 at Florence. "Giovanni and Giacotti Malaspina and their followers included more than thirty on horseback ... and with the Donati boys were the Pazzi, the Spini, and others from their *masnadieri*."[47]

Other words place a greater emphasis upon blood relationships, alliances, friendships, and protective ties. The Doria and Spinola were ruling Genoa in 1309; "the Spinola and their collateral relatives (*con suoi consorti de basso*) held the land with a tyrant's grip".[48] But on 24 September 1339 "the Genoese revolted with a tremendous outcry and drove them and their retainers from the land...".[49] Once again following Villani's narrative, we find that the twelve "principal leaders of the Guelf party who were then in Florence... went with a great company of their friends and retainers to meet the pope" in 1300.[50]

Finally, some more general terms evoke rather the idea of a large number of persons, a mob, or sometimes even a complex, inconstant basis of social recruitment. They convey an impression of the unknown, of lurking danger. The chronicler Landolfo uses the words *seguaci* and *turba* to denote the retainers of Archbishop Grossolano at Milan between 1102 and 1106.[51] Much later, Villani tells us that Florence in 1307 was "full of robbers, foreigners, and farmers, each clan with its *raunata*".[52] He reports that in the little town of San Miniato al Tedesco, in 1346, the Florentine podestà "wished to bring to trial certain criminals who were among the *masnadieri* of the Malpighi and the Mangiadori. But these clans, aided by their armed friends, stirred the countryside to insurrection".[53]

The incessant use of these words to emphasize the power of some person or party suggests that contemporary writers were perfectly well aware of the significance of political clienteles and their decisive role in the life of the city. As officers of the commune, the magistrates could hardly have ignored them, and some sought unremittingly to combat and destroy the régime of factions. An examination of their actions viewed in this light provides decisive proof of this. One of the surest ways to strike at a party was to reduce the number of its clients, to separate the leaders from the collateral relatives whom they were protecting. This explains the civic authorities' interest in measures which were often included in sumptuary legislation to limit mob participation in great family ceremonies or even in the *brigate* of clans or parties during the public festivals.[54] The genuinely public festival, organized by the commune, could thus be a political weapon which would affirm the solidarity of all inhabitants of the city. It was often directed against private festivals which in themselves hardened family and factional particularism.

Other measures were undertaken with a like purpose of weakening the clienteles. In 1328, the Venetian Council of Ten, in an attempt to hinder armed officers from serving private interests, forbade "sons, brothers, nephews, sons of sons or household retainers" to bear arms. The *Signori di Notte* had already instituted this prohibition in 1299.[55] Attacking the *masnadieri* was one of the standard ways of proceeding against the great men at Florence. The Ordinances of Justice foreshadowed the suppression of the idea of collective responsibility of relatives, and Villani expressly emphasized this point shortly after the fall of the duke of Athens.

The Ordinances of Justice noted that previously, when a magnate criminal perpetrated a misdeed against the person of a *popolano*, his entire house or clan would have to pay £3,000 to the commune over and above his own penalty. The Ordinances changed this by saying that it only had reference to his nearest relatives.[56]

This was part of a deliberate policy of loosening the bonds of the family group and disrupting the solidarity felt between kinsmen.

The clientele, formed chiefly by the blood tie but consisting also of protégés, lesser allies, and commended persons of varying status was thus an element of cardinal importance. G.A. Brucker has given a very convincing analysis of this phenomenon in his explanation of certain aspects of the Ciompi revolt at Florence in 1378. He shows that the nobles who were hostile to the party in power were surrounded by a strong clientele of lesser persons, citizens and peasants.[57] If the great clans constituted the basic framework of the political factions, the allies and protégés of all social backgrounds were its necessary human agents.[58] 'Vertical' lines played a determinant role in political and social activity. A final sign which I consider very significant may convince us: in his *Treatise on urbanism*, written from 1537, the architect Serlio, who was originally from Venice, a town where the parties were rather weak, devoted an entire chapter to describing a particular type of house, that of the party leader. It should be fortified, topped with a tower which would serve as the citadel of last retreat, and Serlio stresses particularly that the party leader should place his house at some distance from the town hall, but in the neighbourhood of a clientele toward whom he was to be generous.[59] This last and very late testimony to the strength of the political parties in medieval Italy is truly decisive.

CHAPTER TWO

Town and countryside

Most political histories, even bare narratives of events, civil wars, revolts, and disturbances of all sorts, emphasize the towns and generally ignore the countryside. For the historian, Italy has remained primarily a land of merchant cities which dominated international commerce, banking, and financial activities throughout the West. Despite several excellent recent studies, the countryside is much less well known. The entire Italian aristocracy is still inappropriately identified with the great merchants; in a number of popularizations it is even erroneously called a 'bourgeois' aristocracy. Italian civilization, whether 'medieval' or 'Renaissance' (whatever these words may mean!), is regarded as being first and foremost an urban phenomenon. Agrarian life, *contado* and distant mountain society have drawn scholars' attention only rarely until a very few years ago.

An attitude which has been astonishingly widespread, even among historians, has posited a severe separation between rural and urban society, however improbable on the face of it this may be. They have been considered completely distinct and fundamentally opposed, even hostile. We have been presented with 'capitalistic' or 'precapitalistic' society on the one hand and 'feudal' society on the other. 'Feudal' is a particularly vague word, devoid of precise meaning, which must clearly be re-examined or at the very least severely nuanced. Town seems to dominate the countryside politically, of course, but who actually held power? What were the origins, the bases, the reserves of power of this so-called urban oligarchy or aristocracy?

The town also seems a privileged haven where party fights, violent conflicts, and civil wars can occur with relative impunity. But may we not ascribe this idea to the fact that townsmen composed numerous chronicles and the men of the countryside very few? Urban authors wrote chiefly of what they witnessed each day, and 'modern' historians too concentrate on events which are thus privileged. Hence all conceive of town and countryside relationships in terms of opposition and not of collaboration or even interaction.

Town–countryside bonds and the parties

The great families of the aristocracy, both those of the 'nobility' and their counterparts in the *popolo*, constituted the nucleus and framework of the party. But were clans, which were essentially all-powerful tribes, not settled outside the cities? Did they not have ties with the princes and great magnates of the countryside, bonds with the castellans of the environs? Finally, did their clienteles consist exclusively of townsmen?

We find in fact that many urban families were firmly established in the countryside. This fundamental aspect of the society of medieval Italy, and indeed of the entire West, was long misunderstood or deliberately misinterpreted. Historians always follow sacrosanct theses, in this case the veritable dogma of the profound originality of the urban milieu, of the urban 'revolution'. For several generations they have portrayed an urban aristocracy with no ties in the countryside as present when the towns originated and throughout the early communal period to the end of the fourteenth century. The evidence of their possession of rural lands at the end of the Middle Ages is so plentiful that it cannot be ignored, but the older school has explained this as the result of a desire to withdraw money from unfavourable business ventures during difficult times. There was a loss of the spirit of adventure and a desire to acquire a certain noble character, which in itself was a sign of commercial decline and economic atrophy. This explanation has the further advantage of emphasizing the "economic crisis of the fifteenth century".

Unfortunately, it is totally erroneous.[60] Most families of the fifteenth-century 'urban' aristocracy had no thought of acquiring a patent of 'nobility'; they had enjoyed the status long since. Their lands were not all recently acquired, and they were the antithesis of impersonal financial investments. This is shown by all sorts of private documents, merchant letters, and account books, such as ledger-books or 'Books of Reason' (*di ragione* or *di ricordanze*).[61] Together with books[62] and accounts of possessions,[63] they offer spontaneous proof of a profound and constant interest in or even obsession with affairs of the land, which was a sign of power and a source of profit. The 'Book of Reason' deliberately invokes the rural, by which we may understand seigneurial, origins of the family: the name of the settlement and the more or less legendary ancestors, battles, fortunes, divisions among descendants, and the importance of the domain or ancient patrimony.[64] The 'merchant' always maintained a manor house in this village, with tower, portico, court, well, and outbuildings. There too he tried to lure sharecroppers and extend his landholdings by purchasing numerous domains and patiently assimilating smaller pieces of land. This dominance and continuity, whether real or imaginary, whether created after the fact by an oral tradition or by the invention of the parvenu, shows clearly the political and social importance which was attached to the possession, dating as far back in time as possible, of domains and seigneurial, origins of the family: the name of the settlement and the which is generally held without benefit of serious investigation, rural landholdings far exceed urban both in total numbers and in value in all the Tuscan books. Francesco Datini, the son of a petty shopkeeper and as such a sort of social parvenu, obligingly drew up a balance and estimate of all his possessions in 1407, toward the end of his life. He recorded twenty-seven pieces of property in the town of Prato itself, of which twenty-five were houses and two were *fondachi*, worth a total of 2,948 florins. In the countryside he had a manor house with tower, seven parcels of woodland, two farms operated by sharecroppers, and thirty-five plots of arable land with a total value of 6,992 florins.[65] The example is all the more instructive because Francesco Datini inherited from Marco, his father, only a house in the town and a few very dispersed properties. Francesco bought all the rest from neighbours, lords or peasants. This deliberate policy of extending rural possessions was not peculiar to Datini; it finds confirmation throughout Italy, among persons of all social categories and levels of fortune.

Each city had a group of great nobles whose wealth came not only from lands and seigneurial domains, but also from fiefs and fortified castles. The great houses of Genoa conform to this pattern, from the Fieschi of Lavagna in the Apennines and along the Riviera di Levante to the Grimaldi in Antibes and Monaco.[66] The Tolomei, wealthy bankers and merchants of Siena, held considerable land in the *contado* and kept it even after they had lost power in the city and been expelled from the Council of the Nine.[67] Villani gives numerous precise instances of rural landholding among the great families of Florence, indicating for each of them the power of their fiefs and fortifications and sometimes the geographical pattern of their settlement in the *contado*.

Certain words which were used quite commonly in the great merchant cities emphasize the seigneurial, perhaps even 'feudal' character of the great clans which preserved close ties with the countryside and drew additional power from there even after they had been firmly established in the city. Our texts thus speak of *nobili selvatici* who still possessed a great *selva*, a vast animal run or forest exploitation which was often administered by the entire clan in common. We find them at Pisa[68] and Siena.[69] Giovanni Villani unleashed several denunciations of the disgraceful activities of nobles whom he called *salvatichi*, an adjective which we may certainly, in a deliberate anachronism, translate 'savage', but which Villani also used to mean a person recently arrived in the city or at least a bumpkin who had not yet adjusted completely to the niceties of city life. Hence in 1300 he called the Cerchi "men who are *salvitichi* and unpleasant, as persons who have only recently come to power tend to be".[70] In these same towns and in several regions of the north, the communal officers and later the chroniclers used the names *Cattanei* or *Cattani* for nobles who still held effective judicial rights over their men, relatives, retainers, and clients in both town and countryside. At Pisa, their law court, the *curia Cattanorum* or *corte dei Cattani*, was the vigorous rival of the *curia maleficorum* of the commune in the 1280s. In 1282, twenty-three witnesses stated absolutely that all the dependants of one of these great families were subject to its justice, which was exercised continuously by a number of officers.[71] Several of the oldest clans at Genoa, the Bustarini, Stangoni, Scotti, and Maloni, lived in the old quarter of Sarzano, a nucleus whose history went back to the first period of urban expansion, when it bore the revealing name of the *compagna* of the *castello*.[72] These families united with the della Volta clan in the 1420s to form a single noble house or *albergho*, and they chose *Cattaneo* as their new name.[73] Particularly at such a late date, the use of this name shows the marked attachment to a certain form of power, to seigneurial traditions of obvious rural origins. The Genoese nobles were looking for a kind of symbol. We should note also that only two noble *alberghi* were living in the *compagna* of the *castello* at this time, and that the second bore the equally suggestive name of *Salvaigho*.[74] *Salvaigho* and *Cattaneo* were assumed by these two clans of the old quarter, while many others took names which evoked large scale commerce and maritime adventure (*Mari, di Mari, Usodimare*).

In Lombardy, the della Torre party (the *Torriani*) was attacked and defeated in 1277 by another party called the *Cattanei et vavassores*.[75] A Veronese family which originated in the lower Adige valley and was involved in the interminable conflict between the da Romano and the Este between 1230 and 1250 was called the Cattanei of Lendenara.[76] Much earlier, in the first decade of the twelfth century, a chronicler indicates that a party of *valvassori et capitanei* was formed at Lodi.[77]

Secondly, the clans which were strongest in the city deliberately sought the alliance of more rural families. This occurred most commonly through the marriages of their children, who thus became pledges of future succour with men and property. These numerous alliances were often the fruit of a systematic dynastic policy. Within the short span of a generation or two they could fundamentally alter the balance of power inside the city or even the entire region. This happened with the direct descendants of Romeo Pepoli, the Bolognese usurer and merchant. Their immense fortune enabled them to contract numerous marriages with noble families of the countryside between 1335 and 1350. In this way they became lords of several seigneuries and even entire counties. When Romeo Pepoli was driven from his native city in 1321, he took refuge with his relatives, the Este of Ferrara, before reaching Avignon.[78]

Such a policy might far transcend the framework of simple private bonds between individuals. At Genoa it sometimes brought about the total fusion of two clans, the one primarily urban and mercantile, the other exclusively or mainly 'feudal', master of dispersed seigneuries, lands, and men. Unions between two such different clans or *alberghi* in themselves forcibly introduced a new balance of power. This happened, for example, in the 1440s, when two rich merchant families of the city, the Oliva and the Ceba, were incorporated into the redoubtable Grimaldi clan. On 25 October 1448, sixty-four leaders of the Grimaldi family, certain of them stating that they were acting on behalf of their other close relatives, received seven family leaders of the Ceba.[79] These new solidarities, born of multiple marriages or radical fusions, testify amply to the close union between the urban aristocracy of very diverse origins and the dominant powers of the countryside. In no way did the city remain isolated.

It is likewise impossible to conceive of a 'feudal' seigneurial nobility, isolated in its castles, exploiting its lands, and governing its men while remaining apart from the quarrels and partisan warfare of urban life. Lords of every rank and fortune were deeply involved in the factional conflicts of the city. They constantly intervened with their armies, and the more powerful of them tried to dominate the towns.

Some great 'feudal' dynasts, the lords of the largest seigneuries, particularly those in the mountains, frequently brought all their influence to bear on one or more merchant cities. This occurred most frequently in northern Italy, where the continuation of the old Carolingian 'marches' unified several counties and gave an incomparably great authority and power to the 'marquis'. Such lords tried to establish and consolidate veritable principalities and impose their domination upon the merchant towns, which were sources of the money without which no political or military enterprise could hope to succeed. The forms of intervention of course varied: external pressure could be exerted by armed might and an intelligent choice of allies, or one or more offices of podestà might be usurped for the leading men of the clan or their closest relatives. Such external interventions were among the primary events even of the internal life of the cities throughout the 'communal' period. They were constant threats which complicated and gravely affected the balance of power and the ultimate fate of the parties.

The marquises of Malaspina, the principal 'feudal' house of the countryside around Piacenza, do not seem to have lived in the town themselves. They were lords of vast seigneuries to the south, in the Apennines, and near the border of the district of Genoa. Their territories even reached the sea near Sarzana and Carrara.[80] They nonetheless participated actively in the factional quarrels of Piacenza and other nearby cities, particularly between 1230 and 1260. In July 1249, Bernabo Malaspina entered the little mountain town of Pontremoli "with his own men, a corps of two hundred knights from Piacenza, and the militias of the Taro and Ceno valleys to enforce the domination of this party. They had been summoned by the Pontremoli party, which had already installed six captains". He immediately established his party there.[81] A treaty of pacification sealed at Piacenza in July 1260 between the local 'insider' and 'outsider' parties shows this same Bernabo and his kinsman Frederico Malaspina leading thirty loyal knights, entrenched in the heart of the city as allies of the 'insiders'.[82]

The same was true of the marquises of Pallavicino, whose adventurous enterprises seem to have covered a still larger sphere of action in the heart of Lombardy, from Parma to Como and from Alexandria to Brescia. The leaders of this clan were willing to take control of an entire city or of a party within a town. The career and fortunes of the marquis Oberto Pallavicino afford a remarkable example of a great fiefholder constantly intervening in the affairs of the Lombard commercial centres. Oberto was podestà of Cremona in 1249 and of Piacenza from 1253 to 1257 and, finally and most importantly, the 'signoria' of Piacenza reverted to him in 1261. During this time he had participated in every conflict and peace treaty worthy of note in the area. The author of the *Annales Ghibellini* gave this man a warm funeral eulogy:

He was longtime leader of the entire imperial party in Lombardy and Tuscany ... and was simultaneously lord of the cities of Cremona, Milan, Brescia, Piacenza, Tortona, and Alexandria . . .. He commended his sons to the parties of Piacenza and Parma and to the commune of Pavia.[83]

The image of this colossus was so real that it even took precedence over the emperor's memory or reputation: the party opposed to the Church in these cities was usually called 'party of the marquis' (*pars Marchionis*).

Farther east, in the region of Padua and Verona, where the memory of the powerful counts of the March was still quite vivid, two opposing parties were commanded by clans which were actually great forces of 'feudalism'. The da Romano (*pars Eccelini*, from the name of Ezzelino da Romano) usually favoured the emperor, while the family of the marquises of Este (*pars Marchionis*) fought for the pope. To control or subdue the towns, these great princely clans established their relatives in them. Salinguerra, brother-in-law of Ezzelini II da Romano, became podestà of Verona in 1230 and held Ferrara between 1220 and 1240. Count Sanbonifacio, an ally of the Este, led a strong party of his own (*pars comitis*). Driven from Verona in 1227, he established himself at Mantua and ruled this city till 1272. The Camposanpiero, another great 'feudal' family allied with the Este, meddled constantly at Padua and Verona.[84]

Bologna itself did not escape these sometimes decisive undertakings of the great feudatories. After the Lambertazzi had been driven from the city in 1274, they were attacked before Faenza by a Bolognese army reinforced by contingents from Cremona, Modena, Parma, and other allied cities of the Romagna. But the Lambertazzi in their turn were being helped by the count of Montefeltre, from the distant land of Urbino, and thus they easily vanquished their opponents.[85]

On a totally different level, seigneurial families with less extensive connections often limited their activity to a single neighbouring town. They still carried a certain weight and intervened constantly in the internal struggles of these cities. Bologna also affords examples of lords of this type. The Medicini or Biancucci family, normally called the *Cattanei della grossa terra matildica di Medicina* in the sources written around 1280, held a princely court deep in the mountains which Dante Alighieri visited on several occasions. Their adherents were called *di Medicina* "because they were the *cattanei* and feudatories of that clan". The chronicler Benvenuto da Imola mentions them in saying that "certain noble and powerful persons called the captains of Medicina" ruled there. They were undoubtedly kinsmen of the Medicina nobles of Ravenna. In any case, they were firmly ensconced at Bologna, where they participated in all the great controversies of the age. More generally, they were politically active in the Romagna.[86] Another rural family of the environs of Bologna, the Panico, dominated much of the Apennine range and even held several castles on the opposite slope in Tuscany. They held the title of count and participated actively in the politics of the great city. This brought them honours and offices. Count Ugolino II Panico was chosen captain of the Bolognese highlands in 1292, 1296, and 1300. As rebels against Bologna, they were active in factional strife both inside and outside the city. They supported Lewis of Bavaria against the papal legate in 1329 and favoured the Pepoli in 1342. They helped introduce the government of a despot in the person of Oleggio in 1355, and through Bernardo Visconti in 1356 and 1368.[87] These interventions by necessity entailed a shift in the balance of available power and decisively influenced the fate of the various forces.

The Lombard towns, particularly those near Piacenza, also had to reckon constantly with noble lords of nearby castles whom the chroniclers deliberately called the 'outsiders'. One Obertino de Lando, who belonged to a very active and influential family living in the orbit of Piacenza, affords a fine example of the feudatories who gravitated around the city. His military campaigns and other enterprises between 1268 and 1288 show that he was always an 'outsider' to the city. Yet he intervened in every conflict, using his power as castle lord, redoubling in vain his efforts to enter the town, seeking allies everywhere. The possibility of his intervention thus had serious effects on the balance of power between the factions.[88]

If princes and great lords could dominate a city by holding such positions of authority as podestà, those of lesser rank often served the towns as soldiers of fortune or *condottieri*. Most lords of the Romagna held miniscule territories which were difficult to govern and provided scant revenue. Forced into debt furthermore by an opulent life style, they could only live by the *condotta*, generally as *accomendati* of the great powers of Italy, especially Milan or Florence. This secured them a regular income.[89] Sometimes these captains fought in the proximity of their own castles, thus exerting a powerful influence in nearby cities when they arrived to impose the rule of one of the local parties.

The masses who poured into the streets during the armed conflicts, revolts, and disruptions which bathed the cities in blood did not consist entirely of small guildsmen or even vagabonds or persons on the fringes of society. During the more serious crises, these people were often joined by hordes of peasants brought or summoned to the town. These farmers provided important reinforcements and could rapidly change the course of events. All elements of rural society, noble and peasant alike, thus participated in these factional conflicts.

The townsmen obviously feared most the fiefholders who could arm their men and force the town gates at the head of a horde of followers lusting after booty. The chroniclers took note of their powers and mentioned their fiefs and human resources, including trained regulars under arms as well as the more usual bands of simple peasants. At Piacenza, these *servientes* and *rustici* always accompanied the great lords. The papal legates who wanted to alter town policy in 1266 arranged for the captains and lords of the Fontana party to enter the city "with a great number of armed peasants from the Tidone valley". The rustics encamped in the Buffa palace, but the Church party was defeated by the intervention of Ghibelline troops from Cremona who massacred many of the outsiders.[90]

But the leading families of the cities also had rural clienteles. When the great conspiracy of the Oltrarno families of Bardi, Rossi, and Frescobaldi was discovered at Florence in 1340, their enemies sounded the bells to summon the citizenry to arms. But they also closed the town gates immediately, so that access would be denied to the retainers of the noble clans and their clients in the countryside.[91] Much is now known of the sometimes decisive role of the rural clienteles of the magnates. D. Herlihy has stressed the skill displayed by the great families of Pistoia in recruiting poor peasants to help them. In the most turbulent districts, the nearby mountains, the men who sent troops to help the city were also the poorest, those who had most need of the generosity and protection of some magnate. It was there that the Cancellieri, a family which led one of the two principal factions of the city, found most of their partisans.[92] G.A. Brucker has shown clearly how the great magnates, who were largely responsible for the Ciompi uprising of 1378, had maintained or created multiple ties of protection and dependence in the countryside, thereby gaining the allegiance of numerous farmers.[93] We have already noted the importance within the party of the clienteles of powerful noble clans. They constituted the greatest part of their fighting forces during combat. But they were as much rural as urban, being composed in large measure of villagers from places where the magnates had their manor houses and lands.

The magistrates of the commune in their turn tried to arm their own peasant dependents to oppose the farmer contingents of the *grandi*. The organization of peasant militias seems to have been strongest in Tuscany, where the neighbouring *contado* was closely integrated into city life. In 1250 a series of ordinances established in detail the entire political and military régime of the Florentine *contado*. Political associations were established which were centred around a strong rural parish organization, whose troops were to bear arms during wartime and to come to the city when summoned by the podestà or the captain of the people.[94] Siena had an elite corps of 5,000 farmers in 1302 who were "faithful friends of the holy Roman Church and of the peace of the city of Siena", commanded by *popolani* officers from the city.[95] The Sienese constitution of 1330 devoted fifty-six rubrics (numbers 355 through 411) to societies and companies which had been established to keep order. Special peasant units from the *Massa* or *Cortine*, districts just outside the city, were entrusted with preventing or suppressing acts of magnate aggression against *popolani*.

Social structure, property, and relationships of clientage or dependence thus created constant bonds between town and countryside in an Italy which is generally portrayed as dominated by 'merchant' cities. Many families, which were obviously among the most powerful, maintained dual residence in town and countryside and as such were neither 'bourgeois' nor 'city dwellers', neither 'feudal' nor 'rural', since they were both. These lords were extremely influential and active in both milieus. The two worlds, far from being unfamiliar to each other, were in constant interplay through the alliances and bonds of clientage involved in party activity.

The parties in the countryside

The interaction and close ties between town and country, together with the use of heterogeneous forces in the factional quarrels, made it impossible for the countryside to avoid the bloody party conflicts of the towns. If the principal objective of all these rivalries remained to dominate the town and assume power within the wall, the nearby rural district and the more distant mountains alike were reservoirs of men. They were also quite often strategic crossroads and refuges, providing places of retrenchment for enemies who had lost a battle and been declared 'rebels'. Political and military domination of the countryside moreover assured the cities' supplies of food and tax revenue. Hence various pursuits and reprisals, raids, acts of pillage, assaults, and sackings of villages and castles occurred during the most bitter moments of the party wars.

Giovanni Sercambi strongly emphasizes the devastation of the countryside by the members of the victorious party at Lucca as they pursued the rebels in 1396: "They pillaged the land and burned much of it ...; and they burned more than three-quarters ...; and then they razed the tower of Dallo, destroyed the houses of the settlement, and cut down their vineyards ...".[96] During a campaign of over a year in 1401 and 1402 against the rival Panciaticchi clan, the Cancellieri of Pistoia were particularly avid in devastating the countryside and burning their opponents' villages and castles.[97] Ricciardo Cancellieri, when pursued in his turn by the town militia, had to flee to the mountains and barricade himself in his powerful castle of Sanbuca, where he repulsed all attacks for over two years in the hope that reinforcements would arrive.[98]

For centuries strategic warfare involving fortified settlements and castles was also accepted as a major element in party conflict throughout Italy. The knights of Piacenza, whose position there was very precarious after 1090, fled and reconnoitred "in castles, 'places', and towns of the district of Piacenza". They blockaded the roads

so that no one might enter the town or bring or convey anything there. If they found that someone was transporting goods into the city, they stole his oxen and all that he was carrying, and even cut off his feet and hands.

Thus besieged in the city, the *popolani* began to run out of food and were forced to make a sortie against these fortresses and markets. They captured the 'villa' of San Giorgio, several 'places' and strongholds, took some twenty warriors prisoner, and set fire to the buildings.[99] Somewhat later the marquis of Pallavicino, allied with the urban *popolo*, attacked the captains of the Fontana party and seized the castle of Puglio, where there were "more than thirty knights and many *servientes* of Valdestofola who had come there to serve the knights of Piacenza, together with several local peasants".[100] In 1257 the podestà of Piacenza himself came to besiege the castle of Viciriano, which was held by some exiles from the town. They soon fled, "leaving in the castle some servants and peasants (*servientes et rusticos*) who knew nothing of their departure".[101] Finally, during the great conflicts of 1271, two nobles of Piacenza, Gerardo de Maxerata and Obertino de Noceto, rejoined the party of the exiles (*pars exterior*). They "entered Pietra Scremona with their servants, men of the same party, and the men of Balbi and fortified it . . . they also fortified Ozola". Then, after summoning the forces of allied villages and castles, they launched several attacks or 'cavalcades' against the villages and territories of their adversaries.

On Monday, 4 May, the lord Guizardo de Andito and Razo de Calenzaro marched to Pietra Dueria with about seventy knights who had been at Zavatarello. On Wednesday, 6 May, these knights with their men, together with the men of Gravago, Varxio, and the Sette Sorelle with fifty servants . . . attacked the 'villa' of Tolleric. They pillaged and burned it, and indeed the very countryside itself.

This castle warfare finally led to a pitched battle, a great combat during which the *exteriores* killed many of their enemies and returned to camp with a considerable booty.[102]

Another spectacular example of inter-party castle warfare occurred near Verona in 1233.

The castle of Caldiero was burned. Over two hundred persons died there, both rich and poor. More than a thousand oxen and horses and considerable chattels and food were lost ...; the following day, Messer Ezzelino da Romano entered the castle under heavy guard, with the help of the Monticuli party, the men of Lendenara, and those of the Quattro Venti. He provisioned it with foodstuffs and arms.[103]

Such details show how fortified castles might be centres for sustenance, places of refuge for men and beasts, and victualling depots during periods of open warfare between parties.

The castle and the fortified settlement held by lords and their peasants was obviously a constant danger and a significant threat to adversaries or to men hostile in principle to the party régime. Furthermore, warfare against fortresses was costly, for a castle might hold out indefinitely. It was not always easy to surround one for months at a time with substantial contingents, for financing these required considerable expenditure. The adversaries often preferred to reach a quick settlement by offering peace and paying an indemnity. Many seigneurial fortresses were thus taken "by agreement rather than force" during the factional struggles of northern Italy. It is understandable that, as soon as the town authorities began seizing fortified towers within the city, limiting their height or insisting that they be dismantled or torn down, they also began a systematic policy of opposition to the rural fortresses, in many cases demanding and obtaining their destruction.[104] An example of this in Lombardy occurred at Brescia between 1210 and 1212. When one of the parties emerged victorious and had driven out its opponents, it destroyed their towers and fortified buildings in the city itself, but then attacked the castle of Gavardo, where they had taken refuge. It was conquered by a mob, which dismantled and burned it on St Paul's Day.[105]

In 1316, the commune of Bologna similarly ordered that the three principal castles of the da Panico family (Rudiano, Malfalle, and Panico) be destroyed. Panico was only to fall nine years later. Although it was then completely razed, the victory had been bought dearly and moreover remained incomplete. The da Panico resumed the struggle, relying on the help of the more distant mountain settlements.[106] Collecting the scattered evidence furnished by several chroniclers and authors, Y. Renouard found that fifty-two castles existed in the *contado* of Florence before 1050. Between 1050 and 1100 there were 130, and 205 between 1100 and 1200.[107] These figures show that even at the height of the communal period, seigneurial defences and places of refuge in Tuscany, even those close to the city and under its dominance or even political administration, were being strengthened. The affirmation of communal autonomy and the assumption of power over the *contado* was in no way incompatible with the multiplication of seigneurial fortresses and a stronger military presence of the magnates in the countryside. Only much later, beginning in 1310, did the commune formulate and impose a totally different policy. Villani notes that numerous castles were destroyed at that time on the orders of the town government. After the abortive revolt of the Bardi, Rossi, and Frescobaldi in 1340, the Florentines prohibited "any citizen from acquiring a castle outside their *contado* but less than twenty miles from its border".[108] This ordinance again gives clear proof that rural fortresses were held not only by 'feudal' families who did not live in the city, but also by the citizens themselves. It is of interest to note that this regulation was issued nearly half a century after the famous Ordinances of Justice, whose purpose had been to isolate the magnates and destroy all elements of their political and military power!

Rural life in Tuscany and Lombardy was thus constantly disrupted by factional conflicts which manifested themselves in reprisal expeditions, guerilla warfare, and assaults on strong points or provision convoys. The fate of the countryside was closely bound to that of the cities. Wars there were undoubtedly longer and more devastating in some regions than in others. Armed party conflict in rural Liguria was particularly serious just outside the city walls, in the suburbs and the mountains, and on both land and sea. The goal was control of the Riviera with its ports and the Apennine passes, which would secure marine and land routes or, in the case of the excluded party, the blockade of a besieged town which was awaiting the arrival of ships bearing grain and salt.[109]

Furthermore, the role of parties in the countryside was far greater than merely providing repercussions or prolongation, in a sort of faint echo, of quarrels which began in the cities. The rural districts, however distant from the city they may have been, experienced these conflicts as intensely as did the towns. Rival families struggled vigorously to seize power and profits on a local scale. Whatever the distance from the metropolis and hence the extent of isolation, whatever the type of settlement and the population density of the villages, settlements, or small towns of the area, party struggles of this sort occurred.

Some very small towns which were mere crossroads or fortified settlements on the mountain passes experienced severe and permanent intestine quarrels between rival clans which sometimes managed to surround themselves with genuine political parties. We find this in the small towns of the Romagna, such as Forlì and Faenza, even those of the marches (Fano), and in the lesser settlements and villages of this always turbulent area, where petty lords nearby (such as those of Imola) and their agents constantly had to intervene to settle inter-family conflicts.[110] A similar situation occurred in the Apennines south of Piacenza, on the Ligurian road, and even in Liguria itself on the fiefs of the Malaspina and the Fieschi. At the more substantial settlement of Pontremoli, two clans and their allies, the Filippi versus the Anrighi and Oddoberti, vied to achieve *dominium*. Each party sought distant, powerful allies, the city of Parma or the marquis of Malaspina.[111]

When these conflicts were so long lasting as to appear to be a permanent feature of political life, those involved took over the names of the great Italian political parties of the day. Luca Dominici lists rural villages with their party affiliation as of 1286, when the great rivalry between Whites and Blacks was breaking out in Pistoia.[122] The new quarrel spread to the villages even before reaching the city of Florence. Rural allies and clients thus provided immediate assistance and found themselves engaged in a conflict between magnates who were proprietors of castles and lands.

The two-party régime in specifically rural districts is not peculiar to mainland Italy during the communal period. Corsica had few towns, and even these were small and uninfluential, with no communal organization. Yet in Corsica the same pattern appears: hostile parties whose influence had a considerable geographical range fought throughout the countryside, even in the most remote districts.

Several documents transcribed by G. Santini allow us to examine quite closely these factional conflicts in the mountain district of the Frignano, isolated in the Apennines between Modena and Pistoia.[113] It was the prototype of the valley community, including at various times between thirty and sixty federated primary communities called *pievi*. The *pievi* in turn were of varying importance and size, grouping several hamlets or villages into smaller federations. The generally collegiate government of the Frignano was usually dominated by two podestàs. As it happens, all the documents which furnish information on the internal structure of the valley organization mention two parties. The names varied, but Guelf and Ghibelline were among them. All the *pievi* were divided between these two factions. We find the split in a contract leasing a *selva* to a company of Tuscan herdsmen in 1281; in two peace treaties imposed by the podestàs in 1280 and 1306; in a report concerning the election of the podestàs in 1313; and in all divisions of offices and honours. The *pieve* was a 'solidarity', recognizing only one 'colour' and belonging to a single party. But the peace treaties show that the *pievi* were rivals, caught up in the hostility of two factions which might go as far as armed conflict. The origin of the party régime in the Frignano may have been in a rivalry between the ecclesiastical fiefs, which sided with the Guelf city of Bologna, and the comital fiefs, which were bound to Ghibelline Modena. In any event, a document of 1310 enumerated sixty-one *pievi*, primary federated communes, of which thirty-five were Guelf. This two-party structure was maintained as late as the end of the fifteenth century. A document of 1488 mentions twenty-one communities, including 124 hearths, in the *podesteria* of Montecucculo which constituted the *parte mediata* of the Frignano, and twenty-seven communities including four hundred hearths in the *podesteria* of Sestola, forming the *parte immediata*.

This analysis of a quite ordinary phenomenon underscores the point at which even remote countryside areas with no central town, village, or market, leading only a pastoral existence and thus relegated to severe isolation, might participate just as avidly in the party conflicts as did the great cities. These struggles were not peculiarly urban. We speak more freely of urban political parties, but we are always victims of a distorted viewpoint which leads us to consider primarily the great cities, their merchants and citizens. This error leads us to think that town 'dominated' countryside. The truth is that these two societies were closely intertwined by various relationships, so that all of northern and central Italy participated in these chronic, violent party struggles. The presence of numerous clienteles of farmers in the city reminds us of the importance of this element in the social basis for recruitment of members of the factions. We are doubtless dealing with a vertical social structure, but it was no less complex for that fact.

CHAPTER THREE

The governance of the parties

The political parties of medieval Italy were extremely complex and their institutional structures varied greatly. The historian of institutions finds them difficult entities to understand and even troublesome to approach. They were spontaneous formations which were generally born in the ripening of conflicts which had deep social roots. Then, as the disagreements were suddenly brought into the open by a chance quarrel, the parties were brought into action according to the play of circumstances and precarious balances, with no concern given to the luxury of a rigorous organization. They were *ad hoc* groups of men from all walks of life, masters and clients, city folk and country dwellers, men with necessarily divergent viewpoints and interests and with very different immediate ambitions, who were thrown together in the same political or military venture.

The factions were ungovernable, at least in the early period. They were ruled on a day-to-day basis by the interplay of alliances. The leaders assumed control as a function of their power and prestige and by becoming star performers during the first conflicts. They had no thought at all of creating a regular and stable political institution such as an electoral assembly or a council. Acclamation, not election, created their power. Party government then became interwoven with the fickle and dangerous mobs. No statutes, constitutions, nor even perhaps common practices or customs, were imposed on the party members.

The governors of the political parties had to use the institutional structure which already existed. It could provide a framework which could satisfy immediate needs. The great extended families are one example of such primary structures. Another basis for some parties was a long apprenticeship of aristocratic or 'popular' neighbourhood assemblies, particularly noble 'tower societies' or 'societies of knights', 'merchant societies', or 'gate societies'. Above all, the political party was a fighting unit which subsequently became an organ of political repression used against vanquished opponents, who were naturally called traitors and rebels. The terminology used sometimes shows how much the party structure borrowed from contemporary military and judicial institutions.

Once the party had been established, its fortunes determined its organization. The absolute triumph of one faction, which made the dream of exercising total dominion over the city for many years into a reality, forced the party to create more elaborate institutions which to some degree were patterned on those of the commune or might even be confused with them. It was hard sometimes to distinguish party officials from local magistrates. Finally, the diffusion of party operations into a large area beyond the town or rural district to other cities gave birth to still more varied politico-military or institutional relationships. These might take the form of simple alliances or better organized, more stable regional leagues.

Podestàs and captains

The few precise bits of information which we can find in the narratives, chronicles, and occasional administrative and judicial sources suggest that the administration of the party, which was a political action and pressure group and above all a fighting organization, was extremely rudimentary. It conferred the essential authority upon one or more leaders, who were invested with powers of command and decision-making. A certain hierarchy was undoubtedly established in the more ambitious parties, but it is hard to ascertain the exact division of power. The party usually remained an alliance of primary social structures which were almost invariably families and clans. There was no trace of occasional or regular assemblies, of councils of whatever size, or even of groups of administrators. The collegiate form which was imposed on communal institutions in the early days was not present within the factions, at least during open warfare.

The leaders took various titles, all of which recall legends or were borrowed. Some merely indicate a limited power of representation, saying essentially that the man may speak on behalf of the party to settle some item of business. A house which was ceded to the commune of Bologna in 1287 for the construction of a town hall was actually received by the representative of the party in power, here called *syndic* and *procurator* "of the Bolognese guild and party of the Geremei".[114]

The title used by the head of a party more often denotes effective leadership of a faction. The designation of party podestà was obviously borrowed from the political vocabulary of the commune. The podestà was placed over the councils as leader of the police, supreme judge, and arbiter charged with settling disputes and imposing regulations. Thus, the employment of this word for party chiefs was very significant. It is most often found in Lombardy and northern Italy. The *popolano* party at Cremona in 1197 chose as podestà one Cremosianus Oldoynus, a former consul and hence a knight.[115] Shortly thereafter, in 1200, the *populares* of Brescia formed the Society of San Fausto and chose another noble, Count Narisio, as their podestà.[116] Piacenza too had many podestàs from the *popolano* or knightly parties after 1200, and the authors of the Guelf and Ghibelline annals of the town use the word as a matter of course. From 1220 on, "the podestàs of the people were Grezo Furno and Guido of Crema"[117] On 13 August 1222 the archbishop of Magdeburg as papal legate imposed Gerardo of Dovaria as podestà upon the town. The knights resisted, saying that they would recognize him "neither as podestà nor rector, that they would take no oath to him and would not negotiate with his emissary". Several days later the knights chose as their podestà a man from their own party, the Cremonese noble Giacomo of Borgo.[118] The *populares* elected Belengerio Mastagio, likewise from Cremona, as podestà in 1234, and on 13 December of that year a peace was sworn "between the knights and the *popolo* in a public assembly on the square of the principal church. The marquis Obizzo Malaspina was podestà of the knights and Lord Belengerio podestà of the people".[119] Knights and *populares* alike, the *podestàs* of Piacenza were thus party leaders, governing only a faction, sometimes even in open opposition to the podestà of the commune. The parties' political organization was at least closely related to or directly inspired by that of the aristocratic commune, and in some instances seems to have been copied directly from it. The podestàs of Piacenza, even those of the popular party, were great nobles and knights. Even more significantly, they came from outside the town.

The Guelf Annals of Piacenza also mention "the consuls and knights of the knights' society" during a great assembly of nobles in 1220 which led to one of their trivial scraps.[120] But we do not know the number of these consuls, and we are not even certain whether this word, which had also been borrowed directly from the institutions of the commune, invariably meant persons different from those holding the office of podestà.

Words were also borrowed from military usage. Giovanni Villani shows that each of the parties in Tuscany and neighbouring regions had important officials called *caporali*. In 1303, the pope and the cardinal of Prato wished to impose a peace treaty between the two new factions at Florence. They summoned "twelve of the principal *caporali* of the Guelf and Black party who were in the city". But the cardinal did not trust these men, and accordingly he wrote to Pisa, Bologna, Arezzo, Pistoia, and the Romagna to assemble with all their forces and those of their friends, both infantry and cavalry".[121] Villani again mentions *caporali de' nobili* in 1323, when the Florentine exiles tried to seize the city on the night of 10 August.[122] In September 1324 he shows how "certain *caporali* of the great men and the *popolani* who governed the city of Florence became enemies".[123] Finally, and we limit ourselves only to these few years, while the attainment of an agreement with the Church was being celebrated in March 1326 at Ferma, "the Orsini partisans entered the city with certain Ghibelline *caporali* from the March who disliked the treaty . . . and killed some *caporali* who had furthered it".[124]

The *caporali* were undoubtedly leaders of armed corps within the urban or rural parties. But although their precise attributes escape us completely, they were not responsible for the entire party. They may have commanded the adherents of a single family, clan, quarter, or settlement. The fact that the Florentine Ghibellines in the March had many *caporali* and the Blacks had at least twelve shows a division of command, a separation of the party into primary groups.

The *capitanei* were at a higher level of command than the *caporali* in every party or political society of northern Italy. When Verona approved a monetary loan to the Cremonese in 1234, the contract mentioned "Ungarello della Scala and B . . ., lord of Bonenconto, captains of the party of Monticuli and the Eighties".[125] The two captains of this party were thus acting on behalf of the city. At Piacenza in 1266 we find one Giovanni Palestrello, "who had already been captain of his party [the knights]".[126] During the revolt against the Torriani in 1277 and the troubles which followed, "the people chose two captains at each town gate ... and some of these captains were serving the *popolo* and the knights at one and the same time ...".[127] The meaning of 'captain' in these two instances is close to 'podestà', but emphasizes more military action, maintenance of order, and defence.

The captains were undoubtedly the superiors of the various *caporali* in Tuscany and central Italy. Villani mentions that in 1240 each party had a captain, often chosen from the most powerful family, for each sixth of the city.[128] The entire town thus had only six captains, but the parties had a very precise organization based on topographical, political, and military subdivisions. The institutions of the political party and of the central city administration thus were parallel.

The party and town government

As the party came to conquer and dominate all public offices for many years at a time, it ceased being exclusively a militant political action group with blurred outlines and poorly defined functions. Although they still borrowed from military precepts, the parties became diversified and exhibited a much richer and more complex internal life. To give an imperfect example, the office of the four captains of the *Parte Guelfa* was established at Orvieto in May 1315 to control the town. This was two years after the Ghibellines had been crushed and their property confiscated. It was an action symbolic of the maintenance of the Guelf tyranny over the Ghibellines.[129]

Our best example comes from Florence. After the Guelfs had been driven from the city in 1260, they immediately chose a 'shadow government' by naming a podestà, a party captain, and a council. A kind of anti-commune was thus called into being which presaged the government of the Guelfs after they returned in force to triumph in 1267. After this date, they were masters of the entire city. They imposed a dictatorship of the party which lasted until their own internal conflicts broke out between 1300 and 1303. This domination, which brooked no alternative or division for over a third of a century, had from the start a peculiarly effective organization, a perfectly structured government.[130] First and foremost, the party had significant resources at its disposal, a common treasury, a till filled with booty and the spoils of war, fines, and extortions. The war treasury was managed by Cardinal Ottaviano degli Ubaldini, an influential member of a great Guelf family of the city. The captain of the people was suppressed as a political force when the party organization described by Villani for 1260 was confirmed and reinforced. The party was led by three knights, the three captains of the Guelf party who were chosen alternately for two-month terms by two of the sixths of the town. Their number was subsequently raised to six, and all districts participated in their election. In addition to the captains, who seem to have had considerable discretionary power, there were two councils which met in the church of Santa Maria sopra Porta. The secret or privy council, consisting of fourteen persons, was also called the *credenza*, a word which had long denoted the smallest and most restricted of the communal assemblies in many Italian towns. There was also a great council of sixty persons where party magnates and *popolani* sat together.[131] These two councils chose officeholders from the Guelf faction. They worked full time on party affairs, the battles and survival of the faction, rather than on those of the city. They included the six priors of the party, three magnates and three *popolani*, who were entrusted with the administration of the common patrimony. Another prior kept the party seal. Finally, a *syndic* was charged with uncovering crypto-Ghibellines and preventing them from doing damage to the city at some future time. The Guelf party was thus a much more complex organization than one would expect had it been a mere fighting group.

When narrowly based groups of this sort are mentioned in the sources, nothing is said of the method of recruiting membership, and the Guelf party councils in Florence are no exception to the general rule. Were the councillors chosen by acclamation or cooptation; by primary elections based on topographical circumscriptions; or by direct or indirect designation by the most powerful clans? The party still seems essentially inorganic at this basic level, governed by influence or impulse rather than by regular choice. But the uncertainty, the influence of events, family or neighbourhood groups and the art of manipulating mobs and gaining their acclamation were not peculiar to the political party. Similar conditions occurred in ordinary political life outside the factions: in the choice of the 'ordinary' councils of the commune and of the *popolo*.

The parallel between the commune of Florence and the Guelf party, which was already extraordinary from the first days of the new régime in 1267, was decisively reinforced in 1275, when Rudolf of Habsburg announced his intention to come to Rome to be crowned emperor. The report provoked a general terror which spread into panic and an excess of precautionary measures. The Guelf hold on the city became even stronger. The régime of six Florentines acting as party captains had been given an electoral procedure which could produce some surprises and occasion division or conflict among the rulers. In consequence, these six men were now replaced by a single captain from outside the city who was given extraordinary powers for six months, and later for a year. Thus the Guelf captain, an official with obvious similarities to the podestà, became responsible for the police and for assessing taxes. An abnormal degree of collaboration and confusion developed between party and commune. The Guelfs had new florins struck which were of fine calibre; they were soon to be called *grossi guelfi*. They levied the indirect taxes owed to the commune and even assessed extraordinary levies in the form of a contribution known as the *allibramento*. On the other hand, party decisions were submitted, or rather presented for ratification, to the councils of the commune and the deans of the seven greater guilds. The whole procedure shows how the party had subsumed the organs of the commune and to some extent those of the *popolo*.

The party–commune–*popolo* confusion was eclipsed only in 1279 and 1280, when Cardinal Latino Malabranca, a nephew of Pope Nicholas III, archenemy of Charles of Anjou and his Tuscan allies, assumed power in the town. After three months of delicate negotiations, he forced the parties to make an agreement. Each had to deposit an enormous bond of 50,000 silver marks. Many exiles were repatriated, and all the inhabitants of the town, Guelf and Ghibelline alike, had to swear to uphold a solemn peace on pain of banishment. On 18 January the cardinal promulgated his arbitral settlement and established certain new institutions which seemed to mark at least a considerable weakening if not the end of the Guelf party. The captain general of the party was to give way to a captain of the commune called *gubernator populi*. With this captain, his podestà, and his consuls, the organization of the commune reverted to its earlier form. The podestà as chief justice was assisted by a small council, called 'the Ninety', and a much enlarged assembly of three hundred members which had broad judicial prerogatives. The captain presided over a council of 150 members and another very restricted group, a commission of thirty-six members. These bodies were to approve decisions made by the podestà and his administration. They were to be chosen in equal numbers by the six districts. An exceptional institution, the committee of fourteen, had been established when the cardinal arrived to prepare the agendas which were to be examined in turn by podestà and captain. The auditor of the accounts of all the city officials and supervisor of the communal treasury was to be an officer chosen from outside the city, the "judge, syndic and guardian of the property and money of the commune" (*judex, sindicus, conservator averis et pecunie communis*). He in his turn was to be assisted by another council of one hundred members.

Cardinal Malabranca had thus imposed an extremely complex régime upon the city. It provided a very important role for assemblies of all orders and degrees of importance. He had created a government of committees, commissions and councils rather than of individual leaders or colleges. Careful examination of this new but very ephemeral Florentine constitution leads to several conclusions. First, it had important implications for the political influence of the party in the town. The confusion of party with commune was eliminated. Guelfs and Ghibellines maintained only their own parallel institutions on the fringes of the communal structure. The rise of the councils suggests a political ethic completely at variance with the party régime. Still, for the most important councils, the electoral basis remained the six topographical divisions and not the guilds, an arrangement which had furthered the factions under the old régime. Membership in the councils was expressly divided among Guelfs, Ghibellines, and neutrals, implying that the entire town population was not involved in the party struggle. But the division was to be made proportional to the numerical preponderance of the three groups, and this fact, although vaguely stated and leading to erroneous interpretations, shows that the decisive role of the party was being implicitly recognized as a power and a framework, as the essential political structure of the city.

Secondly, this arrangement was imposed from the outside. The pope, or rather the cardinal, named the podestà, the captain, and all the chief officials. The Church's arbitration was flagrantly imposed, but no power within the town itself seemed capable of attacking the régime and government of the victorious party. When the cardinal left Florence on 12 April 1280 to 'pacify' other Tuscan cities, the Guelfs resumed power by various acts of stealth or violence. The return to the unilateral power of a single faction was hastened by the death of Nicholas III Orsini toward the end of the year. This relative weakening of party government had lasted only a few months.

Subsequently, neither the establishment in 1283 of a college of priors who were named not by the guilds but by the leaders of the sixths, nor the struggle against the magnates whose most notable monument for the historian was the Ordinances of Justice of 1293, was able to challenge the political power of the Guelf party and the permanence of its institutions. These were attested in the 1340s by the construction of a remarkable Palazzo della Parte Guelfa. Giovanni Villani shows that the "captains of the Guelf party and their council" were the most prominent leaders of the troubled city in 1300, at the very time when the split of the Guelfs into White and Black factions was intensifying.[132]

We have already seen that the Guelfs instituted a narrowly exclusive régime after seizing power,[133] and that the party developed several new organs. Treasurers, councils, judges, and various officials were added to the original organization, which was basically military. The Guelfs owed much to the experience of the commune and adapted themselves to it, so that Florence was to know the régime of two closely intertwined governments for many years.

The transcending of the commune by the party

The marked and often spectacular effect of factional quarrels within the city on both nearby and more distant rural areas itself resulted in the establishment of specific institutions and structures which far transcended the urban milieu. This could occur through various *ad hoc* arrangements or by genuine federations or leagues which were much more stable, capable of imposing their wishes upon an entire area. To a considerable degree, such agreements laid the foundation for regional political or administrative unity.

Parties based in one city deliberately espoused or used quarrels between neighbouring towns to determine the configuration of political alliances. Of course, these quarrels might originate in fortuitous circumstances or in sharp rivalries aroused by exceptional circumstances which no one could have foreseen. But the deeper origin of these clashes was almost always a fundamental, virtually visceral hostility which had been exploited by one city or the other for centuries. Two neighbouring and rival cities were thus marshalled against each other. The issue might be an economic rivalry: to dominate routes of communications, ports and tolls, fairs and distant markets, and most importantly hinterlands which were rich in grain and various raw materials. Border strife and generally bad relations between neighbours played their part too, as did the intense competition between cities which were trying to extend their spheres of influence to the point of creating city states which reached far beyond the old frontiers of the contado.

Under such conditions, any fortuitous circumstances might lead to an armed action in which the party felt that it had to intervene. During a famine in July 1250, the Milanese led an expedition ('the army of Caldana') to forage for grain in the countryside around Lodi. They had had an arrangement with the merchants of Piacenza by which the merchants would meet them on the banks of the Po with the food; but the suppliers had not been punctual, and their failure had been responsible for the deaths of more than two hundred Milanese infantry "from dust and even the heat". The Milanese in their turn intended to sell the grain at Parma and avoid giving it to the middlemen; there was thus a dual economic motive. Yet Milanese and Parmegiani continued to purchase grain in the diocese of Piacenza. This communal and intercommunal conflict was evidently created by the action of the podestà of Piacenza, who was related by marriage to a nobleman of Parma who favoured these purchases outside the city. The *popolani* of Piacenza were organized against him. They held several assemblies at the gates and in the churches, rang the bells, and after a long conflict, with many reverses, named their consuls and podestàs and seized power by deploying their forces and their diplomatic maneuvers against Milan and Parma.[134] This episode would seem fortuitous, the consequence of a chance happening, if we did not know that the rivalry between generally Guelf Milan and Ghibelline Piacenza was a constant feature of Lombard politics.

Moreover, these party struggles afforded fine occasions to intervene in the internal affairs of neighbouring cities. The stronger ones took the opportunity to impose their arbitration and thereby prepare the eventual annexation of the lesser towns, which were already included within the political orbit of the great metropolitan areas. Florence deliberately used these disorders as a pretext for intervening in the neighbouring towns of Tuscany. The hilltop settlement of San Miniato al Tedesco, a kind of Ghibelline if not imperial sentinel overlooking the route from Pisa to Florence, controlled the entire strategic Arno valley. It had a Florentine as podestà as early as 1346. But "certain malefactors who were retainers of the Malpigli and the Mangiadori used force to release the podestà's prisoners". These two clans were resolutely hostile to the pretensions of Florence. They wanted to preserve both the independence of their little town and its party régime. They were finally defeated and exiled, and the men of San Miniato then gave "the defence of their town to the commune of Florence for five years".[135]

The incorporation of Pistoia into the Florentine city-state was a longer undertaking, marked by numerous interventions provoked by the complex and interminable party quarrels. The town was a sentinel on the Apennine passes on the route from Lucca. From 1286 on, the Blacks and Whites, parties formed by the Cancellieri and their opponents, sought assistance at Florence and other cities of the area. Contingents from Florence and Lucca helped the exiled Blacks to retake the town in 1306. The Cancellieri settled their internal differences and all were waving the Black banner. But the powerful Panciatichi clan, aided by the Ghibellines, immediately reconstituted the White party and became their rivals. Later, when Giovanni Pianciatichi returned in triumph to his city in 1350, the Florentines intervened unilaterally. With a powerful militia, they retook the city and re-established the Blacks there in 1351. Factional struggles at Pistoia thenceforth crystallized around a new choice: for or against Florence. The great city played its hand with consummate artistry, intervening whenever the occasion seemed propitious, in 1373, 1376, and 1383. The final armed intrusion occurred in 1403, when Ricardo Cancellieri, whom a new turnabout had made a rebel in his city, ensconced himself for two years in his castle at Sanbuca, made peace with the Florentines, and was able to return to Pistoia. Factional quarrels were then appeased as Florentine hegemony was imposed decisively and definitely.[136]

The incessant game of seeking alliances in neighbouring communes thus extended the party squabbles far beyond the narrow confines of the town. It provoked the armed intervention of the great cities and indeed furthered their territorial ambitions and their policies of expansion and conquest. But the great cities were not the only forces in Italian politics which were thus given opportunity for aggrandizement by the party régime. Other parties of citizens were simultaneously seeking assistance and reinforcements from the great lords, counts or marquises of the old marches. This occurred particularly often in northern Italy, where the constant meddlings of the cities were echoed by those of the very princes who were soon to become their tyrants. These alliances sometimes brought about the interference of more distant lords. When the Lambertazzi party was exiled from Bologna to Imola in 1248, they asked and obtained the help of the 'lord' Matteo Visconti, master of Milan, and of Alberto della Scala, 'lord' of Verona, to give them a better bargaining position with their own commune.[137]

In the march of Verona, as far as Padua, two great seigneurial houses led parties between 1220 and 1280 which were called *pars comitis* and *pars marchionis*. These dynasties were the da Romano and the Este, who were constantly at each other's throats. Each wove a web of alliances and clans, both in the countryside and in the great cities, and these clienteles also fought one another. The da Romano installed Salinguerra, brother-in-law of Ezzelino II, who was head of the dynasty, at Ferrara and for a while at Verona. The house of Este could rely upon Count Sambonifacio at Verona and then at Mantua, on the Cattanei de Lendenara at Verona, on the da Camino, and finally on the Camposanpiero. The latter had come originally from Friuli and established their power throughout the region northeast of Padua which commanded the Alpine routes.[138] Throughout the lower Po valley, from Mantua to Treviso and from Verona to Ferrara, political life was thus dominated by two coalitions. They had been established by a series of chance, informal, and in any case fragile alliances which had resulted from personal circumstances and relationships, but they were still capable of imposing themselves as real political powers and of conducting a party feud on a regional scale.

But some alliances were anything but the result of simple appeals for assistance. They were more complex and stable and involved bonds other than those of kinship. True societies and leagues were being organized by formal treaties or even contracts. The words 'society' and 'league' were used interchangeably by contemporary writers. Over a three-year period, the commune of Pavia assumed the leadership of two 'societies' of this type which were engaged in the party struggle or based their power upon it. In February 1270 a pact of *societas* was sworn by Pavia, the 'internal' party of Lodi, the noble lord Bosio de Bovaria, and the 'external' party of Cremona which was led by the Barbarasi.[138] This arrangement thus involved a quite extensive region, the upper Po valley south of Milan, and united a complex group of communes and rival lords and parties, the one holding power in its town and the other in exile from its own home. The second Pavian alliance was sworn in 1273 with the men of Asti and the marquis of Montferrat.[140] This complex alliance complemented the first by incorporating the whole of southern Piedmont. It extended Pavia's network of alliances over the enormous area from the Alps to the Apennines and to Cremona.

Leagues of this *societas* type were then being concluded throughout northern and central Italy. In 1274 the Lambertazzi, who had been banished from Bologna, met their party comrades from Tuscany and the Romagna, who were then camped near Faenza. The Ghibelline army was then attacked, however, by a vast military coalition led by Bologna which incorporated all the armed corps of Guelfs from Modena, Cremona, Parma, and the Romagna.[141] Thus, yet another vast diplomatic and military network had been extended throughout the central Po valley and the great plain south of the river. Spheres of action and fields of competition for these party coalitions thus crystallized.

But for a time at least, other societies and leagues exhibited bolder appeals and more distant ties which even spanned the Apennines. Villani reports that in 1331 the Ghibelline exiles of Pisa established a league with the Lucchese, the Parmegiani, and certain Genoese Ghibellines, whose leader, Manfredo de' Vivaldi, held the powerful coastal castle of Lerichi, which controlled the Gulf of La Spezia.[141] Our hasty enumeration does not allow us to study the structure of this Ghibelline coalition, but it at least gives a good idea of how frequent and normal such arrangements were.

We have much better information about the powerful leagues established by the great structured parties than about those led by communes or exiles. Great Ghibelline leagues were established in Tuscany and at Verona. They collected and organized all their forces in the entire region and held councils. This is especially true of the

Ghibellines, who undoubtedly inherited certain administrative structures from the Empire, such as the offices of vicar and podestà,[143] and whose leaders were at once party captains and representatives of the emperor. Villani describes at some length the general assembly of all Tuscan Ghibellines at Empoli in the autumn of 1260, soon after their victory at Monteperti and their triumphal return to Florence. It was attended by Pisans, Sienese, and the men of Arezzo, but especially by Count Giordano, vicar general for King Manfred "with all other Ghibelline leaders of Tuscany". They held a 'parliament' there "to improve the situation of their party and to levy a forced loan", or in other words to organize an army. The alliance included towns and aristocratic party leaders, great lords of town and countryside: "in the aforementioned parliament all the neighbouring cities, the Guidi and the Alberti counts, those of the Santafiore, the Ubaldini, and all the barons of the environs proposed and agreed, for the welfare of the Ghibelline party . . .". During this assembly, when Count Giordano had to rejoin Manfred in southern Italy, Guido Novella was named vicar general and "war captain in Tuscany". During the following autumn he was to lead an army into the *contado* of Lucca "with the levy provided by the Ghibelline party in Tuscany".[144] We are thus dealing with a major party assembly (*parlamento*), with leaders including a captain general, and with an organization capable of spreading the war effort among the members, of raising armed contingents and placing them under a single command. This spontaneous organization drafted at Empoli was, as it transpired, made more specific shortly thereafter when a solemn act of 28 May 1261 created a true Ghibelline League which united all the parties of the Tuscan towns.

The Ghibelline League of northern Italy still existed as late as the 1320s in the vast countryside of Verona, which was dominated by the Scaligeri. The Veronese chronicles emphasize the role within this league of the hero, Cangrande della Scala, the tyrant of Verona. With a formidable army, which an anonymous author says included 10,000 infantry and 2,000 cavalry, he went in 1320 to the castle of Soncino, in the district of Cremona, where the diet of the famous Ghibelline League of the North was being held. In a "general agreement among the lords of Lombardy and particularly among the Ghibellines", Cangrande was made "captain general of the Ghibelline party, to make war on all its opponents".[145] He reappeared at another party diet four years later, and the narrative provides interesting information on that occasion about the organization and structure of these leagues:

In the castle of Palazolo, in the district of Brescia, a general agreement was made by the lords of Lombardy, namely the lord Cangrande of Verona and the lords of Ferrara, Mantua, and Milan, and all the other lords of Lombardy who opposed the church. They also ordered a bridge to be constructed across the Po to facilitate the movement of goods from Milan to Venice.[146]

This was evidently done to avoid the heavy tolls which the pope or the Church party had been exacting on the Piacenza route. We are thus dealing with a much vaster organization than that of Tuscany. It extended at least from Milan to Verona and Ferrara, thus comprising all of Lombardy and part of Venetia. It had leaders and councils, great assemblies which could make binding decisions, and a military command.

We must consider also the Guelf league. The first Lombard League or society, that of 1167, and the second, of 1226, were actually alliances concluded between towns, not between parties, or vast complexes which united communes, great lords, and even individual party leaders. The leagues of the Guelf party properly so called appear relatively late and do not seem to have had as wide a reception or an organization as well structured as that of the Ghibelline leagues. They became powerful only in Tuscany, the Romagna, and the region of Bologna. Thus, the threat posed by the advent of Henry VII in 1310 revived the quarrels between Guelfs and Ghibellines and provoked, as a spontaneous reaction, the formation of a Guelf league which extended throughout central Italy. It was led by Perugia and included parties and lords of the towns and districts of Lucca, Siena, Spoleto, Gubbio, and even Orvieto. This league was to play a decisive role in conquering Orvieto when the announcement in 1313 that the emperor was approaching provoked a Ghibelline revolt. Bitter warfare raged in Orvieto for three days. The prompt arrival of reinforcements from the towns of the environs and the imperial party gave initial victory to the Ghibellines, but the Guelfs regained the upper hand with the help of substantial reinforcements from the league of Perugia.[147]

A casual reference of Villani for 1319 shows that a Guelf league organized around Bologna was capable of suborning intervention by contingents from towns which were quite distant from the scene of the action: in October 1319 the Florentines, who were members of the league, sent "350 knights, part of a levy of 1,000 knights summoned by Bologna and the Guelf party" to help Cremona. But the reinforcements arrived too late, "for the long war and the disorders had nearly annihilated Cremona".[148]

The *collegati* were well-organized coalitions, leagues of clearly structured parties. By raising armed contingents and intervening in distant places, they undoubtedly show themselves to be forerunners of the powerful political and military leagues, those great blocs of allies which later were to divide northern and central Italy and influence its destiny so fatefully. Of course, we cannot ignore the role of a truly urban diplomacy here, for these leagues united city states from this time on. But the memory of the party alliances remained vivid, as the vocabulary of the agreements and oaths of fidelity shows clearly.[149]

This was the case first of all for peace treaties and agreements between great lords. The oath of fealty which Enrico de Egligen, called della Scala, took in 1367 to Guido Gonzaga, lord of Mantua, and the solemn peace sealed the following year between Amadeus VI of Savoy and Galeazzo Visconti, both take account of many allies. Most of them were not named, but instead were given vague designations such as *vassalli, suddidi,* or *aderenti.* All this sounds very much like personal relations and submissions, a group of clients and thus a party.

The terms of these agreements became more precise somewhat later, when urban leagues and allegiances had become sufficiently complex to include both towns and noble captains. The latter were mentioned by name from this time on, as the concept of a territory over which the city exercised its authority became more exact. Two instances of 1389 show this for regions of central Italy. A league led by Florence was in fact merely a regional organization which was designed to secure the influence of the great city over the others. It was joined by Arezzo, Pistoia, Volterra, Colle di Val d'Elsa, Castiglione Fiorentino, and all the cities "in which the commune of Florence had a certain pre-eminence, authority, or rights of protection . . .". A second, much more comprehensive league was concluded at Pisa. It united many lords and communes, such as Guido da Palenta, Rolando degli Orsini, the lords who then became masters of Camerino, Iesi, Sanseverino nelle Marche, Cingoli, Ancona, Fermo, and Ascoli, together with the cities of Venice, Genoa, and Pisa. These two leagues were thus preparing a decisive confrontation. The second demanded that the alliance be exclusive, a new development: no participant might be involved in any other alliance. But the second pact also specified that "all the lands, towns, castles, and settlements in the Romagna and the march which the cardinal legate of Perugia was governing for the Roman Church" should join the league.

This territorial extension and the care taken to define a geographical frontier rather than a clientele seems still more pronounced in the peace of 8 February 1420 between Milan and Florence. All signatories were named and their spheres of influence delimited exactly. Milan was supported by all her allies and client states "within the borders of Lombardy, the march of Treviso, the marquisate of Montferrat, and the province of Piedmont". The list was quite long. That of the allies of Florence was equally extensive, including among others Bologna and the lords of Imola, Urbino, and Lucca. But the location took precedence over all personal ties throughout. The doge of Genoa was mentioned by both signatories, but was included among the *collegati* of Florence only for his eastern territories: "Sarzana, Livorno, Santo Stefano, Sarzanello, Castronovo, and other places as far as and including the line of ridges above Pontremolo". Similarly, while the marquis of Malaspina and all his possessions were in the Florentine camp, the Fieschi of Lavagna only entered "for all their lands and settlements located up to and including the line of the ridge of the Alps".

This care to define borders shows a very different concept and the end of an evolution. These leagues no longer united only party leaders, but entire states. But just as party and communal institutions might sometimes be intermingled and in any case influenced each other, these diplomatic alliances certainly owed a great deal to coalitions between captains of factions. The Guelf and Ghibelline party leagues thus covered impressive amounts of territory, had organizations and powers of arbitration, and intervened by force of arms over a considerable area.

Notes to Part II*

[1]See above, pp. 33–39.

[2]M. Moresco, Parentele e guerro civili in Genova nel secole XII, *Scritti giuridici in onore di Santi Romani* (Padua, 1940).

[3]Villani [15, VIII, ch. 38, pp. 40–41].

[4]Herlihy [33, p. 202].

[5]Villani [15, IX, ch. 148, p. 242]: per la qual cosa la città di Siena si guarenti di battaglia cittadine.

[6]Hyde [35, pp. 205ff].

* Numbers in square brackets refer to the Bibliography.

[7]Gozzadini [27], for the Lambertazzi [52, ch. 22].

[8]Herlihy [33, pp. 205ff].

[9]Hyde [36, p. 297].

[10]*A.P.Gib.*, anno 1271, p. 551, lines 16ff, cited by Judic [37, p. 234].

[11]Renouard [46, p. 309].

[12]*A.P.Gib.*, anno 1270, p. 543, lines 23–44, cited by Judic [37, p. 70].

[13]Vitale [58].

[14]Gozzadini [27, pp. 212–225] on the Cazzanemici family.

[15]*A.P.Gib.*, anno 1256, p. 507, lines 51ff, cited by Judic [37, p. 78].

[16]*Ibid.*, anno 1257, p. 508, lines 26–34, cited by Judic [37, p. 79].

[17]*Ibid.*, anno 1266, p. 520, lines 1–9, cited by Judic [37, p. 82].

[18]*Ibid.*, anno 1269, p. 535, lines 11–16, cited by Judic [37, p. 84].

[19]E. Dorini, La vendetta privata ai tempi di Dante, *Giornale dantesco*, 1926; A.M. Enriques, La vendetta nella vita e nella legislazione fiorentina, *Archivio storico italiano*, 1933.

[20]Villani [15, VII, ch. 38, p. 41]: e fedito uno di que' del lato de' Cancellieri bianchi, que' del lato dei Cancellieri neri per avere pace e concordia con loro, mandarono quegli che avea fatta l'offesa alla misericordia di quegli che l'aveano ricevuta, che ne prendessono l'amenda e vendetta a loro volontà.

[21]G. della Crossa and P.A. Montegiani, Chroniques remaniées par Ceccaldi, trans. abbé Letteron, *Bulletin de la Société des Sciences Historiques et Naturelles de la Corse* (1888) p. 239.

[22]Waley [59, especially p. xxxi]. This firm division had undoubtedly been anticipated by an earlier concentration within each of the clans, as is shown by the small number of 'noble' families. There were only twenty-seven in 1322.

[23]Gozzadini [27, pp. 286ff], especially for the Geremei family.

[24]For the above and for a brief analysis of these conflicts, see Judic [37, pp. 25–29].

[25]Villani [15, IX, ch. 2, p. 147].

[26]Larner [38, pp. 38–71].

[27]Villani [15, I, p. 219].

[28]Villani [15, VIII, ch. 39, pp. 42–43].

[29]Villani [15, ch. 71, pp. 89–90].

[30]Villani [15, ch. 16, pp. 27–28].

[31]Heers [31 (Eng. trans.), pp. 154–163].

[32]Gozzadini [27], for the Lambertazzi and Geremei families.

[33]Heers [31, (Eng. trans.), p. 149].

[34]Villani [15, XII, ch. 21, pp. 44–45]: il quali con grandi serragli . . .: e cominicato per lo popolo l'assalto manesco a' serragli . . .; e disfecionsi i serragli . . .; e disfatti i loro serragli e forze . . .; e disarmaronsi e disfeciono loro guerigioni e serragli . . .; era si forte e di si grandi serragli. . . .

[35]Villani [15, XII, ch. 17, p. 31]: e di presente fu sbarrata la città a ogni capo di via e di contrade.

[36]Villani [15, VIII, ch. 114, p. 140].

[37]Villani [15, XII, ch. 120, p. 181].

[38]Villani [15, IX, ch. 2, p. 147].

[39]Villani [15, XIII and XII, *passim*] for many examples of this usage or very similar expressions.

[40]Gaspar (ed.), [8, p. 185].

[41]A.P.Gu., anno 1231, p. 452, line 44, cited by Judic [37, p. 48].

[42]A.P.Gib., anno 1273, p. 557, line 53, cited by Judic [37, p. 48].

[43]Ibid., anno 1269, p. 529, line 33, cited by Judic [37, p. 48].

[44]Ibid., anno 1261, p. 513, line 9, cited by Judic [37, p. 49].

[45]Fasoli [24, pp. 24–30].

[46]Soranzo [53].

[47]Villani [15, VIII, ch. 39, p. 44].

[48]Villani [15, VIII, ch. 114, pp. 140–141].

[49]Villani [15, XI, ch. 102, p. 334].

[50]Villani [15, ch. 72, p. 92].

[51]Rossini [48, p. 439].

[52]Villani [15, VIII, ch. 68, p. 85].

[53]Villani [15, XII, ch. 82, p. 120].

[54]Heers [31 (Eng. trans.), pp. 75–77].

[55]S. Chojnacki, Crime, punishment and the trecento Venetian state, in Martines [57, p. 197].

[56]Villani [15, XII, ch. 23, p. 50].

[57]Brucker [19].

[58]The list of Ghibellines condemned in 1268 included many lesser artisans, such as innkeepers, bakers, tailors, and dyers. See Masi [40, p. 12].

[59]Cited by P. du Colombier and P. d'Espezel, L'habitation au XVIe siècle d'après le sixième livre de Serlio (Paris, n.d.), pp. 37–38.

[60]On the nature of these investments in land, see P.J. Jones, Per la storia agraria italiana nel medioevo, Revista storica italiana (1964).

[61]For example, C.M. de la Roncière, Un changeur florentin du trecento: Lippo di Fede del Sega (1285 env.–1363 env.) (Paris, 1973); A. Petrucci, Il Libro di Ricordanze dei Corsini (1362–1467) (Rome, 1965); C. Bec, Il Libro degli Affari proprii di Casa de Lapo di Giovanni Niccolini de' Sirigatti (Paris, 1969).

[62]See, for example, A. Sapori, I libri degli Alberti del Giudice (Milan, 1952).

[63]The account of the possessions of Francesco Datini was fully published by Mèlis [42, pp. 61–72].

[64]Thus we hear from Matteo di Nicholo de' Chorsini, when he returned at the age of forty to Florence after a sojourn of seventeen years in England: Ricordanza ch' io trovai quando tornai a Firenze delle nostre posesione antiche le quale furono di nostro patrimonio: uno chasamento con due poderi posti nel popolo di San Pietro di Sotto del piovere di Decimo comme diremo apresso: Uno Chasamento con torre, corte, colombaia, volta, e pozo . . . Petrucci, Libro di Ricordanze, p. 6.

[65]Mèlis [42, pp. 61–73].

[66]On the extent of possessions and fiefs and on the location of the castles of prominent Genoese families during the 1450s, see Heers [29, pp. 524–554, 592–599] and the appended political map of Liguria.

[67]Waley [59].

[68]Lupe Gentile [39, pp. 22–23].

[69]W.M. Bowsky, Cives Silvestres: Sylvan citizenship and the Sienese Commune (1287–1355), Bolletino senese di storia patria (1965), pp. 1–13.

[70]Villani [15, VIII, ch. 39, p. 42].

[71]Lupo Gentile [39, pp. 29, 34, 35].

[72]On this settlement, see Heers [30, pp. 371–412].

[73]Heers [29, in particular pp. 565–567], after A. Ascheri, *Notizie interno alla riunione delle famiglie in Albergo in Genova* (Genoa, 1846).

[74]See all registers of the *Gabella Possessionum*, Archivio di Stato di Genova, Possessionum Gabella. Nobili. Sala 42/65 B. See also Archivio di Stato di Genova, MS. 88, which gives a list of the members of various councils in which the nobles were grouped by *compagna*.

[75]*Hyde* [36, pp. 297ff].

[76]Rossini [48, pp. 457ff].

[77]Hyde [35, pp. 200–205].

[78]Gozzadini [27, pp. 404ff], for the Pepoli family.

[79]Heers [31, pp. 91–94].

[80]Heers [30, appended political map of Liguria].

[81]*A.P.Gib.*, anno 1249, p. 498, lines 42–44, cited by Judic [37, p. 52].

[82]*Ibid.*, anno 1260, p. 512, lines 2–3, cited by Judic [37, p. 53].

[83]*Ibid.*, anno 1269, p. 531, lines 48–53 and p. 532, lines 1–10, cited by Judic [37, pp. 55–57].

[84]Hyde [35, pp. 200–202].

[85]Gozzadini [27, p. 328ff], for the Lambertazzi family.

[86]Gozzadini [27, pp. 374ff].

[87]Gozzadini [27, pp. 388ff], for the Panico family.

[88]Judic [37, pp. 57–58].

[89]Larner [38, p. 45].

[90]*A.P.Gib.*, anno 1266, p. 519, lines 7–11, cited by Judic [37, p. 66].

[91]Villani [15, XI, ch. 118, pp. 349–350].

[92]Herlihy [34, p. 142].

[93]Brucker [19].

[94]Renouard [46, p. 325].

[95]Bowsky [17].

[96]Sercambi [14, CCCVI, p. 351].

[97]Herlihy [34, p. 141].

[98]Herlihy [33, p. 205].

[99]*A.P.Gu.*, anno 1090, p. 411, lines 7–16, cited by Judic [37, pp. 215–217].

[100]*A.P.Gib.*, anno 1251, p. 505, lines 10–11, cited by Judic [37, p. 102].

[101]*Ibid.*, anno 1257, p. 508, lines 21–22, cited by Judic [37, p. 102].

[102]*Ibid.*, anno 1271, p. 551, lines 16ff, cited by Judic [37, pp. 234–235].

[103]Gasper (ed.) [8, pp. 149–150]. Caldiero is fourteen kilometres east of Verona.

[104]On this point, see below, p. 129 and Heers [31 (Eng. trans.) pp. 197–199].

[105]*Annales Brixienses*, p. 817, cited by Judic [37, p. 155].

[106]Gozzadini [27, pp. 388ff], for the Panico family.

[107]Renouard [46, p. 277].

[108]Villani [15, XI, ch. 118, p. 350].

[109]Vitale [58]. There are numerous references in Villani [15, particularly IX, ch. 97, p. 210, ch. 103, p. 212 and ch. 188, pp. 263–264].

[110]Larner [38].

[111]*A.P.Gib.*, *anno* 1270, p. 547, lines 3–4, cited by Judic [37, p. 51].

[112]Dominici [11, II, pp. 27–28], cited by Herlihy [33, p. 199].

[113]Santini [50].

[114]Gozzadini [27, p. 56].

[115]*Annales Brixienses*, anno 1196, p. 815, cited by Judic [37, p. 153].

[116]*Ibid.*, p. 815, cited by Judic [37, p. 153].

[117]*A.P.Gu.*, *anno* 1220, p. 438, line 13, cited by Judic [37, p. 168].

[118]*Ibid.*, *anno* 1222, p. 438, lines 22–28, cited by Judic [37, p. 169].

[119]*Ibid.*, *anno* 1234, p. 1234, p. 456, lines 47–52, cited by Judic [37, p. 169].

[120]*Ibid.*, *anno* 1220, p. 437, line 36, cited by Judic [37, p. 170].

[121]Villani [15, VIII, ch. 72, p. 92].

[122]Villani [15, IX, ch. 219, p. 283].

[123]Villani [15, IX, ch. 271, pp. 310–312]: certi caporali grandi e popolani che reggeano la città di Firenze vennero in divisione.

[124]Villani [15, IX, ch. 344, p. 259]: quegli d'Orsini concerti caporali ghibellini della marca, non piacendo loro l'accordo entrarono nella città . . . . uccisono de' caporali che voleano l'accordo.

[125]R. Manselli, Ezzelino da Romano nella politica italiana del secolo XIII, in [54, p. 43, n. 2].

[126]*A.P.Gib.*, *anno* 1266, p. 519, line 1, cited by Judic [37, p. 168].

[127]*Ibid.*, anno 1276, p. 565, line 42, cited by Judic [37, p. 171].

[128]Villani [15, I. 252–254].

[129]Waley [59, pp. 95ff].

[130]Renouard [46, pp. 338–339].

[131]Villani [15, VII, ch. 17].

[132]Villani [15, VIII, ch. 40, p. 44].

[133]See above, p. 59.

[134]*A.P.Gib.*, *anno* 1250, p. 499, line 35 to p. 502, line 24, cited by Judic [37, pp. 224–232].

[135]Villani [15, XII, ch. 82, p. 129].

[136]Herlihy [33, pp. 202–207].

[137]Gozzadini [27, pp. 61–62], for the Albari family.

[138]Hyde [35, pp. 200ff].

[139]*A.P.Gib.*, *anno* 1270, p. 540, line 54, cited by Judic [37, p. 43].

[140]*Ibid.*, *anno* 1273, p. 557, line 49, cited by Judic [37, p. 44].

[141]Gozzadini [27, especially p. 330], for the Lambertazzi family.

[142]Villani [15, X, ch. 196, pp. 174–175].

[143]See above, p. 46.

[144]Villani [15, VI, ch. 82, pp. 305–307].

[145]Gaspar (ed.) [8, pp. 197–198].

[146]Gaspar [8, pp. 201–202].

[147]Waley [59, pp. 90–92].

[148]Villani [15, IX, ch. 101, p. 212].

[149]For what follows, see the texts of the agreements as published by Soranzo [53].

PART III
ITALY: FORMS OF WAR AND PEACE

CHAPTER ONE

The town in arms: civil war

Narratives of the factional struggles, some interminable, others brief, fill the pages of all chroniclers of Italian life, for every region. The authors are always contrasting peaceful and prosperous times with periods of disturbances and civil wars, which they invariably portrayed as misfortunes, calamities, divine retribution, or at least ill fortune foretold by extraordinary signs or baneful celestial omens. These were not mere episodes or fortuitous circumstances which were quickly forgotten. On the contrary, warfare, violence, murder, bloodletting, and fear always weighed heavily on the events of daily life and even on the general mood. These disagreements also had ominous implications for the future even from the purely material viewpoint, for they inevitably involved a frightening series of catastrophes and calamities, of arson or acts of destruction by vengeful men. No other region of the medieval West witnessed such frequent internecine warfare. This was one of the most striking aspects of the towns and rural areas of northern and central Italy. While some combats were limited to the streets or avenues which led directly to the city walls, others involved pitched battles in the field or during sieges with troops of a lord or the king. They were not campaigns of the feudal host or mere expeditions, let alone 'feudal' or 'chivalric' warfare.

The manifold forms which these wars might take is frequently demonstrated by the richly differentiated vocabulary of the chroniclers. Villani, who was more imaginative and eloquent than some others, used the common words *combattimento*, *guerra*, or *battaglia*, but he also employed a much more varied vocabulary of words whose meaning is less certain. They undoubtedly connote more confused street fighting and mob involvement. He spoke of *novità*, *mutazione*, *rumore*, or *bellore di popolo*, but he always blamed them on party strife. He noted "certain rumours and drastic innovations which the factionalism of the citizens brought upon the city of Pisa",[1] while "the city of Florence was in such a state of excitement and danger because of the sects and their animosities".[2]

Fights and riots

Apart from the conclusions derived from our brief examination of the vocabulary, a more exact analysis of the forms of civil warfare enables us to distinguish clearly three principal types of street fighting, which diverged considerably from one another as to origins and circumstances, importance and nature of the troops, and even evolution and consequences. But the party, the faction in power and particularly those who were excluded, always played an essential part.

The combat might take the form of a struggle between two factions. Civil warfare came about primarily through a desire to avenge, to cleanse the stain which an insult had left upon the clan, and to affirm the family's unity, power, and social standing. Every assassination by sword or poison involved others in a cascade of homicides. The habit of assembling armed followers near the palace could only produce a very explosive situation. The struggle which the party which was out of power, particularly the Algarda or Algardi, carried on against the Pepoli between 1250 and 1285 at Bologna, was merely a long series of conflicts marked by multiple complications, assassinations, and burnings.[3] In the spring of 1272 the Monaldeschi managed to govern Orvieto for a time, after having waged a series of bitter wars against the Filippeschi. But when four men of the Monaldeschi party were murdered, hostilities were resumed. The murder of a Filippeschi kinsman of the guilty parties avenged the deed, but this in turn gave the signal for open warfare in the city streets between the two factions.[4] A similar case occurred at Pisa in 1323, when the murder, evidently by poison, of Count Ranieri Bergo, who was then 'lord' of the town, united all his relatives and friends. They had already been organized into clans or small allies groups, such as "Count Paffecta and the children of Barosso de Monte Scudaio with their sect". They mobilized several armed *brigate* and thus established a genuine military party:

"and thus was formed the party of the Bergolini at Pisa". The *brigate* attacked the palaces of the other faction, which was led by Count della Roccha, and established their authority throughout the city.[5]

Warfare more frequently originated in an unfortunate but generally fortuitous encounter or provocation which was taken badly and was then exacerbated by a violent act. The peace of the town was thus constantly at the mercy of trifling incidents which were immediately magnified by previous hatreds and appeals for assistance. As Shakespeare shows so well in *Romeo and Juliet*, an ordinary scuffle between servants might thus involve entire clans in feuding. It is striking that the chroniclers seldom blame the feuds on the leaders of the factions, but rather upon their families and collateral relatives, their *compagni* and *seguaci*, and particularly their 'young'. The latter concept must be taken in a broad sense transcending chronological age and suggesting rather a certain degree of "social immaturity":[6] unmarried and unestablished men, pages, and squires who lived in the house and entourage of their prominent relatives. When the culprits directly involved in a first outbreak of hostilities between Whites and Blacks were imprisoned at Florence in 1300, "Messer Vieri de' Cerchi and the other wise men of their own houses" understood "the character and susceptibility of their young men" and for their own part wanted to keep them under control.[7] Villani documents the repeated occurrence during the early months of the rivalry between Whites and Blacks of dramatic brawls and veritable battles which began in accidental meetings and provocations. The problem was due chiefly to a desire to display, to prove one's valour and following in the streets. These street combats thus seem to have been preceded and provoked by an ostentatious show of force, a pleasure in sneering at one's adversary by displaying the strength of one's own party: "it happened shortly afterward that while the two sects were passing on horseback through the streets ...". The author specifies the partisans in these proud parades: "with the party of the Cerchi youth were their *seguaci* and more than thirty horsemen", while "with the Donati boys were ... and still others with their *manasdieri*".[8] It was always the youths, the *seguaci*, the retainers who paraded on the squares and the streets and in front of their enemies' palaces. In such an atmosphere of military parade, the most trifling meeting could result in a call to arms after an exchange of threats and injuries. This occurred at least three times in several months. On 1 May 1300, "as they were watching a group of ladies dancing in the Piazza di Santa Trinità, the parties began to exchange blows and to run at each other with their horses. Several were wounded in the ensuing confusion and melée". One of the adversaries was severely mutilated; "ill fortune caused the nose of Ricoverino, son of Messer Ricoverino de' Cerchi, to be cut from his face . . . and this riot and the bitterness among men had the entire city in arms until evening".[9]

On another occasion, in December of that same year, "Messer Corso Donati and his *seguaci*, together with the Cerchi and their armed *seguaci*", were attending the funeral of one of the Frescobaldi. The two parties met face to face and began to draw their swords. "From this incident, everyone at the funeral arose with a great uproar. All fled to their houses, and the entire city took arms, with the leaders of each party holding large gatherings in their houses."[10] The two factions then sought allies throughout the city, appealing for aid at every palace.

Finally, several days after this incident, a similar encounter on the public street led to a riot. Several Cerchi, returning from their rural domains, found their route into Florence blocked "by the adherents of the house of the Donati, who assembled their partisans at Remole and tried to deny them passage. Each party made several assaults and received injuries".[11]

The commune was able to intervene just in time in each of these idiotic scraps, condemning the guilty to fines and imprisonment, thereby preventing these sudden assaults from mushrooming into civil war. But these instances well show how easily conflicts could occur and how peace was only a precarious and always threatened equilibrium during party struggles.

The factional wars thus began with a gathering of the allies (the *raunata*). In theory, they were limited to 'private' affronts, or at worst were confined to two clans and their followers. The fights described by all the chroniclers – the *anonymi* of Piacenza, Verona, and Pavia, Caffaro for Genoa, Sercambi for Lucca, and particularly Giovanni Villani and all the Florentines – were concentrated around the houses of the party leaders, fortified palaces with high, crenelated towers adorning blind walls which were broken only by narrow machicolations.[12] The tower was at the heart of the combat, a refuge and a strong point from which attacks could be launched. The texts are less eloquent about the towers than a few precious manuscript illustrations. The best is an exceptionally beautiful illumination from Caffaro's

Annals which shows two towers of opposing factions confronting each other, each with warriors in helmets and shields behind the crenels. Men from one tower are trying to set up a sort of mobile bridge toward the other. Two armed men are at the foot of the towers, protected by their coats of mail, helmets, and shields, which bore their coats of arms, and with long broadswords in their hands.[13] We see a similar picture in the watercolours which enrich the manuscript of Giovanni Sercambi. Painted in 1424 and reproduced as sketches in the edition of S. Bongi, these figures all show the town dominated by extremely high towers, of varying number according to the degree of precision of the scene. These illustrations are essentially symbolic, but some show the battles and indicate the particular role of the keeps which arose from the soil in the town itself, by scores or even to a total of two or three hundred: fighters on the towers, towers in flames, wounded or dead warriors falling from tower tops, towers illuminated by fires which were signals of rally or victory.[14]

Let us once again follow Giovanni Villani, our principal guide in this study of warfare between neighbours in the Italian towns and countryside. He notes that factional strife still amounted to siege warfare in 1200: "at this time because of the aforementioned war [that of the Uberti against their opponents] many towns were refortified".[15] This method of fighting was still being used in 1303:

At several places in the city and for several days . . . some towers and fortresses of the city were fortified in the ancient manner (*al modo antico*) to enable the partisans to launch attacks and hurl missiles at one another. A catapult was erected on the tower of the episcopal palace to throw stones on the neighbouring quarters.[16]

These combats were intended in the beginning only to defend oneself and destroy one's immediate neighbours. There was no larger strategy or battle plan. Objectives were confined to the sphere of daily concerns, those of the street and the square or at most of the quarter.[17] These were mere fights between neighbours, very fragmentary and scattered throughout the city. They could also involve sieges, sometimes of considerable duration, with small squadrons which lacked the means to attack walls which were capable of resisting major assaults.

The final victory, after much swaying in the balance, belonged to those who could break free of the towers and launch a cavalry charge against the strong points of the city without encountering other resistance, able as the texts expressed it [to] *correre per la città*. The

first battle between Whites and Blacks at Florence in 1301 was limited
to a simple neighbourhood confrontation between the Cerchi and the
Guigni in a single quarter (*alle loro case del Garbo*). But the Cerchi,
with the aid of the Cavalcanti, were able to break away, "and the
power of the Cavalcanti and the Guerardini then became so great that
they and their *seguaci* ran to the Mercato Vecchio and the Orto San
Michele as far as the Piazza di San Giovanni without encountering
resistance, for their power extended throughout the city and the
contado". "And on that day they assumed primacy over the entire land
and exiled their enemies, the *caporali* of the Guelf and Black party."[18]
The *terra* in this case was the city of Florence. Fanning out from a
single bloc of fortified houses in a single quarter [to] *correre la terra*,
vincere la terra, was then to conquer the entire city and drive out the
enemy.

It has been thought that the street fights of medieval Italian towns
were popular uprisings. But tower combat of parties around the
palaces was the normal way knights and lords with their retainers
fought; this was warfare "in the ancient manner", to use Giovanni
Villani's expression. But at the same time, and indeed from the early
thirteenth century, the towns of northern and central Italy knew a
totally different type of civil war, the riot, when the mobs descended
into the streets to fight openly, bringing the support of their enormous
numbers to a particular cause. This was no longer a mere confrontation
between well-armed knights and retainers, but between guildsmen,
lesser folk, often with no other weapons than those garnered from
warriors who had been taken by surprise and murdered.

The riots undoubtedly imply popular turmoil, an atmosphere of
insecurity, of fear and anguish, perhaps of indignation. The chroniclers
make a distinction between the *battaglie* of the warriors, involving
their *brigate* and *seguaci*, and the more general *rumori* or *bollori*
which affected the entire city. The mood and particular concurrence of
manpower might be provoked and sustained by quite varied
circumstances: economic difficulties, an employment crisis or food
shortage, the spontaneous collective fury which the announcement of
alarming news might bring, or the exactions of a tyrant. But the most
immediate, primordial cause was the great assemblies of large numbers
of people, whether those held regularly or meetings called for a special
occasion. Such were the times when workers left their shops and stalls,
on the occasion of great secular or religious festivals,[19] calls to arms,
revolutionary cries, and the sounding of the town bells.

We know that the bells played an important role in the urban life of western Europe. They punctuated the work day of the journeymen, and most importantly they summoned men to assemble, to help one another. Hence the belfry in the northern European cities and the clock and bell towers of the communes of the Midi and particularly of Italy were enormously significant. The anonymous chronicle of Verona, which only rarely gives hints of daily life in the city before the thirteenth century, nonetheless says for 1173 that "in this year the foundations of the tower of the lord Lambert were laid. It is now called the bell tower, where the great clock of Verona is sounded".[20] The consuls of Cremona had a bell cast and placed on their tower in 1188. This was of course a considerable expense for the community, but it was a symbol which grew into a veritable myth, the town bell which tolled the great moments of destiny. At Piacenza in 1250, "the *populares*, inflamed by what had happened . . . when the bells had been struck with a hammer . . . assembled and sent to the podestà's palace". That official, "seeing the mob of people coming toward him and hearing the bells", decided to release his prisoner immediately. The tolling of the bell became the signal for rebellion.[21] Giovanni Villani examined the division of forces in Florence on the eve of the great conflict of 1343, which was close enough to his own time for him to have experienced and studied it directly, and said bluntly that "the commune and the *popolo* became more powerful by holding the palace and the bell and by controlling all the gates of the city save that of San Gregorio, which was held by the Bardi".[22]

These riots were 'popular' if the criterion is the participation of large numbers of persons, but their essential features might be quite the opposite of what that term usually means. The instigators of mob action, who gave the battle cries, summoned men to arms and surrounded themselves or their relatives with large forces, even the paid adventurers, were almost invariably great men motivated by a spirit of revenge, by unyielding ambitions which were strictly political and not social. In this sense, the riots were part of the larger quarrel between factions, marking another and more dramatic dimension.

The evolution of these events is disconcertingly complex, and it is difficult to isolate significant episodes or unravel the several lines of development. The very objectives of the riot show particular motives which can be distinguished. One was the insurrection against tyrants. The chroniclers often noted this, for such disturbances were very common in all the Italian cities. A perfect example is Villani's narrative of the famous uprising at Florence against the duke of Athens on Saturday, St Anne's Day, 26 June 1343.[23]

Several typical aspects of this riot have been noted. The great men of the city predominated in the early stages. These belonged to prominent families whose property or members had suffered at the tyrant's hands. The Adimari, Medici, and Donati sounded the call to arms on the public squares at the hour when the journeymen of the guilds quit work on Saturday evening. The summons, which had been provoked by the magnates, was really a call for revolution: "Death to the duke and his *seguaci*! Long live the people, the commune, and liberty!".

Secondly, the town was placed virtually on military alert. 'Rumours' filled the air, stirring up the masses. Villani used this word four times ("the duke's men heard the rumous ...; when the aforementioned rumour began ...; when rumour spread ...; how the rumour began ..."). Barricades simultaneously arose throughout the city ("and then the city was barricaded"). Each quarter isolated itself and retrenched. The duke's men were hunted down everywhere and taken by surprise. They were often imprisoned and massacred, or at least disarmed. Horses, lances, and swords passed into rebel hands.

Thirdly, the prisons were attacked as the first discernible goal of the insurgents. There was nothing 'popular' or 'social' about this. The rioters only wanted to release their own people, the kinsmen of the great families. The clan leaders obviously instigated this turn of events, and we find the Adimari leading them ("to release Antonio di Baldinaccio, their relative, the Medici, the Ricci, and others who had been abused by him"). The mob then tried to take the palace of the priors, where the duke was staying. They barricaded the twelve streets leading to it and allowed neither entry nor exit, so that the duke's knights could not maneuver. Another leader, Amerigo Donati, "with his brothers, relatives, and others whose friends and kinsmen were in prison", simultaneously attacked and seized the Carceri delle Stinche and freed the prisoners. The primary objective of the riot was thus to release from jail the members of the clans comprising the faction in revolt.

A further objective was to capture the podestà's palace. This second stage only came when the two groups of insurgents could join forces. The podestà, Baglione da Perugia, fled. The rebels immediately occupied his palace, and as before broke down the gates of the prison, in this case the Vilognanza, and freed the prisoners.

The next stage was to achieve control of the entire town. At this moment, the nobles of Oltrarno, who had retrenched behind their bridges, destroyed their barricades and crossed the bridge in arms, so that the insurgents thus controlled the streets. Villani describes an imposing force of over a thousand cavalry ("their own horses and those which had been taken from the duke's people") and more than ten thousand infantry ("armed with cuirasses like knights"), even apart from "the lesser folk in arms". This was no truly 'popular' sedition at any stage, and it became even less so when three thousand cavalry and four thousand crossbowmen arrived from Siena the next day, followed by the men of San Miniato, and the counts with their peasants.

While fighting continued throughout the *contado* and an *ad hoc* government was installed in the city, the duke held out in his palace of the priors. He was only to surrender formally to the prominent men of the town several weeks later, on 3 August. Three days later he left the city, protected from the fury of the mobs by the leading citizens themselves. A combat of two days duration was thus followed by a lengthy siege and interminable negotiations, during which the leading families of the city acted as a unit to negotiate a peace of the 'wise men'. When reduced to its principal episodes, this 'popular' insurrection against the tyrant shows the omnipotence of the party chieftains at every stage.

Another leitmotif in the history of the urban riot was the uprising for or against prominent men. The leaders of clans or factions quite often bore the responsibility for other 'popular' disturbances which might be directed either against an opposing faction or against the institutions and peace of the commune. Such incitements to revolution and *rumori* imperilled public order and threatened the party in power. They were denounced as 'treasons' by their adversaries, who happened to be in power at the time, and by neutrals who desired above all to preserve the peace and for this reason were hostile to the party regime and the bloody battles which it entailed. In a fifteen-year segment of his chronicle, Villani denounced in this fashion four such attempts at Florence. All were checked, but they show the decisive role of the aristocratic leaders in fomenting insurrections.

The chapter of Villani's chronicle for January 1328 is entitled "Concerning a certain treason which was plotted at Florence but was discovered". Ugolino degli Ubaldini, leader of a very old family and a party leader, gathered "certain men of little account from Florence" in order to seize the city. He named Giovanni del Sega da Carbone as their leader, then summoned (according to Villani) another thousand knights from Pistoia. His task was to create major disturbances throughout the city, then barricade the streets. The entire plot was within the traditional party framework, for he had his numerous *seguaci*, and some Ghibellines went through the town yelling "Long live the emperor!". But the undertaking foundered, "for no men of any consequence in the city answered the traitor's call".[24] Villani seems to be suggesting that an uprising could only succeed if some magnate leaders participated in it or at least encouraged it.

The second instance occurred in 1340. A conspiracy was formed by the great Oltrarno families of Bardi, Rossi, and Frescobaldi, "together with certain other powerful *popolano* families from the far bank of the Arno", against the authoritarian government of the *popolo grasso*. Several prominent families dominated this regime, and they had placed their own friends in all the important positions, inflicting various annoyances and injustices upon other clans, and particularly upon the nobles. Several rural relatives (*consorti*) of the conspirators responded immediately to their appeal. Villani calls them the counts, *i conti* (the Guidi and the Pazzi di Valdarno). They were joined by some leading members of the wealthy families of Prato and Volterra. But the plot was then discovered. The bell of the *popolo* sounded a general call to take arms against the conspirators, who had to take refuge in their quarters. Although they burned the two wooden bridges across the Arno, they had to surrender.[25]

Another conspiracy was discovered in Oltrarno only a few days later, that of the *schiatta* (clan) of Frescobaldi de' Frescobaldi, who was immediately taken into custody. Finally, on that same day, 23 September 1343, separate magnate groups tried to instigate two 'popular' revolts. That of Andreà degli Strozzi ended in front of the priors' palace, when his mob of partisans dispersed after being assailed by missiles shot from the walls. They were also attacked by "people of the neighbourhood, good men of the *popolo* ". A second riot was led by several magnates who tried to derive a sudden advantage from the first disorder and had men running through the streets crying "Long live the lesser folk! Death to the *popolo grasso* and taxes". But once again the party in power defended itself successfully, this time fomenting a mob uprising of its own on the following day. The nobles quickly capitulated.[26]

Each of these riots was bound in some degree to the primary struggle between great families and factions. Although systematically portrayed as 'social' revolts by some historians, they were actually directed by nobles, magnates, and clan and party leaders against other aristocrats who happened to be chieftains of other clans and factions. The Ciompi revolt is certainly the most important example. G.A. Brucker's careful study shows that the real instigators of that famous uprising were Benedetto Alberti, Tommaso Strozzi, Giorgio Scali, Giovanni Dini, and later, in a quite different context, Salvestro de' Medici.[27] They formed an exiled party, excluded in varying degree from power. Most lived on their rural estates in resolute hostility to the party which was ruling Florence. Similarly, William Bowsky's analysis of the 'social' revolt of 1311 at Siena, in which the butchers and smiths launched an attack on the central town square, shows the essential role played by the Tolomei. They were an illustrious and wealthy family who had been excluded from the government of the Nine but still held several magistracies in the city and some castles in the *contado*. The Tolomei had the allegiance of many allies from all walks of life, and Brother Bernardo of the Umiliati, treasurer of the *Biccherna* (public finances), even declared at the time that the revolt had been perpetrated by "as many nobles and magnates as men of the *popolo*".[28] These 'popular' uprisings were thus peculiarly spectacular episodes in the continuing quarrels between the factions.

As to the combats themselves, the strongholds were neither the prisons nor the public palaces, but rather the various fortresses of the great men which were besieged by the mob *in arme e in gelosia*. The nobles and wealthy *popolani* assembled in their enormous dwellings, protected by barricades, and prepared for war. We are told that these fortifications were constructed "more out of fear of other clans than to attack the *popolo*". Street combats during riots generally resulted in repeated mob assaults on the noble quarters of the opposition, against the barricades and fortified houses. The nobles often succumbed to sheer weight of numbers; in 1343, the Frescobaldi, who had strenuously resisted the attacks of their neighbours from the Via Maggio, gave up the fight when the mob arrived from the sixths north of the Arno. A little later on the same day, the Bardi, who had been forced to retreat into a bloc of houses which had seemed impregnable, "when they realized that they were being pressed severely from all sides ... began to abandon some of their barricades between the square and the bridge".[29] The losers were pursued in disorder and had to take refuge with their friends, or more often leave the town. The well-designed mob assault had carried the day.

Another form of urban warfare pitted those in power, supported by their functionaries and particularly by their retainers, against armed troops from the countryside which were thrown into an assault on the city. This was a constant threat, whether from an enemy city, a great feudal lord who was in the opposing party, or more often someone who had been exiled from the town. All authors portray these mighty towns, shut off within their walls, arming quickly, protected by some quickly constructed outer defense lines, closing their gates and positioning their men on the ramparts and at the crossroads of particularly vulnerable routes. The towns were anything but havens of peace within the walls, and they compounded this by attracting many attackers from the outside.

The results of course varied. The 'external' party of Milan, that of the captains and vavasours under Archbishop Simone de Lercario, began their campaign in November 1276 by investing Como easily and exiling the della Torre. Shortly thereafter they attacked the large fortified settlement of Dezio, where the podestà of Milan and his party (the della Torre) had retreated. The story of this siege caught the attention of the author of the *Annales Ghibellini* of Piacenza, who describes how the crossbowmen and cavalry who had dismounted fought in the moats for the brattices. The siege was finally successful on 21 January 1277, and since Milan could thus no longer defend itself, the 'exterior' party entered the city unopposed.[30] Salimbene reports that in the same year the knights' party of Parma, which had been exiled by the emperor but still had considerable political power, arrived from Piacenza and entered the city on 15 June, immediately expelling the imperial partisans.[31]

Giovanni Villani gives lengthy descriptions of two dangerous enterprises which came up against the opposition of the local citizens and resulted in resounding defeats. He entitles his chapter for 20 July 1304 "How the Whites and the Ghibellines came to the gates of Florence and departed in defeat". This operation, which made a vivid impression on the Florentine imagination after the fact, was prepared by a lengthy mobilization effort in the countryside. Written appeals were sent to all the leaders of the Ghibellines and White Guelfs who had recently been expelled from the city. The letters told them that "the city was weakened and open at several places" and that the conspirators could rely on the aid of several Black *caporali*. After the first armed contingents had left Pisa, they were joined by others as they progressed, usually secretly and under cover of darkness, until they got control of the roads and were able to intercept all messengers en route to Florence. But the 'external' conspirators' party did not realize that the Florentine government knew all about their plan and had summoned reinforcements from Bologna and assembled its own troops on the Piazza San Giovanni. The attack was broken as soon as the invaders had passed through the suburbs and breached the wall. The attackers, although Villani claims that they outnumbered the defenders, could neither maneuver nor find water for their horses and thus had to flee. A mob of footsoldiers and crossbowmen had thus defeated a powerful army of knights in street combat.[32] A similar instance occurred on the night of 10 August 1343, when a group of exiles, "with the help of certain nobles to whose houses the exiles belonged" – in other words, assisted by persons within the town – attacked the city, but they were defeated by the reinforced communal defences and had to flee the scene.[33]

Thus the great city had many weapons which enabled it to defend itself: strong defences and guards, a substantial militia, and even its mobs which could be used for street fighting. It could gain a complete victory over a force of knights coming from outside the town. Indeed, attacks by an 'external' party could succeed only when reinforced by strong, well trained contingents from other places, and when the way had been prepared by a powerful cell inside the city which was disloyal to the régime in power.

Collective psychology. Massacres and acts of cruelty

These civil wars demonstrate the existence of original features in the general mentality which are quite distinct from the traditional image of the chivalric combats of the 'feudal' era. Thoughtful contemporaries perceived the warfare very differently, as somewhat shameful; the emotions which moved the antagonists owed much to the exasperation produced by party discords and hatreds.

These were conflicts involving neither honour nor heroes. The vendetta of course was intended to wash away the stain of an affront, to redeem the honour of a member of the clan or the party, ally, or relative. The collective feeling of honour was very powerful and demanded either that blood be spilled or that peace be bought dearly, with heavy penalties and significant compensations paid by the adversary. But we have seen that even the act of exacting vengeance respected no code of honour. The avenger tried to catch his foe by surprise. He would be just as likely to strike at a close or even distant relative of the culprit, preferably a weak, isolated, unarmed, or imprisoned individual incapable of defending himself.[34] The commune of Florence jailed several Cerchi and Donati for street fighting in 1304. "Then one accursed Ser Neri degli Abati managed to get into the prison, had dinner with them, and brought them a pudding (*migliaccio*) as a gift. They ate it", and six thereafter died of poison.[35] The vendetta was thus the very opposite of the duel, for there was neither risk nor open combat.

The same was true of the group fighting in the city, which too was often inspired by an acerbic, festering hatred. Warfare between rival factions was a true civil war, with neighbours fighting each other. Men who knew one another well, were jealous, and had learned to associate and often to hate for long years, seized the opportunity to settle old grudges.

Another characteristic of the collective social ethic is inherent in the participation in these bloody struggles not only of veterans who had abandoned professional soldiering, men who might be able to respect a certain code of behaviour or at least traditions, but also of amateur fighters: guildsmen, artisans, merchants, and at times the poor, foreigners, and mercenaries who profited from the warfare. All were involved in the vendetta. This was group warfare, in which numbers were of paramount importance. The multitude could carry everything before it, and the valour of the individual was trampled under by the mob.

Actually, there are few references to the courageous individual. The annals and chronicles mention no hero or champion, no individual exploit, but rather convey the impression of an opaque, gray confusion, of anonymity. Although the authors mention the leaders' names before the battle, when the alliances were being formed, and then the names of the executed or exiled losers, they were much less interested in individual exploits and very rarely noted them. I can discover only one heroic figure in the work of Giovanni Villani, in a single significant episode. The Guelfs of Reggio in 1263 appealed to the exiled Guelfs of Florence for help in fighting the Ghibellines of their native city. The latter were led, however, by the redoubtable and already half legendary Caca de Reggio, a man who incorporated all the force of his party: "he was great because he was a virtual giant and had marvellous strength, with fists of iron . . . and the entire battle was delayed because of him". But the sequel, which was told carefully and even so scarcely covered his opponents with glory, should be noted. They named twelve 'paladins' [*sic*] who attacked the ferocious hero with knives. They finally killed him, and "when the Ghibellines saw that their champion had fallen, they fled from Reggio in defeat".[36] This was the bitter end of a battle which had neither virtue nor honour, but epitomized the triumph of sheer numbers.

Finally, this was a merciless struggle for total victory, for the opposing party had to disappear or perish. All of this was aggravated still more by the element of surprise, the suddenness by which troops were raised, by fear and anguish, the confusion which made all doubt everything, the suspicion of the moment, and the brutality of the combats in which the fate of the city, the parties, and their leaders might be thrown into the balance within a few hours. For all these reasons, there was nothing chivalrous about this warfare. It appealed only to hatred and deceit. It inspired neither poets, troubadours, nor authors of chivalric romances, neither an epic narrative nor *chanson de geste*. These were two different worlds.

All the chroniclers also denounced the civil wars as ruinous, for they left the town exhausted, half burnt or otherwise destroyed. The devastations were sometimes perpetrated by the combatants themselves: relentless party men moved by their thirst for vengeance, overcome by envy (*gelosia*), and just as much by the elemental desire to obliterate every trace of a despised opponent and to rehabilitate their own partisans, or at least their memory. When the podestà's palace was seized by the opponents of the duke of Athens in 1343, the entire judicial archives were burned:

All the charters and writings were taken and burned . . . and then they broke the doors of the chamber of the commune, and took nearly all the books in which sentences of banishment and treason had been written and burned them. They did the same to all acts of the *officio della Mercanzia* . . . .[37]

These acts of pillage can be attributed to political motives, and regarded as episodes of the party struggle. But they were much more often the deeds of street mobs and even of professional ruffians whose rapacious, dirty troops descended on the city as soon as one party was defeated and its houses destroyed and thus given over to the greed of anyone who happened along. When the della Torre were driven from Cremona and subsequently Milan by the opposing party in the winter of 1276–1277, one of their leaders, Caxonus della Torre, returned unexpectedly to Milan to try to save his property there ("he went to his house and drove many plunderers away"). But after his party had been defeated shortly thereafter, "many lesser folk entered the houses of the della Torre. They pillaged and then destroyed them almost totally within a few days".[38] Villani gives a much more precise and realistic description of the various disorders perpetrated by the aroused street mobs after the defeat of the Bardi and their allies in 1343. The city of Florence was delivered to the tender mercies of a mob intent on rapine and destruction (*furia, gelosia*). Conditions were so bad that all property, whether chattel or not, and even merchandise of any value in the shops, was threatened. "Those who had valuable property and merchandise hid it in churches and holy places." The spectacle of convents and churches serving as places of refuge and of shops standing fortified in the city centre recalls the abbeys or fortified churches of Italy or France at the time of raids by Saracens, mercenary troops, or highwaymen. We know from other sources the importance of the urban religious establishments as depositories for precious objects and books, even if these were only the commercial records of the great Tuscan families. The church as a haven of peace or at least an asylum and a safe place was not at all peculiar to the 'feudal' world, but also was true of urban civilization. The merchants were certainly not being overcautious in 1343, for Villani continues: "All the houses and palaces of the Bardi, from Santa Lucia to the square before the Ponte Vecchio, were ravaged by all sorts of lesser folk; for not only men, but even women and children, could not get their fill of rapine or control themselves". Then came the professionals, outlaws or at least rootless persons, a multitude of semi-nomads thrown together as bands of looters: "more than a thousand marauders gathered to fight the Visdomini and rob them". These people of course tried to explain away their actions and misdeeds as political acts, attacks on the property of traitors and rebels, but Villani concludes with brutal candour that "they just wanted to steal".[39] The social phenomenon of 'popular', temporary banditry and the professional robbery of the marauders thus inevitably accompanied party warfare, which was always animated by an ineluctable hatred and by *a priori* justifications for destruction and rapine.

The chronicles and annals convey an even more dramatic impact with tales of arson. Fire was a horrible scourge of the time, particularly in the towns, where houses were crowded together. Touched off by simple carelessness, lightning, or sheer accident, fire was almost invariably used as a weapon in civil warfare. It was a convenient way of perpetrating vengeance and systematic destruction, individual criminal deeds, or even unilateral acts of despair, as when the Bardi burned their own houses in 1343 rather than leave them open to the ravages of their enemies and the despoilers.[40]

Fire also figures prominently in the occasional pictures of city warfare which have survived. Among the great works, we need only evoke here the "bad government" panel of Ambrogio Lorenzetti's mural of 1338 which adorns the town hall of Siena. But the miniatures illustrating the chronicle of Giovanni Sercambi of Lucca demonstrate the constant fear of fire felt by the artists and other men of this period: pictures of two armed *brigate* fighting and setting fire to houses, scenes in which a tower in flames is seen in the background.[41]

The chroniclers too give frequent and detailed descriptions of fires which were peculiarly dramatic or were novelties at the time. Arson might even be a call to arms. For the exciting and devastating day of 13 November 1343, Giovanni Villani lists all the fires which broke out in the city, and also notes that "wherever a fire was set, the entire city was thrown into an uproar, as everyone took arms and readied his defences".[42]

Fire was always a severe threat, and too often the result of a deliberate criminal act, a deed of vengeance committed outside formal combat or more often after victory. It was a weapon habitually used in armed party struggle, as well as a means of humiliating a weakened or defeated adversary still farther, of ruining him or running him out of town. The anonymous chronicler of Verona relates that in 1173 "their violent quarrels led the citizens to burn the entire town", while at Vicenza in 1325 "there was a great fire which lasted ten days and destroyed a quarter of the city".[43] G. Gozzadini's study of all the great families of Bologna who owned towers and fortified palaces in the thirteenth century shows that their houses were frequently destroyed by fire.[44] As the party in power at Fermo in 1326 was concluding an agreement with the papacy, their exiled opponents, the Orsini party, "entered the town . . . and set fire to the city hall while the council was deliberating the agreement, and many men of property died or were severely burned".[45] Giovanni Sercambi relates that the new Gerbolini party at Pisa burned the houses of the della Roccha in 1323.[46] Finally, Giovanni Villani devotes an entire chapter ("How Florence experienced still another fire which consumed a substantial part of the city") to the acts of arson which ravaged the town as the disturbances and fights between Whites and Blacks were beginning in 1304. The man accused, Piero Scheraggio, was a "worldly, bellicose, and dissolute man, a rebel and enemy of his own kindred". He came from a rich family and wanted desperately to avenge himself against the members of his clan. He began by setting fire to their houses near the Mercato Vecchio in the quarter of Orto San Michele, whence the fire spread throughout the city with astonishing rapidity; "for the accursed flames were furious and impetuous and were spread by a strong north wind . . .". Villani reports that a total of 1,700 houses in the city were consumed and destroyed on that single day. The fire had visited the merchant quarters particularly severely, and as a result the shops were soon open to all. The people had been so excited by the civil wars that the merchandise which had not been burned "was stolen by the malefactors who were fighting in various parts of the city". The dual scourges of fire and the subsequent pillaging ruined several powerful families: "numerous companies, clans, and families were decimated and even impoverished by this arson and thievery". Some clans, including the richest and most influential, then lost their wealth, clientele, and political power. They included the Cavalcanti and particularly the Gherardini, who were even party leaders ("captains of their sect"), but who "lost their vigour and station and were driven from Florence as rebels after their houses and those of their *seguaci* had been burned".[47] Fire, a dramatic consequence of the civil wars, was indeed a political weapon.

The fury of the victorious party could be appeased only by destructive vengeance. Such passion was particularly strong among collateral relatives, clients, protégés, and the *seguaci*; and its results were especially loathsome just after the conclusion of neighbourhood warfare. The intense exasperation which was produced by implacable hostility toward the enemy led to brutal executions, and even more to gratuitous acts of collective cruelty. The unleashing of homicidal fury seemed commonplace, indeed inevitable. It was the price of victory which had to be paid in blood to the party followers. Thus when the Veronese Mastino della Scala obtained the lordship of Brescia in 1332 by arrangement with several Guelf nobles of that city, he gave them what amounted to total license for three days to pillage and massacre their enemies: "and the Guelf party was given free rein to spend three days hacking the Ghibelline party to pieces inside and outside Brescia".[48] These wholesale massacres were often deliberately perpetrated under the worst possible circumstances with neither risk nor glory, and chroniclers writing about them many years later still shuddered at the memory. Such incidents occurred under the sponsorship of different parties in two neighbouring towns. The Ghibelline conquerors of Spoleto in November 1319 put "the Guelfs into a prison to which they immediately set fire. Everyone inside was burned in this act of villainous cruelty".[49] When the Guelfs of Rieti drove their enemies from the town in August 1320, "over five hundred were killed. They even drowned them in the river, which became red with blood".[50]

Individual acts of bestiality and torture might also be visited upon an imprisoned tyrant or one of his officials, or even on any skulking dignitary who was spotted by chance and thereby became a focal point for mob rage. Villani mentions no heroes in the combats leading to the fall of the duke of Athens in 1343; this was group warfare perpetrated by nameless mobs. But in two long pages he relates the horrid fate of the men who were seized by these mobs and sent to their fate. The duke's officials were treated worst. Simone da Norcia was found guilty of torturing the wrong persons and "was cut to pieces". A Neapolitan soldier who was thought to be an infantryman of the duke was recognized and seized at the Porta Santa Maria and "was completely hacked to pieces by the people". One Ser Arrigo Fei, "who superintended the gabelles", was discovered at San Gallo as he fled disguised as a monk. He was put to death, "and then the boys dragged his naked corpse through the city, hanged it by the feet in the Piazza dei Priori, and quartered it like a pig". A last gruesome example is the case of Guiglelmo of Asciesi, "who was reputed to be a supporter of the duke's tyranny". He was seized with his eighteen year old son and handed over to the people and to the relatives of his former victims, the

Altoviti and the Medici. The young man was killed and cut to pieces in his father's presence ("and they chopped him into tiny pieces"). Villani then concludes with this frightful, grisly scene: "the father in turn was killed, and everyone carried a piece of the corpse on lances or swords through the town. Then they were so cruel and enraged to such animal fury that they ate the raw flesh".[51] Once again, the unleashed fury of the mob joined the vengeful spirit of the parties, of relatives and allies bitterly fighting their enemies, to perpetrate these barbarous acts.

Thus, abandoned to passions and refinements of cruelty after the abortive coup attempted by the Bardi and their allies, Florence only recovered its equilibrium later in 1343 through the sometimes brutal intervention of neutrals ("the vicinity, with many men of property in arms") and an authority transcending that of the factions ("the mercenaries of the commune"), and even by the quite effective action of foreigners, cavalry from Siena and Perugia. Pillaging was ended only when the soldiers got the upper hand and took the malefactors into custody. The latter were immediately condemned to lose their feet and hands. "And thus", Villani concludes, "the wild and angry people, intent on rapine and evildoing, were calmed. Shops began to reopen, and everyone returned to his own affairs".[52]

CHAPTER TWO

The losers' fate

The end of the fighting, pillaging, arson, massacres, and bestiality merely proclaimed the absolute, insolent triumph of the victorious party. The losers then became the victims of acts of vengeance and violence which were no longer spontaneous outbursts, but rather involved condemnations, various extraordinary measures involving their persons or property and making them outlaws or second-class citizens who were deprived of a substantial part of their political rights. Factional warfare and insurrections incited by a great family or group of allies led inevitably to the establishment of an absolute power which was capable of imposing its will by force. This could be either the victorious party, a tyrant, or a political coalition not involved in the party conflicts.

Magistrates or officials with discretionary powers were often placed in charge of the repression, the purpose of which was to exclude the enemy from political affairs and responsibilities and to exercise a careful surveillance to prevent him from returning to power. The spirit of vendetta inevitably prevailed, involving a total intolerance, a refusal to have anything to do with the adversary in the city. A concept of collective responsibility was also intertwined with this. It led the victors to strike at all members of the defeated clan or party. Opponents had to disappear, whether through the death or exile of their leaders, financial ruin, or by constant blows to their social prestige.

These manifold and frequently applied measures merit attention. With an unabating rhythm, they syncopated all urban and rural life in northern and central Italy. They were a major preoccupation of the régime in power. With significant and often dramatic consequences, they engendered new economic and social situations. Finally, the losers' fate was also an important source of contemporary literary inspiration.

Condemnations and executions.   Reprisals against property

No study of the 'trials', or, better stated, political condemnations has
ever been made. We still know little of procedure, how victims were
chosen, the exact nature of the indictments brought by the judges or
justiciars, 'judicial' customs, how the guilty were judged, and penalties.
Our texts say little of imprisonment, concentrating instead on executions and banishments.

Capital penalties were always handed down in a climate of absolute
hatred and violence as soon as the combats had ceased. These were acts
of pure vengeance and on-the-spot executions rather than real punishments imposed by judicial tribunals. They arose from blind fury. After
the Ghibelline victory at Florence in 1249, the Guelf leaders, such as the
wealthy Count Ridolfo di Capraia and Rinieri Zingane de' Buondelmonti, were initially spared and were taken to Apulia with the imperial
armies. But their enemies in Florence were soon bombarding the
emperor with letters, urging him to impose cruel penalties which would
furnish an example to others.

And they plucked out the eyes of all members of the great noble houses of Florence, then
beat them to death and threw their bodies into the sea. Only Messer Rinieri Zingane was
spared, for he was considered wise and magnanimous. They did not want to kill him, so
they merely blinded him, and he finished his days as a monk on the island of Montecristo.[53]

Several weeks after the battles and the victory, eyes were thus torn out
and men thrown into the sea! These were reflections of an implacable
hatred, of passions unleashed. Such coldly planned and executed acts of
vengeance clash strangely with the idyllic concept of the town as a
haven of peace and home of justice.

Another Tuscan example of brutal and arbitrary capital punishments
visited only on a few leaders comes from San Miniato al Tedesco. The
party of the *grandi*, led by the Malpighi and the Mangiadori, had been
excluded from power, but finally gained the day in 1308 with the
assistance from friends outside the town and defeated the 'popular'
party.

And they seized and killed many of them. Certain leaders were decapitated, and they
burned all their ordinances. They buried the bell of the *popolo*, and the *popolo* was thus
harshly suppressed until the *grandi* families began having disagreements among themselves.[54]

As soon as public peace and the authority of the state had been re-established after an abortive clan or party uprising, retaliation followed swiftly. The captured leaders were immediately executed as criminals. When the Uberti family led the Ghibellines in a fruitless effort to seize power at Florence in 1258, two of their most important leaders were seized, and, following an indecently hasty trial, were decapitated at Orto San Michele. In September of that same year, the abbot of Vallembrosa, a gentleman reputed to be from the Pavian family of the Beccheria, was suspected of Ghibelline sympathies and accordingly hanged on orders of the commune.[55] These convictions and executions were preventive measures, totally outside any openly declared conflict. At Florence too, the rising in 1343 of the great Oltrarno families of Bardi, Rossi, and Frescobaldi provoked a lively reaction against their allies, the Counts Guidi, who were lords of castles in the Tuscan countryside, as soon as the triumph of their opponents was certain: nine Guidi captains of this faction were sternly condemned.[56] Verona was the scene of an unsuccessful revolt in 1354. It had been fomented against Cangrande della Scala, who was then absent from the town, by party of allies including the Gonzaga of Mantua, Frignano, the tyrant's natural son, and the exiles. The rebels controlled the city for several days, but were then annihilated in a bloody battle which ended in several lynchings near the belfry in the main town square. The anonymous chronicle of Verona names twenty-two rebel leaders who were hanged and exposed to the mob in the heart of the city. The authorities obviously intended to make an example of the rebels. Indeed, the author continues, "he [the tyrant] had a mural painted for the chamber of the *procuratori* in the town hall. It showed these traitors hanging from the gallows, so that the memory of their ordeal would not be lost".[57]

Losses and confiscations

Yet, spectacular though they were, the executions and acts of cruelty committed on the orders of the victorious party affected only a few leaders. Their main significance is their illustration of a spirit of vengeance. They were committed to settle personal scores rather than out of a deliberate will to weaken or annihilate the entire opposing party. This desire existed, of course, but it gave vent to different measures, a calculated and consistently pursued policy which had more serious consequences than the political executions.

First, the members of the opposition might be ruined economically through the destruction of their houses or the confiscation of their property. Razing the house of anyone, but particularly of a noble, was a seal of infamy. It was a decisive and particularly heinous affront to his honour and that of his ancestors and his entire clan, who were made sport of by the action.[58] Criminal fugitives were often punished by the demolition of their houses in cases having nothing to do with the factional conflicts. G. Gozzadini has published a unique notarial act of October 1272. It records the proceedings of a consultation with several master carpenters and masons undertaken at the request of the podestà of the town. The scion of a noble family who had been indicted and punished for murder had been found to be the owner of half of one house and one-third of another. The guildsmen were asked to determine which parts of these buildings should be destroyed. They ascertained the extent of his possession (from one wall to another, as far as such and such a column). They retained a door for the parts of the houses which would be left standing, and proposed that a roof be built to protect these segments. They gave instructions for consolidating the pillars of the great hall, roughly half of whose area was to be destroyed.[59]

During party conflicts in all Italian towns, the houses of the losers, particularly the wealthiest of them, were systematically destroyed. The chroniclers speak of this continually as an ordinary and generally admitted state of affairs. To the damages caused by battles, arson, and pillaging were added those which were deliberately planned and carried out on the orders of the victorious party officials. Giovanni Villani's chronicle once again furnishes innumerable and varied examples. Even as early as 1215 at Florence, shortly after the first bloody party conflict had ended in a Guelf defeat, "some thirty-six Guelf fortresses, both palaces and great towers", were razed to the ground.[60] Such demolitions were occurring more frequently a century later in all the cities. The prevalence of the phenomenon can be illustrated by the number of cases mentioned by Villani alone over a span of a few years. The victorious Whites drove the Blacks from Pistoia in 1301 and "destroyed their palaces and possessions, among them a splendid group of palaces and towers called 'Damiata' which belonged to the Cancellieri".[61] The Blacks suffered a similar fate that same year at Lucca, for "they destroyed their houses and set fire to the quarter of Fondo di Porta San Gervasio, burning more than one hundred dwellings".[62] The Grimaldi returned in triumph to Genoa in 1309, expelled Ubizzino Spinola and his party, and established themselves as lords. "The only change which this entailed was the destruction of Messer Ubizzino's fortified palace of Luccoli at Genoa."[63] The party led by the Querini, which conspired to overthrow the power of the ca' Gradanigo at Venice in 1310, received similar treatment after its failure, but Villani remarks, with the astonishment of an outsider, that the town had been spared such destructions of houses until that time: "and when they destroyed their palaces, this was the first such incident which had even occurred in Venice".[64] After the party of the Lanfranchi, the Sismondi, the Capronesi, and the Gualandi, supported by Count Nieri de' Gherardesi and one Coscetto del Colle, had failed at Pisa in 1322, "fifteen leaders of these families were executed as rebels and their property was destroyed".[65] Finally, in a last episode which Villani knew well, for it occurred only a few years before his death, we note the penalties visited on the rebel families of the Florentine Oltrarno in 1340: "their palaces and properties in both city and *contado* were furiously attacked and were dismantled and destroyed even down to the very foundations".[66]

All the annals and chronicles of the period, and even the later histories of Italian towns, describe just as many houses torn down as we have implied here, in a continuing drama which everyone might experience at first hand several times during his life. The *Annales Genovenses* show that this was the case at Genoa;[67] other evidence demonstrates it for Ferrara;[68] at Bologna, where Gozzadini's study frequently notes houses torn down and in ruins;[69] and at Lucca and Pisa according to the chronicle of Giovanni Sercambi, in this case illustrated by several sketches of both Guelf and Ghibelline houses being destroyed.

It would be pointless to cite still more examples of this practice and impossible to compile an inventory of them. In each case which we have noted it affected only a few families or a single quarter. It accomplished the vengeance which was the goal of the feud. But other more catastrophic and systematic undertakings show a more comprehensive intent to annihilate an entire party, an opposing political force, or even a whole city. This practice may have been conceived or at least spectacularly given legitimacy by Frederick Barbarossa's destruction of Milan in 1162. All the houses within the city walls were completely razed and all who wished to remain had to withdraw to the suburbs. To make an even greater impression on the townsmen of Lombardy and to abase Milanese pride still further, the emperor ordered stones to be taken from these houses and ruins to the hated rival town of Monza, where he was constructing a palace. Milan was only rebuilt in 1167 in a veritable resurrection under St Ambrose's patronage. The event is immortalized in a bas relief carved on the Porta Romana in 1171: the myth of a rebirth which defied the opposing party and assumed the significance of a true miracle.

The rigidity of the emperor, who demanded that the town which dared oppose him be razed, was demonstrated by other less spectacular but equally significant enterprises. Frederick II insisted on mass destruction after he had taken Verona in 1239: "the emperor immediately ordered the destruction of the houses and all the towers of the Landenara, the Chalchabusani da Montagnana, those of the men of Pesena, of San Quirice, and many other towers in Verona".[71] Another chronicler attributes the deed to his envoy, Piero della Vigna, but says that "the plenipotentiary had nearly all the towers of Verona ruined, above all those of men suspected of being part of the Monticola faction".[72] The same thirst for total destruction, a very powerful tradition among the leaders of the imperial party, was still being demonstrated by the heirs of Frederick II. When the famous and sadly celebrated Ghibelline 'parliament' was held at Empoli in 1260 after the victory over the Florentine Guelfs, all the Ghibelline leaders, the Counts Guidi, the Alberti, the partisans of the Santafiore and the Ubaldini and all the barons "proposed that the city of Florence be destroyed completely and reduced to a village, so that it could not retain its ancient condition, renown, prestige, nor power".[73] This proposition was only rejected thanks to the energetic intervention and refusal of Farinata degli Uberti.

The flight of the Guelfs from Florence on this occasion was followed immediately by the destruction of their houses, and the register of indemnifications which were made as soon as the Guelfs returned to power in 1267[74] gives an exact idea of the stupefying extent of this demolition. We see entire quarters razed and piled with rubble, streets passing through a scene of ruins, with only public buildings and churches keeping an isolated watch over a desolated landscape. A total of 103 palaces, 580 houses, and eighty-five towers (most of which were destroyed "with houses"), or at least seven hundred important residences of various types were thus demolished. Many castles of the *contado* were similarly dismantled or completely destroyed, and not even peasant villages were spared. Of a total value of damages estimated at £132,350 Florence, properties in numerous places outside the town in the *contado* represent roughly half.

The same systematic policy and lust for destruction are found at Bologna in 1280, when the Lambertazzi, defeated after a long struggle, were driven from the town. The victorious party itself compiled a register of enemy property which was destroyed. Although only a fragment survives, it lists "250 acts of damage, of houses belonging to the Lambertazzi which had been destroyed".[75] At Siena, when the 'popular' revolt led by the magnate Tolomei clan had been crushed, the accounts of the Office of the Nine noted £317 paid to the "masters and labourers who destroyed the goods and properties of the traitors who had troubled the peace of the commune of Siena". These wages were paid "to have the houses and palaces of the aforementioned traitors razed and their vineyards cut down".[76]

Thus, an entire town or large and important quarters thereof might be reduced to rubble, affording a reminder for many years of the violent hatreds, of the insane desire to pursue the opposing party and humiliate it still further and prevent it from recovering its prosperity or any standing in the community. Without great palaces, without *loggie*, with no place of assembly, shelter, or refuge in time of danger, the defeated party immediately forfeited the tangible symbol of its power, its prestige, and all possibility of keeping the loyalty of a large clientele of faithful followers or "persons who were maintained".

But these wanton acts of destruction could offend wiser persons, for they caused the good name of the city to suffer. They were the dramatic reflection of its internal conflicts and to some extent of its weaknesses. They brought the victors no material gain. This is why the victors occasionally took the rebels' property for themselves, rather than destroying their houses and palaces. Veritable offices of confiscation were established which seem to have been quite active. During the civil war at Orvieto between the Monaldeschi and Filippeschi parties, sixteen Filippeschi leaders were condemned by the podestà, followed by a second group of twenty in December of the same year. In each case fines of up to £7,000 were assessed, preferably to be paid in land. Fines which had not been paid were commuted by an agreement of December 1273 for a lump sum of £21,000, of which two-thirds was to be paid immediately. The Filippeschi assumed these obligations.[77] The Guelf victory of 1310 at Orvieto was the signal for large scale confiscations. A *balia* or special commission was entrusted with the task of compiling a list of all Ghibelline property. It was revised several times and constituted a veritable cadastral survey of the palaces and houses of an important segment of the town population. A fragment of this register has survived and shows clearly how totally the victors appropriated the lands and buildings of the losers, particularly in the quarter of Fabro, where the Filippeschi had considerable valuable property. These notorious confiscations finally provoked so many abuses and scandals that all of these property transfers were re-examined in 1314.[78]

The return of the Guelfs to Florence in 1267 was accompanied by the immediate confiscation and sale of the lands and houses of their enemies. The commune, the Guelf party, and those Guelfs who had been ruined by their losses in 1260, each received one-third of the profit from these sales. This suggests that the confiscations of 1267 and 1268 far surpassed the value of the destructions of 1260 and 1261. It also implies a massive alteration among property owners and residents, together with wholesale expropriations.[79] Still, when Corso Donati and the Blacks who constituted the radical wing of the Guelf party returned to their city on 4 November 1301, Florence was pillaged for the next five days and Charles of Valois derived considerable financial profit from the confiscated properties. They were so significant, enormous, and complex that the commune ordered special scribes to compose a separate register, the *Libro del Chiodo*, in which all confiscations and fines were listed.[80]

Finally, some expropriations on a smaller scale redounded to the profit of the commune alone. Stones from demolished houses could be used to build or reinforce the city wall. The land on which destroyed palaces had once stood might become a public square. At Florence, in 1265 and 1266, two Bolognese podestàs who had been summoned to pacify the city ordered the destruction of the houses of the Uberti, who had been fomenting discord. After they left, the commune constructed the Palazzo della Signoria on the same site, but to a design which would avoid any construction on the soil which had been declared accursed.[81] Villani too mentions the construction of this palace in 1298 and gives details: "on the site of the aforementioned palace, the houses of the Uberti, who were Ghibelline rebels of Florence, had formerly stood. A square was made where their neighbours' houses had been, so that they could never be rebuilt".[82]

Thus the private, family or partisan vendetta, the desire to abase the adversary by destroying the houses which symbolized his clan and power in the minds of contemporaries, the imperial policy of razing insubordinate towns, monetary needs or conquerors' rapacity, and the desire for free and open space to build the town hall or maintain a great public square all were traditions and collective feelings which combined to extend the demolition and ruins far beyond the damage caused by the combats themselves. Whether limited to a single group of houses or systematic and massive, these acts of destruction were an essential, primordial aspect of urban life in the Middle Ages. They and the fires, with the reconstruction which necessarily followed, in large measure brought about a continuing evolution and sometimes a decisive alteration of the urban landscape. Towers and fortifications gradually disappeared before new architectural styles and fashions, and gradually too before the new social functions of the aristocratic dwelling.

Exile

Sentences of exile were also very frequent and were perpetrated on a vast scale. Many men from rich and powerful families had to leave the town and wander about seeking a new home. These condemnations, in my opinion, were an essential aspect of urban life whose astonishing extent and serious consequences must be noted by historians.[83] Exile greatly influenced the destiny of all cities. It might be of considerable duration, for banishment obviously quickened the desire to return to power and avenge oneself. It thus prolonged the course of party warfare indefinitely. This was naturally a dangerous threat to the countryside. One faction monopolized power, while the members of the other were forced to live outside the city, using all means at their disposal to return to political power. On the other hand, exile shows in harsh outline the bonds between town and countryside, human migrations and thus population movements, commercial activity, the victualling trade, means of recruiting companies of knights, collective mentalities, and the themes which inspired works of literature.

A rich and at times very specific vocabulary used constantly by all contemporary authors shows the frequency and significance of political banishments. They use these words with such facility that each of them undoubtedly perceived clearly the gravity of the phenomenon and reflected their time accurately. Throughout their narratives, the Tuscan chroniclers, particularly Giovanni Sercambi and Giovanni Villani, devote long chapters to the exiles and their activities. Villani's very titles show this interest clearly: "How the Ghibelline party was driven from Fano"[84] or "How the Genoese exiles retook the dependent villages of Genoa".[85] This holds true not only for Florence and the great Italian cities, but also for little settlements in the *contado*, such as Colle di Val d'Elsa.[86] Statistics on these titles and chapter contents would be tiresome to compile, but would undoubtedly show the extreme importance of the exiles' activities as contemporary Tuscan chroniclers perceived them.

Of course, various words might be used. Villani employs several: the expression *ai confini* and the words *sbanditi*, *rebelli* or *rubelli*, and particularly *usciti*. In December 1343, "because of a certain discord which the *grandi* wrongfully provoked at Florence, Enrico de' Bardi and four of the Frescobaldi, together with . . . were sent to the borders (*ai confini*)".[87] At Pisa, the Bergolini drove the Raspanti from power on Christmas night, 1347, but "did them no other ill than robbing and burning the houses of their adherents and sending the counts and their *seguaci* to the borders".[88]

Sbanditi (the banished) were persons excluded from political life and not permitted to live inside the town's jurisdictional area. They obviously hoped to return, and accordingly fomented all kinds of trouble. One chapter is entitled "Concerning the great changes which some *sbanditi* caused at Florence". In 1322 three *sbanditi*, hoping to become *ribantidi*, sent eight of their captains to the city to negotiate their repatriation.

The words *rebelli* or *rubelli* were used very frequently to mean persons with clearly aggressive intentions: "rebel and newly arrived, carrying a banner deployed against our commune" or "having entered our lands".[90] The rebel was thus a person who invaded the territory of the commune from exile, crossed the frontier armed, and did not respect the borders beyond which he had been exiled.

Finally, the word *usciti* was used for all towns and circumstances. It was the most ordinary and current term and best translates the city dweller's need to take constant and habitual account of the presence outside the town of a numerous and often dangerous body of citizens who had been deprived of their rights and part of their property.

The vocabulary current in the north Italian countryside was somewhat different, of course, but it reflects the same mental outlook. The concept of exile was if anything more prevalent in the rural areas than in the towns. The Veronese chronicles ordinarily juxtaposed *estrinseii* and *intrinseii*,[91] while other authors mention the *parte di fuori*. The Ghibelline *Annals* of Piacenza frequently use the expressions *pars extrinseca* and *pars intrinseca* for Piacenza as well as for the other Lombard towns, such as Brescia, Cremona, and Milan.[92] This vocabulary undoubtedly suggests another concept which was more precise than that of Tuscany: the awareness of a firm contrast between power and exile, for all persons living in the city, both those holding power and ordinary residents, constituted only a single citizens' party.

But when we direct our attention to those excluded by the victorious party and the commune, in addition to noting the organically developed vocabulary, we perceive clearly the importance of these political exiles for the fate of the city. An administration and special officers had to be established to count and oversee the exiles and keep the lists up to date. The chroniclers reproduce the essential features of these enumerations. Banishments were immediately visited on many people, for the victors intended not only to strike at a few powerful opponents, but to weaken an entire party by removing every active and dangerous member from the political scene. Sentences were pronounced publicly in a dramatic, solemn ritual, and were intended to leave a vivid imprint on the imagination. In 1277 the party of the conspirators who tried to seize power at Verona from Mastino della Scala was defeated, then subjected to a harsh, merciless repression. The principal leaders, who had signed the pact and fomented the revolt, were executed, while the others, who had fled, "were sentenced to exile for life, at the sound of the bell, by the voice of the people of Verona assembled on the square at the public pillory . . . on condition that neither the rebels nor their descendants might ever again live at Verona".[93] Exile in perpetuity was thus decreed spectacularly at the sound of the bell, on the main town square before the mob. No appeal was possible from this draconian judgement. It could only be reversed by the equally spectacular means of returning to the city with a magnificent display of force, which in its turn would involve exiling their own enemies in turn.

Some banishments were even preventive measures, precautions taken as suspicions were raised of dangerous 'popular' unrest orchestrated by the other party. When several members of the great families of Florence had to leave the city in 1343, "to remove all suspicion from the *popolo* and to flee its wrath, they went into the *contado*, leaving the city to live in their villages".[94]

The reference to persons leaving the city and going to the countryside to live on their domains, in the villages of which they were the masters, is extremely significant. Most fugitives or exiles who were not sent beyond the borders of the city's jurisdictional area (*mandati ai confini*) were able to repel all pursuits simply by taking refuge in their castles.

The Guelfs who were driven from Florence in 1248, the nobles "and others, some *popolani* of that party, took refuge on their domains and with their friends in the *contado*". The leaders then evidently intended to assemble, "some in the castle of Montevarchi in the Valdarno . . . and others in the castle of Capraia".[95] While the factions of Orvieto clashed between 1334 and 1354 in magnificent confusion, the exiles were gradually occupying much of the *contado* closest to the town.[96] The same thing occurred on the Ligurian Riviera and in the mountains, where substantial areas were always being controlled by Genoese *usciti* or *ribelli*.

The practice of taking refuge thus explains the prestige and power of the great seigneurial clans who resided both in the town and the countryside. Castle lords could easily play an extremely prominent role in the political life of the city, for they had many friends and protégés there who could influence their political fortunes. The desire to maintain a hideaway in case of exile or other ill fortune, such as economic failure, certainly led many families, noble and other, to acquire and maintain rural domains, fortified manor houses with stone walls and towers, with lands and sharecroppers to ensure the food supply, which in any case would provide resources adequate to maintain them when they were away from the ordinary mercantile concerns of the city. City dwellers acquired possessions in the countryside not only as investments and to further their social ambitions, but also as precautionary politics.

Other losers had to flee to more distant places, totally beyond familiar horizons, and thus experienced a real exile from their homeland; they often had trouble supporting themselves. Sometimes leaders were received by the heads of the party in a different town. These were men already linked to them in many cases through business, the textile trade, financial dealings, or by matrimonial alliances which at some point had made them kinsmen. Such settlements far from the mother city were often extended and might be terminal, for these men would take their families with them or marry in their adopted land. Thus, the influx of new blood, real interminglings of populations which are inadequately understood but were still significant, occurred constantly in every town, brought about by changes of fortune and the dangers of political life. One of the most spectacular examples of such displacements of large numbers of persons was the mass exile of Milanese from their ruined town in 1162. They sought refuge in neighbouring cities and were well received in all the towns which somewhat later constituted the Lombard League, but some went farther across the mountains toward the sea. They swelled the size of the Milanese quarter of Genoa, that of San Ambrogio, which had been founded five centuries earlier by other exiles from the Po plain who were fleeing the invading Lombards. The Milanese presence and more generally that of many artisans, merchants, bankers and wholesalers who had come from the towns of the north, particularly Piacenza,[97] was to have considerable influence on the commercial future of the Ligurian city. The dramatic exodus of the enemies of the imperial party facilitated the quick settlement of the new town of Alexandria at the same time, between 1167 and 1170. Although founded on the spur of the moment, Alexandria was rapidly elevated to the rank of a city in a veritable act of defiance of the German armies and the Ghibelline party.[98]

Such displacements and intermingling of populations were evidently occurring much more frequently a century later, during the bitterest of the struggles between Guelfs and Ghibellines, particularly in central Italy on both sides of the Apennines. A careful study with good maps would undoubtedly enable us to determine a geography of these human movements and to ascertain certain recurring themes. In addition to the fortified castles of the countryside, some towns became places of refuge which were often populated by exiles from the larger cities of the neighbourhood or even farther away. Salimbene de Adam noted that exiles whom the emperor expelled from Parma in 1267 found homes in Piacenza.[99] The members of the Lambertazzi party, who had been declared rebels at Bologna, settled at Imola in 1274.[100] When this party was exiled again in 1298, some of its adherents went to Faenza, others as far as Padua.[101] Florentine exiles too went to distant cities and established themselves in great numbers, occupying entire quarters and constituting a powerful nucleus of resident immigrants. During their exile between 1258 and 1260, the Ghibellines preferred to reside at Siena, where they did their utmost to reconstitute a powerful army by burrowing money and by pawning several of their *rocche* (fortified castles) to the Salimbeni company for a loan of 20,000 gold florins. When eight hundred of Manfred's horsemen arrived, a great spontaneous celebration broke out in this city, which was so hospitable to Ghibelline emigrés: "and all the Ghibellines of Tuscany drew great strength and arrogance from that fact".[102] When Manfred won his great battle several months later, the Guelfs who were exiled from Florence were generally rebuffed. They found refuge only at relatively nearby Lucca, where they joined forces with all other Tuscan exiles "and established their residences at Lucca in the suburb around San Triano, the church in which the Florentines had their *loggia*".[103] Thus, they needed an entire suburb to establish temporary residences, a common parish church, and a *loggia* for daily assemblies or the political meetings of the leaders. Lucca had obviously become quite suddenly the protector of a refugee camp, an entire party with its institutions and ambitions.

These mass movements, often involving major displacements and intermingling of populations, were virtual enterprises of colonization. Whether temporary or permanent, they obviously left a deep and original imprint on conditions of life, economic activity, and at times the culture of the Italian towns and countryside.

The exiles were not all from the propertied classes, and despite the hospitality shown them in their new homes and notwithstanding bonds of all sorts, not all were treated in the same way. Some led a difficult, nomadic life, seeking a permanent establishment in vain. Salimbene de Adam gives an excellent description in a few lines of the knights of Parma who were exiled by the emperor in 1267. They "were stouthearted men, robust and strong, very competent in the art of war, but they were bitter, for they had to go from house to house seeking refuge, even those who had come from great families".[104] Not all the Tuscan Guelfs who migrated to Lucca after the exile of 1260 could stay there for any length of time. In 1265, Count Guido, leader of the Ghibellines and imperial vicar, threatened the town with a large Pisan army and forced the Lucchese to promise to expel the exiles. "The unhappy Guelfs who had been exiled from Florence and elsewhere in Tuscany had nowhere else to turn. Thus they and their families had to leave Lucca and its *contado*." This entire affair lasted only three days. The second exile was naturally much more dramatic than the first. Now driven completely out of of Tuscany, miserable groups of outlaws tried to reach Bologna over the Apennine passes or had to seek a difficult road which involved many stops and improvised encampments. "And harsh necessity forced many noble ladies who had been exiled from Florence to give birth to their children on the peak of San Pellegrino, between Lucca and Modena."[105]

Some sought to recover their fortunes in more distant places, in trade and the money market. Still speaking of the Tuscan exiles who were fleeing Lucca, Villani shows that some went beyond the Alps for 'gain'. He calls these the first 'factories' of the Tuscan merchants outside Italy, for "this had not been customary before, but it brought Florence considerable wealth".[106] This is perhaps too categorically stated, but it is still possible that political exiles considerably furthered the diaspora of Tuscan businessmen in France, Flanders, and England, just as had occurred with the Milanese and the citizens of the other Lombard towns after the victories of Frederick Barbarossa. They were not agents of great companies, but were small businessmen and financiers, moneychangers who loaned small sums and were involved in the various petty trades of usury and banking. Characteristically for foreigners residing in a particular city, these men tried to gain acceptance by rendering various services while enriching themselves in the process and making a mark on their new social environment with their newly acquired wealth. Thus they devoted their most strenuous efforts to loaning money at interest, a business which brought them at least the possibility of associating with important persons and of confiscating lands in case payments were defaulted. Thus, they could become wealthy landowners in the environs of the town, even if they obtained little in the short run. The foreign minority was often narrowly exclusive, and its members were far enough from their homelands to be able to shake off all social taboos quite easily, readily forming colonies of moneylenders and petty financiers.[107] The connections between usury and political exile thus seem obvious, and Italian moneylenders quickly became the active competitors of the Jews. This explains why the 'Lombard' usurers of the years between 1160 and 1200 were followed nearly a century later by the needy Tuscan financiers, particularly Florentines, Sienese, and Pistoians, all of whom were still normally called 'Lombards'. Many of them were political exiles who had been driven out by their party's downfall.

Large scale banking kept all its privileges nearer Florence, and the exiled leaders of the great Tuscan companies tried to maintain their businesses as well as was possible under the circumstances. We have already seen how after the Guelf defeat of 1260 Pope Urban IV managed in 1263 and 1264 to threaten the merchant companies which remained at Siena and Florence. He compelled them to deal exclusively with him and even forced their leaders to leave their city and thus, against their own inclinations, to join the Guelf exiles. These men established themselves at Radicofani and Chiusi in the papal states, where the Sienese in particular remained in constant contact with their offices and their English clients. The Florentines preferred to send their leaders to Ostia and Rome to finance the papal expedition on behalf of Charles of Anjou.[108] They also set up operations at Pisa. Later, in 1304, the White Cerchi who had been driven from Florence by the Blacks "retreated into the extensive Florentine business network which exiles had developed at Pisa a century earlier".[109] Pisa's prosperity was declining, for its businessmen, who tended to be shippers and seamen rather than financiers, seem to have withdrawn from large scale international commerce. But the settlement of the Florentine exiles there made Pisa once more a very active banking center, at least for Italian concerns. This development may have paved the way for the eventual economic conquest and later the political rule of Florence over Pisa. Genoese bankers too came to Pisa: as late as 1325 the communal government was borrowing money "at interest from the Genoese exiles who were living at Pisa".[110] The fugitive Genoese financiers and merchants were also established along the entire Ligurian Riviera, particularly at Levante, between Genoa and Pisa. When in February 1322 the lords of Genoa successfully repulsed the assault of the exiles who were then living in the Riviera villages, they took many prisoners and a splendid booty "of personal effects and property which they found in the villages, worth more than 20,000 Genoese lire, for these exiles were living with their households, practising their occupations and trades just as they had in the town".[111]

These armed exiles, who sometimes held fortified castles and could count on help from their peasants, could constitute redoubtable, aggressive, and dangerous threats on both land and sea, particularly for the Genoese. Indeed, they were a constant menace which held the entire countryside in a state of military alert. Some of them were semi-nomadic wanderers seeking position and fortune, and these were much more dangerous than more established persons.

The bands of exiles were often led by noble knights who found security and fortune in the profession of arms. The Tuscan Guelfs had scarcely established themselves at Bologna when they were suddenly summoned to Modena to fight the Ghibellines there. As conquerors in their turn, they confiscated all the Ghibelline property, arms, and horses at Modena: "these exiles from Florence and other territories of Tuscany were much enriched by these confiscations, acquiring the horses and

arms which they so desperately needed". All, even those who had
obviously been poorest, could then equip themselves and fight from
horseback once again (*e tutti s'incavallano*). The horses were not only a
considerable booty, but also gave to the new owner the opportunity to
acquire military equipment and establish himself in the profession of
arms. The Guelfs obtained another windfall shortly thereafter by
capturing property from the Ghibellines of Reggio. They immediately
formed a fine company of four hundred mounted men at arms.[112]

Others became brigands. Establishing economic blockades was very
profitable, for the exiles could then attack convoys of foodstuffs going to
the town which had expelled them, or ambush merchant caravans and
ships. This running war on the mountain passes and along the islands and
the rocky coasts was extended by the presence of so many exiles. In
1304 the White Cerchi exiles waged a continuous war of subsistence
against Florence, intercepting convoys taking food to the city.[113] The
Genoese exiles imposed such an effective blockade on the city in 1320
that there was widespread starvation: "Genoa was running out of food,
for the exiles of the city were privateering along the Riviera with
seventeen galleys, seizing ships and cogs and other boats which were
carrying food to Genoa". To alleviate this constant menace, the
Genoese had to arm twenty-seven galleys which attacked the rebels and
corsairs at Cerici.[114] But in December of that same year "fifteen galleys
maintained by Genoese expatriates raided along the Riviera and got as
far as the village of Chiàvari, where they robbed and burned everything".[115]

Piracy in Italian waters was very often linked to political exile. As late
as 1462 the exiled doge and archbishop of Genoa, Paolo Fregosi,
seized four ships in the port, then gathered others under his command.
Finally, established in several pirate ports in Corsica, he seized
everything that came within his reach. Aided by his brother Pandolfo
and five hundred men at arms, he even defied the entire Genoese navy.
To defeat him, the Genoese had to go to the considerable expense of
arming a special fleet of three large vessels. Conquered and deprived of
his best ships, Paolo Fregosi, although forced to live the rest of his life as
a pirate exile, nonetheless was able to live on the fruits of his
conquests.[116]

Like group hatreds and the vendetta, like the anguish of civil war,
exile left a profound imprint on Italian minds in this period. Every
aristocratic family experienced at least once such a flight in disgrace

from the city, withdrawing to their rural property or even establishing themselves on distant foreign territory. The *Libri di Ragione* speak of these banishments of fathers or more distant ancestors as being among the most essential features of the family's past, on a level with war and alliances. They were decisive stages, constant reminders of the common clan tradition.

The exile as a social type was also a person who incorporated or symbolized a long struggle on behalf of others. He was a victim who attracted compassion and sympathy. Quite naturally he embodied the spirit of vengeance in the hearts of his family and their friends. This tragic but by no means hopeless situation was sometimes underscored still more by the dramatic, spectacular nature of the departure. Like an execution, it could be staged to make a vivid impression on the minds of the assembled multitudes. During an interminable conflict between the factions at Orvieto in 1313, the Guelfs began by sending their women and children out of the town. Then, after a three day civil war during which they were annihilated by a hastily assembled Ghibelline force from the nearby imperial towns, they were driven out in their turn. They left their city in long processions *plorantes et clamantes* through the Porta Santa Maria and the Pertusa.[117]

Such an exile was a brutal scission in one's life, the rupture of most of one's social ties and daily habits. The man became a foreigner who, far from his city, nursed his memories and a strong nostalgia for the past, for the quarter and streets where he was born and had lived, for the dialect of his city. Exile probably strengthened the attachment of many outlaws to their fatherlands and their pride in their cities. An entire literature of exile suggests this, and banishment was a major theme of all poetic and dramatic inspiration. The lofty, harsh, and sensitive figure of the exile, his feelings and regrets, his pride and his sometimes piercing sense of isolation, his implacable hatred of the party in power and his insatiable hunger for vengeance dominated and animated a considerable number of literary works of all types: tales, short stories, poetry, and dramas.

Exile was often the basis for a surprising satirical spirit which expressed perfectly this feeling of superiority and nostalgia by biting critiques or burlesques of the manners and customs of the foreign area which had in fact received the author as a fugitive. The acid wit of these poems reflects the particularism of each urban milieu and is also a valuable source of knowledge of the conditions under which the exiles were living. The critique is always coloured with a strong tint of nostalgia. Even when he was happy, well fed and clothed, the exiled poet could not abide the idea of spending his entire life in this foreign land and wept for his own. He affirmed his will to return to his city, which he embellished with every beauty and virtue. Hence Pieràccio Tebaldi, exiled from Florence to Faenza, could write:

> Well clothed, shod, and the stomach quite full,
> I lack nothing that I need.[118]

But he nonetheless lamented and hoped with all his might to return to Florence:

> and I am never at peace
> Staying so long here in the Romagna,
> For it is real torture for me.
> I want to leave the countryside now
> And return to the delightful locale
> Of the noble city, happy and strong.[113]

Dante Alighieri wrote in a style totally different from these minor poets, but at about the same time. His very life, his emotional reactions, the hatred with which he pursued his enemies show that he was above all else a poet in exile, so attached to the situation and mental attitude of the expatriate that he refused to return to Florence even when he had the opportunity. His refusal to accept pardon and forgiveness cannot be explained merely by the comfortable circumstances of his life, protected by wealthy patrons; the crystallization of his entire life and emotional being around exile must have been important too.

Born in 1265 of a noble but not particularly prosperous family, he had been a member of several communal councils even as early as the 1290s. He sided with the Cerchi and the Whites against the Donati and the Blacks, who had been his earliest neighbours and protectors. He was prior in 1300, and when Charles of Valois handed Florence over to the Blacks in 1301, he was in Rome on official business. Dante Alighieri did not return to his native city, and in January 1302 he was condemned *in absentia* to a heavy fine and a two year exile. This sentence was changed in March to death. Exiled, he went in turn to the della Scala at Verona, to the Malaspina and the Lunigiana at Bologna, and finally to Ravenna, where he died in 1321. The *Divine Comedy*, begun in 1304, is permeated with the passions of the partisan and the exile, with the vengeful violence which motivated all clans and parties of the time. But it also expresses a kind of veneration, a desire to exalt the native land and city.

A few lines of *De vulgari eloquentia* perfectly express this pride and homesickness:

The world has become my fatherland, just as the ocean is the fatherland of the fish. But my thirst has been quenched only by the waters of the Arno from my earliest years, and I love Florence so fiercely that because of this very affection I suffer an unjust exile.[120]

Banishment was thus responsible for many important migrations of peoples, for many initiatives undertaken by Italian merchants and financiers in distant lands, and for numerous acts of brigandage and piracy. But it also inspired contemporary poets, even the most illustrious of them. Exiles, intransigence, exacerbation of hatreds and hopes for vengeance produced by the party struggles thus obviously affected all aspects of the social, economic, and even intellectual life of the time.

CHAPTER THREE

Peace and the people

Factional conflicts, which were so deeply rooted in the minds and political mores of the day, were not easily allayed. Civil peace entails the intervention of new decisive forces. On the one hand, we find a perceptible spiritual movement of minds and hearts to reconcile enemies, abandon the vengeance which was often symbolized by reverence for one's ancestors, the leaders of the clan, or the collective solidarity. This desire often corresponded to individual religious aspirations, an original mysticism controlled to some degree by the Church, but sometimes virtually or absolutely heretical. This mysticism was the fruit of individual initiatives, of preachers deeply involved in political activity, or mass movements. On the other hand, peace also implies the intervention of a public power outside the party structure which could impose its authority, break the power of the factions, and force them to respect a lasting peace, a power which could prevent and then forbid acts of vengeance. This could be an absolute lord, a tyrant, another political unit which escaped the dualism and the influence of the parties, with their strange and tenacious Manicheism, a power which rested on totally different foundations. This entity, at least in Florence and the Tuscan towns, was the 'people' or *popolo*, in a political meaning which does not correspond to the modern social sense of the term.

Peace and peace movements

Even during peacetime, party leaders could avoid bloodletting and collective vengeance, the dramatic confrontation of their clients, only by handing over the culprit immediately to the other side. The Cancellieri of the Black party at Pistoia feared the reprisals of their White relatives in 1300. "To secure peace and concord with them, the Cancellieri submitted those who had committed offences to the mercy of their victims, who could thus exact penalties or take revenge as they pleased."[121] But the chronicles suggest that such acts of deliberate renunciation of the collective solidarity were extremely rare. The peace of the town was generally at the mercy of any trifling incident. Civil war then occupied the energies of the clan and often of the entire faction.

The vendetta could be appeased only by a peace treaty which was negotiated and solemnly proclaimed between the clans and the parties. These frequent accords syncopated the internal life of the cities. Established after long consultations and haggling, reinforced by financial compositions or matrimonial alliances, sanctioned by oaths sworn on the Gospels and by kisses of peace, they brought a more or less permanent pacification, or at least a change in the political and social climate.

Some treaties, however, were not generally accepted and involved complex political activity extending over several years. Keeping the agreements was another source of conflict in itself, and peace terms, penalties, and even the exile of certain persons were the object of discussions extending over several negotiating sessions.[122]

We know furthermore that throughout the West, particularly in certain regions of the Auvergne and upper Languedoc, bishops in the eleventh century were summoning peace assemblies of knights, clergy, peasants, and townsmen to oppose the devastations of brigands and robber barons. All who attended these meetings took an oath to support the peace. They drove out and condemned those who fomented disorder, levied taxes to support militias, and were thus often one origin of representative political assemblies on both the municipal and provincial levels.[123] In the Italian towns, the bishop declared himself the principal guardian of the peace and intervened constantly by persuasion and the use of spiritual weapons. He preferred, however, to bring public pressure to bear in the interest of re-establishing peace, thereby reconciling the parties spectacularly in a wave of virtually mystical enthusiasm.

When the quarrel between the Avogadi faction and that of the della Volta and di Castro at Genoa took a sudden bloody turn in 1169,

gravely threatening the peace of the city, Archbishop Ugo, perhaps at
the instigation of the ruling consuls, had the bells sounded at sunrise to
call all citizens to a *parlamento* on the public square. They arrived to
find the archbishop surrounded by his entire clergy in solemn garb, on a
platform illuminated by torches. They were displaying the relics of St
John the Baptist from the church sanctuary at the foot of a cross. Ugo
gave a long and virulent address on the Christian obligation to
reconcile, and entreated Rolando Avogado, leader of one party, to
swear to keep the peace.

As they approached, Rolando tore his clothing and fell weeping to the ground. He called
out to those whose deaths he had sworn to avenge, whose honour did not allow him to
pardon their murderers. Since no one could make him come forward, the consuls, the
archbishop, and the clergy approached him. Renewing their pleas, they finally won him
over and had him swear on the Gospels to forget past hostilities.

Then the crowd and the clergy went to the houses of the della Volta,
whose leaders had not appeared at the assembly, and forced them in
turn to take oath and give the kiss of peace to the leaders of the
opposing party. The bells were rung loudly and the archbishop ordered
the chanting of a *Te Deum*.[124]

Somewhat later, in 1201, the Milanese archbishop and the prior of
the Camaldolites managed to establish peace between two parties
which had long been fighting: the Milanese and the Piacenzans against
the Pavians and Lodians.[125] The patriarch of Aquileia himself arranged
an accord at Brescia in 1209 between the knights and the opposing
party, that of the *popolo*, who were aided by the Cremonese. "He freed
the prisoners, and the two parties agreed that the lord Ottono Bono of
Genoa would become podestà in the city."[126]

Another very famous instance of prelates leading the masses in
extraordinary measures to restore peace was the action of the nephew
and legate of Pope Nicholas III. On 4 August 1279 he temporarily
ended the wars between the Lambertazzi and Geremei at Bologna.
While sitting on a *cathedra* covered with gold brocade which had been
erected near the town hall, he presided over an assembly in the public
square, which was festooned with banners and flowers. Surrounded by
the bishops and archbishops of the entire region, he forced fifty nobles
from each party to swear on the Gospel to uphold peace. This
ceremony, culminated by long celebrations, was well designed to strike
the imagination.[127]

Peace was an essential theme of popular preaching throughout northern and central Italy at this time. The attacks of the preachers against civil war were as vigorous as their condemnations of unchastity, wealth, various vices, and sometimes even heresies. These themes were used particularly well by the Mendicants, who were quite cognizant of social and political problems. Many were even active in such causes as fighting poverty and leading the masses. Several new orders, such as the *Humiliati*, joined the Franciscan and Dominican friars. They were more limited than the latter in their geographical range, but they were much closer to the situation of the common man and to lay activity. Some monks became heroes of the peace movement, achieving a striking renown as fighters for peace and leaders of men.

The Dominican friar Giovanni da Vicenza first became famous in 1233, when his sermons at Bologna led the two local factions to compose their differences. Buoyed by his success, acclaimed by the multitudes, carried in triumph in a sacred cart, he then sent to Monsèlice and all the towns of the march of Treviso, to Treviso itself, Belluno, and Feltre.[128] Preaching the peace, he visited the great lords of the region, the counts and marquises of San Bonifacio, da Romano, Camino, and Cornegliano, extracting promises and oaths from them. A little later in that same summer of 1233, he pacified Vicenza, Mantua, Brescia, Padua, and Ferrara before going in late August to the plain of Paquara, on the banks of the Adige, to preach to three thousand Veronese. Masses of people came there to hear him from all the towns of lower Lombardy, Venice, and even Bologna. The chroniclers claim enthusiastically that hundreds of thousands were there, grouped around their banners.[129] He had them swear on holy relics before all the bishops of the towns to keep the peace, and invoked various maledictions on those who broke their word, even condemning their animals to mortal illnesses and their crops and vines to sterility.[130] This peace agreement concerned two parties primarily, the San Bonifacio and the Lendemara, also called the Eighty: "and they exchanged kisses to seal a good and lasting peace. A noble marriage was arranged between Rainaldo, the marquis of Este, and a daughter of Alberico da Romano".[131]

Some attributed powers of healing the sick and raising the dead to Giovanni da Vicenza, but the peacemaker was also a politician and a redoubtable tyrant. Wherever he went, he had the city's statutes handed over to him for modification. He had obedience sworn to himself and demanded hostages from the towns, villages, and great families as guarantees of peace and their submission. He obtained total power with the titles of duke and count at Vicenza. He exercised a veritable dictatorship at Verona and had sixty persons burned alive on the river bank on his personal accusation of heresy.[132] But he was unable to maintain his power at Vicenza, for another monk, brother Giordano, prior of the convent of San Benedetto of Padua, had aroused the resentment of the citizens against him, with the help of a strong contingent of Paduan knights.[133] He finally had to withdraw into a convent at Bologna, leaving the entire countryside suffering "from the many wars caused by his preaching".[134]

In that same year 1233, Leone, a Minorite friar, began by making peace between the knights and the *popolo* at Piacenza, then tried to divide offices and profits between the two parties. He destroyed the organizations of these two groups.[135] At about the same time three Dominicans, Pietro da Verona (later called Peter the Martyr), Rolando da Cremona, and Leone da Perego, who later became archbishop of Milan, went from town to town, preaching for peace and against heresy before large crowds.[136] Finally, during the struggles surrounding the Pepoli at Bologna in 1285, the Dominicans preached reconciliation, and at the end of December had a hymn of peace, a *laudo*, composed by the jurist Egidio Foscarari. They thus imposed a peace which was sealed by kisses and matrimonial alliances between the party leaders, Cipriano Algardi and Giovanni Pepoli.[137]

These preachers for peace became leaders of the rural and urban masses, reformers who yearned for a kind of primitive purity. But they were also political leaders who were driven by strong personal ambitions. The harshness of the party struggles and the desire of many to defuse them thus explain the sudden rise of popular tribunes, tyrants who lasted for a few days while they condemned and burned the enemy. These strong personalities were one of the most original features of the political life of medieval Italy. These men were in the tradition of the clerical or lay tribunes of Rome, such as Cola di Rienzo.[138] To some extent they presaged Savonarola of Florence.

From the very beginning of the factional conflicts, peace seemed a miraculous gift of God. Armed warfare between the knights and the *popolo* of Piacenza in 1090 had been going on for several months when, the chronicler reports, "a divine judgement of our lord Jesus Christ so moved the knights with pity and mercy that they recognized their own wickedness and insanity. Moaning and wailing in tearful voices, they cried 'Peace! Peace!'". The *populares* too wept and beat their breasts with their hands, recognizing their evil and bestiality, "and shouted 'Peace! Peace!' And the knights left the town and made overtures to the *popolo*, and amidst general weeping and moaning they began to behold one another ... and thus they entered the town, and concord and peace were made between them throughout the town and district of Piacenza".[139]

This divine peace could be achieved only by fervent collective supplication. Only if sin were renounced, purity were fostered, and battle waged against vice, luxury, and social injustice could the end be attained. Hence preachers who proclaimed their own purity had an appeal which can explain the emergence of several spontaneous 'popular' movements enjoying mass support. They often involved at least temporary renunciation of temporal concerns as well as an often critical attitude toward hierarchies. Some indeed bordered on the heretical.

The great peace movements were rooted in an ancient ideal which was flourishing with renewed vigour from about 1230. The most powerful and numerically significant of them would triumph in the 1260s. Some were clearly on the fringes of episcopal or pontifical authority. Some were openly hostile to it, while others received their rules from the papacy and were tolerated. The general search for peace was thus an essential cause of the formation of these somewhat idiosyncratic or heretical groups of religious peripatetics who were so characteristic of the spiritual and social life of this period.

We note first the famous Alleluia or Great Alleluia movement of 1233. It was founded by a certain brother Benedetto, "who was called a brother of Cornetta", a simple but literate man who was innocent and morally pure and a friend of the Minorites. His story is recounted by Salimbene. Starting from Spoleto or Rome, he went from one town to the next, from Pisa to Parma, with a long beard, an Armenian-style cap, black clothing cut like a sack, and a toga adorned with two big red crosses. He also carried a trumpet with a peculiarly piercing blast to attract the masses. He preached on church squares, between tree boughs and lighted torches before assemblies composed primarily of the very young (*quem sequebatur maxima puerorum multitudo*), who at his invocations responded in chorus *sia lo Spiritu Sancto* and

"Alleluia! Alleluia! Alleluia!". This movement spread through all the towns of Italy, and the general euphoria brought about a pacification of the factional disputes.[140]

The Flagellants appeared somewhat later in northern Italy. Also coming from the south, they progressed through all the towns of the north Italian plain: "naked men beating themselves with whips started coming from Rome. Invoking peace and the Holy Virgin, they got as far as Bologna". Actually, they merely went from their home town to the next one down the road: the Bolognese Flagellants went to Modena, the Modenans to Reggio, and the men of Reggio to Parma. This pattern held true also for Cremona, Piacenza, and Pavia despite the hostility of the local authorities, who had "gibbets erected at all borders of the diocese of Cremona and decreed that anyone who entered flagellating himself would be hanged on the spot. No Flagellants dared enter Milan for fear of the gallows. Nonetheless, they did bring about a period of peace among enemies, and many good things were accomplished".[141]

These spontaneous and powerful movements were surprisingly successful everywhere within a few weeks, but they evidently remained poorly structured, even chaotic. They are in striking contrast to some societies which were founded by leaders who could impose rules, a kind of administration, and even a hierarchy, always in the services of peace. The most famous of these was the Bolognese nobleman Loderingo Andalò, who was related by marriage to the Salinguerra of Ferrara. He founded a religious order in 1260 to combat factional quarrels: the *Ordine dei militi di Maria Vergina gloriosa*, also called the order of knights *gaudenti* or *del gaudio* (joy, happiness).[142] Loderingo became its first *maggior generale*. The institution spread astonishingly quickly and was very successful within a short time. It was received in fifty-four different towns and sixteen *terre* (rural districts), and Loderingo was invited to become governor or podestà of six great cities, including Bologna and Modena. But when factional fighting was resumed in 1265 and threatened Bologna, two knights *gaudenti*, the Ghibelline Lodisio Andalo and the Guelf Catalano Catalani, each a member of a powerful family, assumed control of the town government. They brought the parties to an agreement and based their power on a special corps of 1,200 armed citizens who served under the banner of *Maria Vergina gloriosa*. They were then summoned to Florence to establish peace there, and fought the Ubaldini party. Driven out briefly, they returned victorious, but as pacifiers, to the city, accompanied by two other *gaudenti* brothers.

The knights *gaudenti*, who often included members of the most illustrious families, of course had to renounce the idea of holding public office themselves. But in fact they were carrying out a political program which transcended the factions. They were established just as firmly at Padua as in Tuscany. Enrico Scrovegni, who owned a palace built on the site of the Roman amphitheatre, was forced to join the *gaudenti* and promise to build them a chapel. In no other way could he make his peace with the Church and enjoy unchallenged the inheritance of his father Reginaldo, a notorious usurer whom Dante placed in Inferno.[143] He made the donation no later than 1277. This chapel, called *di Scrovegni* since that time, was dedicated in 1304 and adorned with frescoes by Giotto in 1304 and 1305. It remains one of the most noteworthy monuments of Italian painting from this period.[144] The *gaudenti* were opposed to the parties and the spirit of fighting and vengeance. They were naturally hated or at least scorned by the exiled Dante Alighieri, who saw things quite differently and belonged to another intellectual world. He called them hypocrites and misers, people whose judgements and actions were wrong.[145]

These great spontaneous outpourings of mysticism maintained their strength for some time and enjoyed a revival in central Italy much later, in 1399 and 1400, with the *Bianchi* brotherhoods. This movement may have originated in the Dauphiné (some say Spain, England, or Scotland). It first appeared in Italy at Genoa, where 20,000 persons marched in procession. Then it entered Tuscany via Lucca and Pistoia. The *Bianchi* were responding to a vision of Christ which had announced that one-third of mankind was about to perish. They invoked the Virgin as their procession moved from town to town in nine-day marches, crying 'Mercy!' and 'Peace!' They could not change their white raiment nor sleep in a bed or inside a walled town. Received enthusiastically everywhere, they confiscated weapons and ended quarrels. At Pistoia they enthusiastically arbitrated an accord among the families and factions. Luca Dominici, who gives a long list of the families thus reconciled, notes that "countless peace treaties" were concluded. The commune was to nominate four special officials, the *Pacioli*, to enforce these arrangements. Exiled criminals and debtors were to be repatriated. Luca Dominici reports that at this news the

Florentine captain of the town fell to his knees crying "peace and mercy", "and thus the entire council cried out with one voice which could be heard through half the town".[146] But the worst factional quarrels that the town had ever known were to break out beginning in 1401.

Peace was ardently desired and was sometimes realized in the emotion of the moment, but it was imposed on parties which were always attached to their institutions and ready to resume fighting. These momentary enthusiasms and religious movements undoubtedly provided a favourable environment, a guide, a standard for peace arrangements, but they had little practical effect. They were spectacular incidents in the life of the city, mystical rites which in the last analysis were inconsequential. A more lasting peace could only be produced by a consistent political policy: by immediate interventions by a superior power, generally the commune, and particularly by establishing new political institutions.

Political activity and institutions on behalf of peace

The commune, by which we mean the various forms of public power in the town, tried to escape this interminable cycle of quarrels either by weakening the clans and parties or by taking the easier route of avoiding collisions, provocations, and occasions for fighting. Its sumptuary laws[147] forbade overly numerous assemblies of relatives, friends, and clients at private ceremonials, particularly marriages, funerals, public ceremonies, and festivals. It prohibited parading on horseback through the city and appearing armed in public. Sometimes the commune even forbade members of one party to pass the houses and palaces of their rivals on horseback. It vehemently prohibited the shouting of rallying cries, calls to arms, and insulting epithets, and even the use of party names, which in themselves had a kind of bellicose magic and incited violence.

Peace measures imposed at Orvieto in 1322 included an absolute prohibition on "yelling or shouting in a loud voice 'Long live . . .' or 'Death to' in reference to another person".[148] When Gil Albornoz tried in 1357 to reorganize the papal states and pacify the factions there, he began by prohibiting the use of the names Guelf and Ghibelline "or any other party name as a reproach . . . or even to invent a totally different name which might lead to the formation of a party". Furthermore, no one was to yell 'Long live!' at any person or group unless it were "Long live the Church".[149]

Such measures, particularly arbitrations, could only be imposed by a power outside the parties which was strong enough to force them to observe the rules and truces. This necessity led to the installation of podestàs in many Italian towns as guardians of the peace, chief justices, and military leaders. The podestà was chosen from outside the town for the short term of six months or a year, and as a single ruler was better able to impose stringent measures of order and peace than the more diffuse and tolerant régime of the consuls. He prosecuted criminals, troublemakers, and 'rebels'. A miniature in Caffaro's *Annales Genovenses* shows the town podestà presiding over the destruction of the fortified house of a noble rebel.[150] We even find him intervening to negotiate or impose general, difficult, and complex peace arrangements between opposing parties, restoring them to tranquillity and reason, seeing to it that punishments were carried out. We shall cite only one very instructive case, from Orvieto, between 1240 and 1286. The Berardini, who were members of the powerful Monaldeschi party, sought redress in 1272 from the Filippeschi, who led the city's other faction and had refused to pay a fine. They had been assessed this penalty in 1264, eight years earlier, when a peace had been arranged to settle a conflict which went back at least to 1240! This in turn had been the origin of a long series of acts of aggression followed by peace treaties of varying degrees of efficacy. Four Berardini were assassinated by the Filippeschi in the spring of 1272. One of the assailants was killed shortly afterward, and general warfare erupted between the two parties. A compromise peace imposed by the podestà condemned sixteen Filippeschi to outlawry, with heavy fines and destruction of their lands and houses. Then twenty-five leaders of each faction were exiled, and a final intervention of the podestà in December punished the Filippeschi more severely. An agreement signed by the two parties in 1273 in the podestà's presence and evidently on his orders entailed the temporary exile of several Filippeschi leaders, who were to undertake pilgrimages to St James of Compostella or the Holy Land. The parties then kept the peace until strife resumed in 1286. This in turn was ended by a ceremony of reconciliation of the representatives of the two factions on the town square, before the bishop, the clergy, and the entire population.[151]

But these repeated interventions could only be efficacious if the podestà had real power which he could exercise for more than a single year. The limitation of his term of office meant that his government could be terribly authoritarian and tyrannical while it lasted, but thereafter conditions might revert to 'normal'. A certain Brancaleone di Andelo was a member of a wealthy and respected Bolognese family. He agreed to go to Rome as podestà in 1253 only on condition that his term of office be no less than three years. He also demanded that thirty youths from leading Roman families be held hostage at Bologna for his safety. When these terms had been accepted, he carried out an extremely vigorous police action at Rome, besieging the fortifications and towers of unruly nobles and hanging rebels from their palace windows.[152] He was imprisoned during a riot led by the Annibaldeschi party and owed his safety to the steadfastness of his compatriots holding the Roman hostages at Bologna. He was released, and two years later returned to Rome to exact stern vengeance on the Annibaldeschi. He had 140 towers and fortresses destroyed and forced Pope Alexander IV to submit by making an armed attack on his native land of Anagni.[153] Brancaleone died at Rome in 1258 of a horrid disease. His position was given immediately to one of his relatives. His head was placed in a costly urn on top of a marble column. We know that shortly after this another di Andelo, Loderingo, was to found the order of the *gaudenti*, the peace knights, while a third member of the clan was a peacemaker at Florence.[154]

The duke of Athens tried to pacify the families and parties of Florence, but Villani tells us that "this was the best thing that he did, but he and his men were plentifully enriched by bribes from those who appealed to them."[155] Their simple services were not rendered *gratis*. On balance, the podestàs and tyrants were able to impose only limited, precarious truces, for the party régime was permitted to remain. At times they even relied on the support of one of the parties, and their action was not invariably free of a certain partisanship.

Only new political institutions whose foundations were different and which were outside the direct influence of great families and factions could launch an effective struggle against the political dualism of the two party system, against the Manichean mentality and desire for vengeance.

Contemporary jurists and chroniclers who were able to draw lessons from their observation of political customs realized that there were in the last analysis two means of governing a city. Factions with clienteles and friends could rule, but another possible form involved the inclusion of the entire urban community through a division of honours and offices among the various social categories or primary political communities, which were then called upon to play a considerable role in naming officials for the entire city. Writing of events which had occurred only shortly before, and which he had personally experienced, Giovanni Villani vigorously criticized the *popolani grassi* who were in power in 1340 but "gave no share to the grandi or those of middling or lesser wealth, as would be necessary for good communal government" (*come si convenia a buono reggimento di comune*).[156] This expression seems to reveal an opinion quite singular for the time about the proper form of city government.

For another region, the chronicler Rolandino da Parma gives a very precise notion of this difference of political styles and régimes. He shows that in 1238 the Paduans were being governed "by the party, not by the commune".[157] Similarly, the government of Ezzelino da Romano in 1282 was established "not by justice, but by the parties".[158] Government by faction is the antithesis of the more just and equal system of a true community. The commune or community of course rested on an extremely vague concept which indicated only that its members perceived a common interest, which could be demonstrated under various political régimes: government by consuls, a podestà, or a tyrant. But one form of government seemed to incorporate the ideal particularly nicely: that of the *popolo*, at least in Tuscany and particularly for the Florentines. The word literally indicates 'people', but it can have quite varied shades of meaning.

The word *popolo* was often used very vaguely to indicate the entire urban community, if not all inhabitants of the town. It was frequently used at Pisa and Florence in political slogans and the rallying cries uttered during revolts, particularly those planned and led by the grandi: "Long live the *popolo*!" or "Long live the *popolo* and freedom!".[159] At Florence and Siena, but also in the papal states as far south as Viterbo and Orvieto, the sources deliberately use *populus* or *popolo* as a synonym for *comunitas* or *civitas*. It was the commune in the broadest sense of the term.[160]

But the *popolo* was also the mob, those who rampaged in the streets during civil strife. Villani constantly uses the expressions *a rumore di popolo* or *a bollore di popolo* in describing the agitation and street fighting. The word also had a social connotation of a particular group constituted essentially of persons who were in trade and derived much of their income from it. Official sources and chronicles often contrast these *popolani* to the knights or magnates, the *grandi*. But we have already seen how arbitrary these distinctions could be and how difficult it is to define and separate the two aristocracies.

From a political and social standpoint, the *popolo* was also a political organization, a regrouping of the masters of the *arti* which permitted them to exercise real power in the city in this capacity. The Ghibelline party leaders created the institutions of the Florentine *arti* between 1180 and 1190. The guilds were subjected to the authority of two and later three captains of the *popolo*, of whom one was a knight, one a judge, and one a *popolano*. The association of the *popolo* thus incorporated a wide social base and was placed above the *arti*.[161] The organization hardened and became more precise in 1283. Each of the *arti*, which were associations including one or more trades, had its banner and chose a leader, the gonfalonier (bearer of the standard, the gonfalon). The gonfalonier was assisted by four councillors. All the *arti* were subordinated to a directorate of six priors who were led by a "captain and defender of the *arti* and the artisans, captain and keeper of the peace of the commune of Florence". Later he was to be called simply "captain and defender of the *arti*".[162] The new titles are renewed evidence that the government was anxious to maintain peace. Thus the *popolo* might be a certain political force, that of the aristocratic master artisans who had enrolled in a guild, thereby escaping more felicitously the hold of the clan or faction.

But the most original concept involved in the word *popolo* was something quite different from this, at least in Tuscany. The vocabulary of the Tuscan chroniclers contributed significantly to the elaboration of the meanings peculiar to this extremely complex word. The final meaning was more political than social, and it has not always attracted the attention of historians as much as it deserves, for they are too concerned with the modern, more social connotation of the word.

From the beginning of the urban and rural communities alike, the Tuscan *popolo* was above all a territory with an autonomous political and military organization. It was a political cell which could defend and rule itself. In the diocese of Florence, the Christians had been divided from the time of conversion into *pievi*, basic circumscriptions around a baptismal church.[163] There were fifty-eight *pievi* in the Florentine *contado* in 1295, together with a single urban *pieve*, that of the cathedral church of Florence itself. The rural *pievi* were subdivided into a number of *popoli* of very unequal importance. The urban *pieve* of Florence comprised thirty-four *popoli* which were more usually called *contrade* or *vicinanze*. The *popoli* near the gates had their own larger organizations which were also called *vicinanze*. These political units were active and showed a marked particularism. They were anything but simple topographical, administrative, or fiscal circumscriptions; rather, they were active, strong, differentiated political forces which were very conscious of their autonomy.[164] As social and political groups, the *popoli* were administered according to well defined customs, the *usus terrae*, which were interpreted by elected magistrates called *boni homines* (or *portinarii* in the towns) who could impose punishments and heavy fines.

The primary identity felt by every Florentine even as late as the 1350s was as a member of a given *popolo*, whether of the town or the countryside. Villani's statistical inventory of 1338 noted 110 churches, "including fifty-seven parishes with *popolo*".[165] The *popolo* was thus a larger circumscription than the parish, sometimes including more than one church.

Such neighbourhood political and military organizations are found in many other cities of northern and central Italy.[166] Salimbene speaks of the *vicinie* of Parma at the time of the Great Alleluia movement in 1233: "and each *vicinia* in the city of Parma wanted to have its standard to carry in the processions which were then occurring".[167] At Verona and neighbouring towns, men assembled on the *brolo*, a square before or near the parish church. This word became synonymous with *arengo* or *concione*, and later came to be applied to the assembly itself and thus to the political unit.[168] The *broletto* subsequently became the place of assembly, the palace of the commune or the *popolo*, throughout northern Italy.

Much later still, a Genoese notarial register recorded the transactions of the assemblies of the *vicinia* of San Donato, in the quarter near the Porta Soprana. When it was founded in 1447, it included the heads of 102 families. They met in the *logia nova* of the town square, across from the church, and chose four *principales* to rule and particularly to keep peace among themselves for a six-month term. The proceedings show that this *vicinia* was active until at least 1470.[169]

Thus Italians in both town and countryside were acquiring some degree of administrative, military, and political experience, albeit within the narrow but clearly defined framework of a neighbourhood association: *popolo, vicinanza,* or *vicinia.* It is very doubtful if the *popoli* or *vicinanze* ever covered the entire city or included all the rural subjects of the great towns. The influence of these political units of course clashed in many quarters with the power of the extended families and thus of the parties. In this sense we may adopt a certain schematic picture of the town: on the one hand neighbours of equal standing, and on the other the network of clients and protégés of the great families. They constituted two political systems which were mutually hostile and diametrically opposed in every way.

The leaders of these associations hoped to extend their political system, organization, and style of public life throughout the city. The success of this program was certainly the major political event of the thirteenth and fourteenth centuries. For this period witnessed the passage from one political system to another. The Florentine and Tuscan chroniclers call this governance by *popolo* or more simply refer to "making a *popolo*". Sercambi and Villani constantly say *facere uno popolo,* and Villani even used it commonly as a chapter heading, such as in 1250, "How the first *popolo* was made in Florence to regroup and repair the damage done by the Ghibellines". This was the action of *boni homines* who began meeting in the church of San Firenze, naturally a very meaningful and symbolic choice of locale. When expelled from there, they met at Santa Croce. These armed men began by attacking the houses of the nobles, the Anchioni di San Lorenzo, and immediately "they chose thirty-six leaders of the *popolo*". This action was carried out very efficiently: "they seized power from the podestà who was then ruling Florence . . . and then organized themselves into a *popolo*". They chose a captain, twelve ancients (two per sixth), and then, in their first important undertaking, they reinforced the city walls with stones taken from towers of the nobles which they had destroyed. Finally, "to strengthen the *popolo* even more", they had work begun on the first town hall "behind the Badia and on the Piazza San Pulinari".[170] The *contado* was similarly reorganized into ninety military associations centred around a parish, each with its gonfaloniers and rectors. These organizations in turn were grouped into regional leagues. In each parish or group of parishes a *popolo* was established, each with one or two rectors chosen by the captain and the ancients of the *popolo* of Florence.[171]

Villani indicates that this was done also in the other towns of

Tuscany. The expression *facere* or *fare un popolo* did not change and recurs constantly in the sources. In the tiny town of Colle d'Elsa in 1322, after the town exiles had failed to regain power, "the men of Colle made a *popolo* with the arms and cross of the *popolo* of Florence".[172] The example of the great city was contagious, spreading to the nearby village. This might even occur outside Tuscany. On 24 September 1339 "the men of Savona made a *popolo*" which expelled the Doria and the Spinola. Three days later, the Genoese

arose in a great uproar and deposed the captains, driving them, their families, and other powerful persons from the land. And they made a *popolo* and in the Venetian manner chose as doge one Simone Boccanegra, a member of the middle group of the *popolo*.[173]

The word *popolo* is used in both a political and social context in this passage. Villani says further that in February 1339 "nearly all the territories of the march made a *popolo*, and they killed Marcennaio, who had been lord of Fermo . . . and then exiled those tyrants whom they could not kill".[174] Finally, after the conspiracy of a *grandi* party had been checked in 1343, a second *popolo* came to power at Florence: "How the *popolo* of Florence threw the *grandi* out of the palace and reformed the land along the lines of a *popolo*". This was not a total overthrow of municipal institutions. The change was more subtle, as new magistracies were created which would complement and supplant the others: three councillors of the priors from each quarter, gonfaloniers of the companies of the *popolo*, and councils of the *popolo* with sixty-five members from each quarter. This procedure led Villani to say that "through this kind of dissimulation, the government of the city was reformed and placed under the power of the *popolo*".[175]

The installation of a *popolo* thus marked an important change in the political structures of the city: the transfer from the régime of the *grandi*, assisted by their clients and the parties, to that of the *popoli*. There was an obvious and even violent political opposition among *grandi*, magnates, and *popolo*. Two political concepts were in conflict, and quarrels, retreats, and sudden strokes marked a political climate in which the opposing forces might 'unmake' a previously established *popolo*. Villani gives an instructive example of "How the *grandi* of San Miniato abolished their *popolo*". This action was a raw test of strength. They had desired to act "because the *popolo* had controlled them so stringently that they could not dominate the land as they wished". As conquerors, the *grandi* tried systematically to destroy the *popolo.* They condemned and had executed some of its leaders, thus "keeping the *popolo* thenceforth in harsh subjection".[176] To avoid such counter-revolutions, *popoli* everywhere issued ordinances, significantly called 'Ordinances of Justice', against the magnates and the parties. These decrees limited the political and social horizon of the *grandi* and forced them to respect "the peace of the commune" or "the peace of the people". From 1272 the commune of Pistoia exacted a monetary bond from the *grandi* to insure their respect for the "peace of the commune". In 1292 a *Liber securitatum nobilium* was compiled which recalls the earlier Sacred Ordinances of Bologna and the Ordinances of Justice of Florence. It prohibited all breaches of the peace under pain of heavy fines.[177]

The *popolo* often achieved power as the result of a brutal conflict. It was a newly triumphant political force symbolized by a more general consultative role for the citizens, by the bell which summoned them to meet and defend themselves, and by a new palace, often called the *Palazzo del Popolo*. This fortress deprived the clan strongholds of much of their social importance and their political and military power. The alteration was indeed profound. The most spectacular aspect of this evolution, and its principal lesson for us, is not the removal of one aristocracy from power and its replacement by another. The *popolani* were often powerful persons, and the *grandi* cannot be defined easily. The rise of neutrals, however, men who were not involved in the party struggles, is of cardinal importance. With the end of party bipolarity, a new basis was found for the distribution of public offices, and the success of the *popoli* in Tuscany involved political groups and entities which can be defined territorially and topographically. Finally and of particular importance, this development meant that social ties between masters and their clients were being broken as the extended families grew weaker.

But we must analyse all the aspects of this evolution and keep them in proper perspective. We may note that the conflict and political evolution did not reflect a class struggle or even involve well defined social categories. We do not even find a real 'social' conflict within the aristocracy. The social and political meanings of the word *popolo* must be kept distinct. Secondly, the triumph of the *popolo* was not always permanent. It often occupied only a brief moment in the political history of Italy. It was threatened by reversions to the old party system, such as occurred at Florence between the first *popolo* of 1250 and the second of 1343. The *popolo* moreover often paved the way for another form of government to come to power: personal lordships, tyrannies of a single man.

The *popolo* did not triumph in every city. Genoa experienced a gradual victory of the party régime in the fifteenth century, with a systematic division of public offices. Even after the sixteenth century, this strong, populous city, which had important industries in shipbuilding and in weaving and dyeing woollen and silk cloth, allowed only minimal political participation to the *arti*. They were permitted to choose three of twelve members of the council of the ancients. They were not even unified into a *popolo* or coherent political organization. The Genoese trade guilds remained under the strict control of the commune, most of whose officers represented the great families, clans, and factions. The *popolo* as a local political unit (called the *vicinia* at Genoa) did not become part of Genoese political custom. Genoa did not "make a *popolo*", but continued to be governed by Whites and Blacks.

As we terminate this essay on Italian political parties during the communal period, let us emphasize various aspects of a particularly complex and confused political and social life. First, the race for offices was determined primarily by questions of internal politics, not by allegiance to Empire or Church. Secondly, bonds between towns and countryside were important and substantial, characterized by multiple social overlappings and constant reciprocal interventions. Town and countryside really formed a single political world. Thirdly, institutional evolution was extremely fluid and uncertain, so that it is difficult to be very precise about the nature of political structures. Public life reflected the constant overlapping of different forms of government. The Italian commune was always in process of evolution. Finally, social bonds and structures were of decisive importance, greatly influencing political life and conflicts which could not have been caused only by economic rivalries between persons of different levels of fortune or ill-defined social classes. Indeed, the very existence of these classes seems rooted not in the sources, but in the views of certain authors whose works have been or should be supplanted.

Notes to Part III*

[1]Villani [15, IX, ch. 153, p. 244].
[2]Villani [15, VIII, ch. 42, p. 46].
[3]Gozzadini [27, pp. 74–75] for the Algarda family.
[4]Waley [59, pp. 50ff].
[5]Sercambi [14, CXXXI, pp. 93ff].
[6]Toubert [55, pp. 737–738].
[7]Villani [15, VIII, ch. 41, p. 46].
[8]Villani [15, VIII, ch. 39, pp. 43–44].
[9]Villani [15, VIII, ch. 39, p. 44].
[10]Villani [15, VIII, ch. 39, pp. 45–46].
[11]Villani [15, VIII, ch. 39, p. 46].
[12]On the towers and the fortified structures owned by private citizens in the Italian cities at this time, see Heers [31, pp. 174–201].
[13]Bibliothèque Nationale, Paris, MS. Latin 10136, f. 111v, reproduced as a drawing on the cover of Heers [31].
[14]Sercambi [14, I, pp. 11, 95, 201, 239, and II, p. 193].
[15]Villani [15, I, p. 196].
[16]Villani [15, II, p. 84].
[17]Villani [15, I, p. 196].
[18]Villani [15, VIII, ch. 71, p. 90].
[19]On the social and political role of the festivals, see below, pp. 269ff.
[20]Gaspar (ed.) [8, p. 124].
[21]A.P.Gib., anno 1250, p. 499, lines 35ff., cited by Judic [37, p. 225].
[22]Villani [15, XII, ch. 20, p. 44].
[23]For all of this, see Villani [15, XII, ch. 27, pp. 31ff].
[24]Villani [15, ch. 114, p. 109].
[25]Villani [15, XI, ch. 118, pp. 345–350].
[26]Villani [15, XII, ch. 20, pp. 43–44].
[27]Brucker [19].
[28]Bowsky [17].
[29]Villani [15, XII, ch. 20, p. 44].
[30]A.P.Gib., anno 1277, p. 564, line 46 to p. 566, line 43, cited by Judic [37, pp. 239–244].
[31]Salimbene de Adam [16, I, p. 271].
[32]Villani [15, VIII, ch. 72, pp. 92ff].
[33]Villani [15, IX, ch. 219, pp. 282–283].
[34]On this point, see Enriques [23].
[35]Villani [15, VIII, ch. 41, p. 46].
[36]Villani [15, VI, ch. 87, p. 311].
[37]Villani [15, XII, ch. 17, p. 32].
[38]A.P.Gib., anni 1276–1277, p. 564, line 46 to p. 566, line 43, cited by Judic [37, pp. 240–243].
[39]Villani [15, XII, ch. 20, p. 64].
[40]Villani [15, XII, ch. 20, p. 64].
[41]Sercambi [14, I, p. 95].

* Numbers in square brackets refer to the Bibliography.

[42]Villani [15, X, ch. 205, pp. 182–183].
[43]Gaspar (ed.) [8, pp. 124, 203].
[44]Gozzadini [27, passim].
[45]Villani [15, IX, ch. 344, p. 259].
[46]Sercambi [14, II, pp. 93ff].
[47]Villani [15, VIII, ch. 71, pp. 89–90].
[48]Gaspar (ed.) [8, p. 213].
[49]Villani [15, IX, ch. 104, p. 213].
[50]Villani [15, IX, ch. 125, p. 228].
[51]Villani [15, XII, ch. 17, pp. 35–36].
[52]Villani [15, XII, ch. 21, p. 48].
[53]Villani [15, VI, ch. 36, p. 258].
[54]Villani [15, VIII, ch. 98, p. 132].
[55]Villani [15, VI, ch. 65, p. 286].
[56]Villani [15, XI, ch. 118, p. 350].
[57]Gaspar (ed.) [8, pp. 226–228].
[58]On this point, see Heers [31 (Eng. trans.), pp. 104–105].
[59]Gozzadini [27, doc. no. 79, p. 581].
[60]Villani [15, VI, ch. 33, p. 255].
[61]Villani [15, VIII, ch. 44, p. 48].
[62]Villani [15, VIII, ch. 44, p. 49].
[63]Villani [15, VIII, ch. 114, p. 141].
[64]Villani [15, IX, ch. 2, p. 147].
[65]Villani [15, IX, ch. 153, p. 244].
[66]Villani [15, XI, ch. 118, p. 118].
[67]Caffaro, Annali Genovesi... [7].
[68]Chronica parva Ferrariensis, ed. L. A. Muratori. Rerum italicarum scriptores, VIII (Milan, 1726).
[69]Gozzadini [27, passim].
[70]Sercambi [14, pp. 43–44].
[71]Gaspar (ed.) [8, p. 160].
[72]Della Corte [10, p. 424], cited by Gaspar [8, p. 160].
[73]Villani [15, VI, ch. 82, p. 306].
[74]See especially O. Brattö, Liber estimatiorum anno MCCLXIX (Göteborg, 1956).
[75]Gozzadini [27, p. 335].
[76]Bowsky [17, pp. 251ff].
[77]Waley [59, pp. 50ff].
[78]Waley [59, pp. 93ff].
[79]Renouard [46, p. 338].
[80]Renouard [46, p. 506].
[81]Cited by Gozzadini [27, p. 77] for the Andalo family.
[82]Villani [15, VIII, ch. 26, p. 29]: e cola dove pussono il detto palazzo furono anticamente le case degli Uberti, rebeli di Firenze e ghibelini, e di qué loro casolari feciono piazze accioché mai non si rifecessono.
[83]In 1971 D. Cavalca announced a forthcoming study on banishment in the communes of Florence and Bologna.

[84]Villani [15, IX, ch. 140, p. 237].

[85]Villani [15, IX, ch. 101, p. 212].

[86]Villani [15, IX, ch. 148, p. 242].

[87]Villani [15, XII, ch. 28, p. 55]: per alcuna gelosia mossa in Firenze per gli grandi e non vera, furono dati i confini a Enrique de' Bardi, e a quattro de' Frescobaldi, e a . . . .

[88]Villani [15, XII, ch. 120, p. 181]: senza fare altro male nelle personne, se non di rubare e mettere fuoco nelle case de quegli della parte Raspanti, mandanto a' confini i conti e loro seguaci . . . .

[89]Villani [15, IX, ch. 219, pp. 282–283].

[90]Villani [15, XII, ch. 79, pp. 127–128].

[91]Gaspar (ed.) [8, many references, in particular p. 188, n. 5].

[92]Judic [37, in particular pp. 28, 234, 238].

[93]Gaspar (ed.) [8, p. 189].

[94]Villani [15, XII, ch. 28, p. 55]: per levare sospetto al popolo e fuggire la furia, se n'andarono in contado agli loro luoghi ad abitare, e lasciarono la città . . . .

[95]Villani [15, VI, ch. 33, p. 254].

[96]Waley [59, p. 140].

[97]P. Racine, *Les Placentins à Gênes à la fin du XIIIe siècle*, unpublished doctoral thesis, third series (University of Strasbourg, 1970).

[98]M.E. Viora, *Statuti e consuetudini in Alessandria* (1969–).

[99]Salimbene de Adam [16, I, 271].

[100]Gozzadini [27, p. 328]: Hi sunt banniti et inobientes de domibus magnatum et de Nobili progenie. . . . Sub hoc titulo continentur nomina eorum qui positi fuerunt in banno comunis Civitatis Bonomie occasione rebellionis qua pars Lambertatiorum civitatem ipsam discipare molita est.

[101]Gozzadini [27, p. 61].

[102]Villani [15, VI, ch. 77, p. 296]: e tutti i ghibellini di Toscana ne presono grande vigore e baldanza.

[103]Villani [15, VI, ch. 82, p. 305].

[104]Salimbene de Adam [16, VI, ch. 45, p. 271].

[105]Villani [15, VI, ch. 86, pp. 309–310].

[106]Villani [15, VI, ch. 87, p. 310].

[107]On this point compare the study of a similar situation in L. Poliakov, *Les Banchieri juifs et le Saint Siège du XIIIe au XVIIe siècle* (Paris, 1965), especially pp. 27–87.

[108]Renouard [46, pp. 333–335].

[109]Renouard [46, p. 506].

[110]Villani [15, IX, ch. 188, pp. 342–434].

[111]Villani [15, IX, ch. 188, pp. 263–264].

[112]Villani [15, ch. 87, pp. 310–311].

[113]Renouard [46, p. 506].

[114]Villani [15, IX, ch. 107, p. 215].

[115]Villani [15, IX, ch. 117, p. 223].

[116]A. Giustiniani, *Annali della reppublica di Genova*, 2 vols. (Genoa, 1935), pp. 441–452.

[117]Waley [59, pp. 90–93].

[118]Masséna [41, XXIII, p. 294], cited by N. Guglielmi, *Modos de marginalidad en la edad media: Extranjeria, pobreza, enfermedad* (Buenos Aires, 1972), p. 9.

[119]Masséna [41, XXIV, p. 295], cited by Guglielmi, *Modos*, p. 9.

[120]Dante Alighieri, *De vulgari eloquentia.*

[121]Villani [15, VIII, ch. 38, p. 41]: per aver pace et concordia con loro, mandarono quegli ch'avea fatta l'offesa alla misericordia di coloro che l'avea ricevuta, che ne prendersono l'ammenda e vendetta a loro volontà.

[122]On peace arrangements in the cities of the West, see Heers [31, Eng. trans.), pp. 105–7 and 120–1], with bibliography. For a particular case, see G. Cecchini, La pacificazione fra Tolomei e Salimbeni, *Quaderni delle' Accademia Chigiana*, II (Siena, 1942).

[123]On the peace assemblies, for two examples see R. Bonnaud-Delamare, Les institutions de paix en Aquitaine au XIe siècle, *Recueils de la Société Jean Bodin*, XIV (Brussels, 1962), pp. 415–488; and R. Grand, *Les paix d'Aurillac. Etude et documents sur l'histoire des institutions municipales d'une ville à consulat (XIIe–XVe siècles)* (Paris, 1945). See also T.N. Bisson, *Assemblies and representation in Languedoc in the thirteenth century* (Princeton, 1964).

[124]*Obertus Cancellerius Annales Genuenses*, pp. 324–327; *Uberti Folietae Genuenses historia*, L, II, 278, cited without reference to edition by Sismondi [52, II, 141–143].

[125]*A.P.Gu.*, anno 1201, p. 422, lines 8–9, cited by Judic [37, p. 11]: facta et firmata est tregua sacramento . . . per domnum archiepiscopum Mediolani et priorem Camalduli.

[126]*Ibid.*, anno 1208, p. 424, line 49 to p. 425, line 2, and *Annales Cremonenses* [2], anno 1201, p. 804, line 5, cited by Judic [37, p. 14].

[127]Gozzadini [27, p. 51], for the Abati family.

[128]Rolandino [13, ch. 7]; Salimbene de Adam [16, p. 102].

[129]Several authors cited by Sismondi [52, II, 461]; Gaspar (ed.) [8, p. 152].

[130]Cited by Gaspar (ed.) [8, p. 150].

[131]Gaspar (ed.) [8, p. 153].

[132]G. Solinas, *Storia di Verona* (Verona, 1964), p. 118.

[133]Rolandino [13, anno 1228, II, ch. 17, p. 197].

[134]Sismondi [52, II, 467].

[135]*A.P.Gu.*, anno 1223, p. 455, line 43, cited by Judic [37, p. 10].

[136]*Memoire della città e campagna di Milano*, anno 1233, LI, pp. 478–483, cited without reference to edition by Sismondi [52, II, 454].

[137]Gozzadini [27, pp. 74–75], Algarda or Algardi family.

[138]E. Dupré-Theseider, *Roma dal Comune del popolo alla signoria pontificia (1252– 1377)* (Bologna, 1952), pp. 517–649.

[139]*A.P.Gu.*, anno 1090, pp. 411–412, cited by Judic [37, p. 217].

[140]Salimbene de Adam [16, pp. 98–102].

[141]*A.P.Gib.*, anno 1260, p. 512, lines 34–38, cited by Judic [37, p. 208].

[142]Gozzadini [27, p. 77], Andalo family; D.M. Federici, *Istoria dei cavalieri gaudenti* (Treviso, 1787), in particular I, pp. 187, 289.

[143]Dante. *Inferno*, XVII. Reginaldo Scrovegni.

[144]See *The Arena Chapel frescoes* (New York, 1969).

[145]In the *Inferno* the poet encountered Loderigo and Catalani, "*gaudenti* brothers of Bologna", crushed by the weight of their capes, which were "dazzingly golden on the outside, but within were made of lead". *Inferno*, XXXIII.

[146]Dominici [11, p. 50], cited by Herlihy [33, p. 198].

[147]A. Fanfani, *La legge suntuaria fatta dal Comune di Firenze l'anno 1335 e volgariz- zata nel 1356 da Ser Andrea Lancia* (Florence, 1851); C. Mazzi, Alcune leggi suntuarie

senesi del secolo XIII, *Archivio storico italiano*, ser. 4, V (1880); E. Verga, Le leggi suntuarie milanesi; gli statuti dal 1396 al 1498, *Archivio storico lombardo*, ser. 3, IX (1898); G. Bistort, Il magistrato delle pompe nella republica di Venezia. Studio storico, *Miscellanea di storia veneta della Reale Diputazione di Storia Patria*, ser. 3, V (1912).

[148]Waley [59, p. 105].

[149]E. Emerton, *Humanism and tyranny* (Cambridge, Mass., 1925), p. 249.

[150]Miniature in *Annales Genovenses*. Paris. Bibliothèque Nationale, MS. Latin 10136, f. 42.

[151]Waley [59, pp. 50–65].

[152]Matthew Paris, *Chronica Majora*, ed. H.R. Luard, V (London: Rolls Series, 1880), anno 1254.

[153]*Raynaldi Annales ecclesie*, anno 1258, cited by Sismondi [52, II, p. 168].

[154]Sismondi [52, II, p. 000].

[155]Villani [15, XII, ch. 15, p. 17].

[156]Villani [15, ch. 118, p. 346].

[157]Rolandino [13, XIV, col. 908], cited by Mor [43, p. 101].

[158]Rolandino [12, p. 40], cited by Hyde [36, p. 282].

[159]Thus, at Pisa on 24 December 1347, when the Bergolini hoped to attack the Raspanti and expel them from the city government, they had the cry "Viva il popolo e la libertà!" shouted in the streets. Villani [15, XII, ch. 120, p. 181].

[160]Waley [59, p. 9].

[161]G. de Vergottini, *Arti e popolo nella prima meta del secolo XIII* (Milan, 1943); Renouard [46, p. 320].

[162]Renouard [46, p. 348].

[163]On the *pievi* throughout Italy, and especially for the marginal regions at some distance from the cities, see Santini [50], with a particularly fine bibliography.

[164]On forms of political life within the framework of the Tuscan *popolo*, see B. Stahl, *Adel und Volk im florentiner Dugento* (Cologne and Graz, 1965).

[165]Villani [15, XI, ch. 95, p. 324].

[166]P. Sella, *La vicinia come elemento constitutivo del Comune* (Milan, 1908); G. Luzzatto, Vicinia e Comune, *Revista italiana di sociologia*, 1909.

[167]Salimbene de Adam [16, p. 109].

[168]Gaspar [8, p. 36, n. 2].

[169]Archivio di Stato di Genova. Notario Giovanni Vernazza, filza 1, no. 85.

[170]Villani [15, VI, ch. 39, pp. 261–262].

[171]Renouard [46, pp. 323–324].

[172]Villani [15, IX, ch. 148, p. 242].

[173]Villani [15, XI, ch. 102, p. 334].

[174]Villani [15, XI, ch. 107, p. 336].

[175]Villani [15, XII, ch. 19, pp. 40–42].

[176]Villani [15, VIII, ch. 20, p. 12].

[177]Herlihy [33, pp. 200ff].

PART IV
POLITICAL PARTIES OUTSIDE ITALY

Factional struggles in other countries of the medieval West have not received the attention which historians have devoted to those in Italy. With a few exceptions, such as the famous conflict between Armagnacs and Burgundians, and the Wars of the Roses in England, political parties seem virtually unknown outside Italy, or else they have played only a negligible, episodic role, party warfare being merely incidental to the great lines of political development.

It is possible that this unobtrusiveness is the result of a series of circumstances and situations, or of particular political institutions. The power of the state in France, England, or Aragon may explain the weakness of the factions, rendering it impossible for them to maintain a clientele sufficiently numerous to dominate political life. But it is also possible that this distinction between Italy and other lands is only illusory or at least is less profound than the general histories would lead us to believe. We must remember that the much sparser documentation and the paucity of modern treatments of the subject outside Italy can distort and may have led to hasty and erroneous conclusions.[1]

There can be no serious doubt that political parties existed in various social milieus of the medieval West outside Italy. Factions struggled constantly to seize power, assume responsibilities and offices, and install their clients and protégés in positions of authority. This is why their rivalries seem particularly strong, active, and bitter and their fighting so well organized in times of anarchy, when governmental institutions were in a state of chaos and the authority of the central, sovereign state was weak or divided.

This leads us to examine in order three forms of group political action outside Italy. One of these involved parties trying to assume power in the towns. This type of activity, hitherto studied only for the Italian merchant cities, also occurred in many other urban milieus of diverse character and involved various types of economic activity of varying degrees of complexity. These conflicts can be observed particularly clearly in two periods. The first was the age of urban expansion, which corresponds to the early communal era in Italy. This was a period when institutions and structures were still fluctuating and poorly defined. During this time too the new monarchies were still unable to take decisive action to impose public peace, order, and law. This age of gestation and metamorphoses occurred in the eleventh and twelfth centuries. The second occurred toward the end of the medieval period in the great merchant cities. Thanks to their economic power or often to their location near the borders of the kingdom, virtually outside royal authority, they were able to maintain or obtain a kind of administrative autonomy or sometimes even virtual political independence. The towns of Germany and Catalonia and even Bordeaux are good examples.

The standard explanation for these two cases and periods completely ignores the role of genuine socio-political parties. Modern authors consistently provide a purely economic causation: the disorders and civil wars were provoked by conflicts between socio-economic categories or even 'classes'. During the early communal period this was a struggle between the merchant and 'feudal' worlds; later it became a battle between a more or less stable oligarchy and the 'people'. These pat explanations have been forcefully propounded. We have seen that they are worthless for Italy, however, and the same is true for trans-Alpine Europe. Their clarity and simplicity can lead us astray, but they end by boring us with a hopeless monotony and an indolent and comfortable conformity. They are abstractions which reflect insufficient notice of structural complexities and take little account of the relationship between society and politics. Fundamentally, they disregard phenomena of collective psychology.

A second type of party political activity involved great noble clans, in border areas where the king's power was weak, in a violent confrontation to dominate the countryside. This form of political life was quite traditional and was maintained in anarchical regions or those lacking a sovereign state power, such as mountainous areas which preserved their political and economic isolation. We find such a situation throughout northwestern Castile, where the king was able to intervene only occasionally to impose a peace that came too late to matter. Even more characteristic was the Basque country of Spain, where the division of seigneurial clans into two hostile *bandos* dominated all political life until the 1480s. Similar conditions undoubtedly prevailed in Andalusia. Even after the king was in control in Estremadura, the conflicts between noble *bandos* were extended into city administration by the regular division of all municipal offices between the two parties.

A third type of party united allies, leaders, and protégés during dynastic quarrels in an attempt to seize central power in a monarchical state. Ill-regulated succession quarrels often opened the door to bloody confrontations or even civil wars. The claimants based their power on gangs of nobles and followers, but at times they also had a geographical and regional base, as provincial particularism reinforced the bonds of fidelity. These dynastic factions assumed their leaders' names. They engaged in bitter quarrels between princes for a crown. Each side was aided by an entire party of lords, clerics, prelates, towns, and public officials. The feuds between these dynastic parties became widespread in France and England from the fourteenth century. During the early days of the new Valois dynasty in France, a Navarrese party was formed around Charles the Bad,[2] while others formed regional parties and militias of Normans, Burgundians, and men of central France who succeeded each other at Paris in the royal entourages of Philip VI and John II, exerting considerable influence on the conduct of affairs.[3] There was also a party struggle at this same time between the two dynastic factions of Brittany who vied for the succession of Duke John III of Brittany after his death in 1341. They were led by John IV of Montfort and Charles of Blois, and the latter was supported by the king of France. The French civil war between the Burgundian and Orléans (later called Armagnac) factions occurred later. Hostilities were begun by the assassination of Louis of Orléans in 1407. They were to be prolonged, with innumerable reverses of fortune, by a later confrontation between the parties of the dauphin (later King Charles VII) and the Burgundian dukes. The situation lasted until the Peace of Arras was concluded in 1435 between Charles VII and Philip the Good of Burgundy.[4] The last great dynastic conflict of the medieval West was the Wars of the Roses in England; two strong princely parties, York and Lancaster, vied for power between 1455 and 1485, when the decisive victory of Henry Tudor ended the conflict. Both parties owed much of their power and cohesion to the bands of retainers who wore the prince's livery, and to family ties which were consolidated by a systematic policy of marriage alliances.[5]

The study of political factions outside Italy can undoubtedly provide

new and very interesting elements, together with some original explanations for political events. It will certainly shed new light on the history of
the disorders, revolts, and civil wars. In the present state of documentation and secondary literature, we must nonetheless limit ourselves to a
detailed analysis of a few special cases which are relatively well known,
then draw comparisons with the Italian situation. The essays which
follow are thus intentionally limited in scope. Even for the dynastic
parties of France and England it seems useless for me to give a detailed
recital of events or even to attempt a comparison with Italy. I have only
noted the dynastic quarrels in the last part of this book for purposes of
studying much less well known collective phenomena, symbols, and
mentalities.

CHAPTER ONE

The urban parties

The early communal period

The period from the beginning of the eleventh century was troubled by riots, revolts, street fighting, civil wars, and levies of troops. Virtually all historians have linked these disturbances to a triumphant communal movement. The commune was an association which was then achieving the 'liberation' of the infant towns from the 'feudal' yoke of count or bishop. It had developed from the rise of a completely new social category, the merchants. There was supposedly a struggle between the 'feudatories', rich landlords of the countryside who were unfamiliar with the town, and the merchants, who were new men or even adventurers and were in any case hostile to the seigneurial and rural world. This explanation has a disarmingly childish simplicity. It involves a kind of Manicheism of evil against good, the champions of oppression against the defenders of liberty, but it is based on a totally erroneous social analysis. The presence at this time of a strong landed aristocracy composed of fiefholders, knights and therefore warriors within the towns has been proven beyond shadow of doubt, even in northwestern Europe, for example in Normandy and at Paris. Many merchants in turn had clienteles of relatives, friends, and allies. They held rural land and even seigneuries. The two classes which historians have considered so distinct were actually closely related.

This explains the erroneous interpretations heretofore propounded of the conflicts and revolts of this period. Their origins were undoubtedly very complex and diverse. But among the many causes we must certainly assign an important place to the quarrels between powerful parties, often two groups dominated by powerful persons with substantial clienteles. These were not socio-economic conflicts, but were rather political confrontations engendered by private, personal rivalries.

Factional collisions in the early period of town life might assume various forms; a few exceptional cases which are well known can provide insights here. Some of these involved dynastic rivalries within the county, when at least one party sought allies in the largest city of the region, such as occurred in the case the commune of Le Mans of 1070. According to the *Acts of the bishops of Le Mans*, this affair was more than a simple merchant uprising against the town lord: the circumstances leading to the birth of the commune sprang from a purely partisan conflict.

The duke of Normandy had conquered Maine, but he had been detained in England after his victory at Hastings in 1066. During his absence "the powerful men of Maine agreed with the people" to offer the office of count to a certain Atho, who was then in Italy and had married Gerconda, daughter of Herbert, who had been count of Maine. The Normans were driven from all their castles and Atho was victorious. This situation was complicated still further by the ambiguous attitude of the bishop, who went to England to swear fealty to William the Conqueror. All his property at Le Mans was pillaged during his absence, and when he returned he could only re-enter the town after ratifying an agreement which his clergy had negotiated with the inhabitants. Two political parties were thus assuming somewhat clearer outline in Maine: that of the Normans and Duke William and that of the local men of Maine with their new count. But Atho, who was short of money, lost his following and returned to Italy, leaving his wife and son Hugh under the guardianship of Geoffrey of Mayenne. A rebellion followed against Gerconda and Geoffrey. A commune or sworn association was formed which committed "innumerable crimes". Its members launched an expedition against the most powerful of the lords, Hugh of Sillé, but a siege of his castle was unsuccessful. This was undoubtedly a communal movement, but it was also party warfare, for the 'communards' were supported by the bishop. Their army indeed was led by the bishop and the priests of the town churches, "bearing the cross and the banners of Christianity".[6]

Vaguely defined political parties seem to have been formed as well during the famous uprising which followed the assassination of Count Charles the Good of Flanders in the spring of 1127. The assassins were the Erembald clan, led by Bertulf, provost of the church of St Donatian of Bruges and chancellor of Flanders. According to the notary Galbert of Bruges, the count had learned that the Erembalds had originally been servile, but had been concealing their status by marrying into lesser noble families. Faced with the count's threat to degrade them, the Erembalds plotted murder. Their party originally consisted of their own clan and in-laws and other *ministeriales* from the lesser aristocracy, supported by many citizens of Bruges. The count favoured the adherents of Thancmar, leader of the van Straten family, who were nobles of the environs of Bruges and were cordially despised by the townsmen. After the assassination, the Erembalds tried to hunt down the van Straten and the intimate councillors of the late count. The quarrel at this stage was personal, as the Erembalds attempted a palace coup, with party loyalties determined by momentary interests, not by class consciousness of any sort.

But the Erembalds soon lost control of the situation in Bruges, as the nobles allied with some town leaders and surrounded the castle in which the murderers were barricaded. The Erembalds had obviously expected help from both quarters, for Galbert tells us that "they believed the barons of the realm were their accomplices in crime and bound to them in faith and friendship". During the siege some of the barons or peers, whom Galbert strictly differentiates from the knights or lesser nobles, maintained contacts with those inside the fortress. After the siege had carried, some intervened on behalf of one of the survivors.

Why then were the Erembalds not supported by their own class? Flanders, in common with most regions of northern Europe, had a large group of knights, men of modest means but with grandiose social aspirations, and a smaller body of nobles or peers. Both groups lived by landholding and warmaking, but were distinguished by social rank and extent of wealth and influence. Obviously, the one was a source of biological replenishment for the other. Galbert's narrative makes quite clear that Count Charles had been conducting sworn inquests on a massive scale into the question of the servile origins of persons who were claiming free standing. It is absolutely inconceivable that the Flemish knights who had married nieces of the Erembalds were unaware of their class. Charles the Good was obviously undertaking a policy which could embarrass many Flemish nobles, and the Erembalds naturally thought that they could count on their fellows to help them quash the meddler.

But the great Flemish nobles had no desire to have themselves tainted by association with persons now admittedly servile. The Erembalds were sacrificed to a united front of nobles and townsmen; no source after 1127 mentions the presence of *ministeriales* in the Flemish nobility. The party quarrel had thus pitted *nouveaux* against the townsmen who found their pretensions offensive and the great nobles who considered them an embarrassment.

But no sooner had the Erembalds been defeated and hounded down than the towns and nobles began to split. Territorial parties began to form as the Brugeois made a pact with the men of the Franc or castellany of Bruges for common action in choosing a new count. With the support of King Louis VI of France, the barons chose William Clito, grandson of William the Conqueror of Normandy and England and pretender to the English crown. The towns accepted William at first, in return for charters of liberties. But they soon fell out with him, generally over his attempts to impose a comital administration over them, and chose as the new count Thierry of Alsace, cousin of Charles the Good. He eventually prevailed, and Galbert shows that the large towns in fact imposed him on the other elements of Flemish political society, although conflicts continued until William Clito died in battle in the summer of 1128.

The events of 1127–1128 thus show elements of a two-party struggle of nobles and townsmen. But their worlds were hardly distinct, for Galbert makes plain that the burghers and nobles had family ties in common. Only after the fall of the Erembalds did the towns and nobles divide their previously united front. The Erembald affair was the catalyst for the development of two mutually antagonistic estates in Flanders, which together were able to limit severely the power of the counts of Flanders. Once again, momentary interest created alliances or parties which could not last and which had only an artificial social basis.[7]

Other conflicts involved rivalries among the clergy. Prelates and clergy did not necessarily present a united front which could rule the town and impose their influence upon it. Sectarian conflicts, doctrinal rivalries in times when heresy was in the air, conflicts between the bishopric and the great abbeys or the cathedral chapter, all of them more personal rivalries, provoked grave schisms within the clergy which led to the collision of two church parties. These were composed only of clergy in the beginning, but they were soon seeking allies among the townsmen and the great lords, or even foreign princes.

Cambrai furnishes a good example of quarrels of this type which lasted for several centuries. They began in 1103 with a divided episcopal election, with opposing parties favouring the candidacies of Gaucher and Manassès to the bishopric. Factions supporting each candidate arose in the town. Gaucher got the emperor to support him, while Manassès relied upon Robert the Frisian, count of Flanders. Besieged in Cambrai, Gaucher won the inhabitants to his side by giving them a communal charter, but it was annulled by the emperor Henry IV in 1105, and the fact that it was granted had nothing to do with an irresistible, violent, and triumphant communal movement. It was obtained only as an accident of a war between two episcopal parties. From this time until the 1340s political life in Cambrai was continually dominated by the quarrels between two church parties, those of the bishop and of the canons of the cathedral chapter. Both obtained powerful followings in the city as they sought allies among the inhabitants and thus assembled clienteles.[8]

These two situations – competition between two rivals for the episcopal see and hostility between bishop and canons – were in no way exceptional. The urban history of the West affords many other examples. If episcopal schisms seemed at the time regrettable accidents which men tried to settle as best they might, the rivalry of bishops and canons occurred as a matter of course. It was a constant feature of political life even in some towns which were least divided between the two parties.

Another form of conflict occurred between a united episcopal party and a merchant faction. To cite only one of many possible examples, Cologne knew such a disturbance in 1074. The *Annals* of Lambert of Hersfeld give a fine account of the circumstances. Violence began with a fortuitous circumstance. The archbishop of Cologne had received a visit from his friend, the bishop of Münster, and wanted a fine ship to take the visiting dignitary home. His people thereupon forcibly seized a vessel which belonged to a wealthy local merchant, and some fights broke out. The merchant's son was quite popular, for he was strong and bold "and was related to all the leading families of the city". He hastily assembled his servants and "all the young men of the city whom he could find". Then, continues Lambert of Hersfeld, "the friends of the two parties took arms and came to their assistance". Despite the belated efforts of the archbishop, who surrendered in a gesture which he hoped would restore peace, the youth continued to create disturbances. He stirred up the inhabitants against the prelate, whom he accused of arrogance, injustice, frauds, rapine, and acts of violence, and reminded the men of Cologne how their neighbours of Worms had expelled their bishop.[9]

The social analysis is obviously different here from our previous cases, for the leaders of the two factions were not engaged in the same occupation in the city. But the difference between them was undoubtedly less great than one might think, for each of these bishops belonged to an aristocratic family and had to maintain numerous allies among the nobles. At any event, although the text is unfortunately brief, it allows us to make several important points. Parties and their clienteles – young men, servants, followers, and friends – were present. A great aristocrat was prominently involved in beginning a supposedly 'popular' riot. Civil war was not breaking out from economic malaise nor social discontent. Nor was it a conflict between professional interests nor a class struggle, but a simple private conflict between retainers acting in their masters' interest. Finally, each of the competing parties was led by a great family. Were such internal conflicts unusual or common but not known to us? It is difficult to conceive of the merchants presenting a perfectly united front and not being, like comital families or the upper clergy, profoundly divided by personal, family, and factional quarrels. The conditions which were so common in the Italian towns could hardly fail to arise by force of circumstances in other parts of the West: economic rivalries in trade, local conflicts and hatreds, affronts to honour and the desire for vengeance, and particularly the will to dominate and monopolize all offices.

Contemporary sources and particularly the historians tell us very little about such conflicts, at least for the early communal period. Only one significant example comes to mind. The city of Rouen was split in the 1190s between two clearly defined parties, the *Pilatenses* and the *Calloenses*. One leader, Clarus Pilatin, lived in a castle granted him by the abbey of Jumièges and located near the city wall. His son of the same name had acquired lands near the town. This was certainly a merchant family, but its members lived like knights who had settled in the city in a fortified dwelling, and their lands yielded them a considerable revenue.[10]

Most of the characteristics which we have noted for the Italian cities thus reappear north of the Alps during the eleventh and twelfth centuries, the first communal era: parties dominated by an aristocracy and gathering clienteles; a strong family structure; conflicts whose ultimate goal was the seizure of the town offices; and extremely close ties between the city and the countryside.

The period of the great merchant cities

During the three centuries between 1000 and 1300 social structures were neither revolutionized nor even subjected to extreme changes. The towns were still dominated by aristocracies whose members held important landed properties and even seigneuries, but also traded in many commodities. Social bonds remained equally strong. But several elements which greatly influenced urban development seem more prominent now than in the early communal period. The rise of national monarchies meant more frequent and decisive interventions by the king. The rise of certain industries inflated the numbers of retainers and created mobs which could make the armed conflicts seem more dramatic. Conflicts between groups or parties at all events remained essential elements of political life in many cities. Two examples from quite different environments seem to merit particular attention.

The political and economic situation of Bordeaux was quite unique and can be described easily. The city was an economic capital whose 'bourgeois' lived in the city while owning vineyards, often at some distance from the town. They managed to monopolize a great overseas wine trade with England.[11] Bordeaux was also an important centre of naval armaments, an arsenal for constructing ships of small and medium size to transport wine.[12] Finally, Bordeaux was the political capital of Guyenne, and even at times of the duchy of Aquitaine, a centre of English administration[13] where the king and his great functionaries intervened constantly. But neither province nor town totally escaped the jurisdiction of the French crown, which revealed its ultimate aims there by seizing upon various pretexts to intervene and seek partisans, and even inspired the formation of an anti-English faction. The economic health of the city, and to a lesser extent the competition between foreign powers, may explain the considerable degree of autonomy enjoyed by Bordeaux.

The party conflict is first mentioned in 1243, when the English king forbade the men of La Réole, Saint-Macaire, and Langon to go to Bordeaux or permit any person to go there "to help any citizen fight another in the city". Innumerable subsequent texts indicate that the parties always bore the names of the same two families, the Soler and the Colom. A little later, in 1249, Henry III gave semi-official recognition to these parties, declaring solemnly that "since there are two rival factions in the city, an equal number of echevins shall be chosen annually from each party".

On 26 June of that year, the Colom, who were protégés of Simon de Montfort, earl of Leicester and seneschal of English Gascony, incited a violent revolt. They undoubtedly did so to influence the municipal elections which were to take place shortly. Simon de Montfort summoned the leaders of the two factions and had them hand over twenty hostages apiece. Fifteen men from each party appeared at his court, but only the Solers were condemned and thrown into prison.[14] Their leader, Rostan de Soler, was then placed under surveillance and his house destroyed. A few months later, in 1250, the two parties swore an agreement in the presence of the archbishops of Bordeaux and Auch, the Gascon barons, and the entire community of the town. A total of two hundred men of the city and the environs took an oath to keep this peace, which forbade anyone to bear arms in the town or to band together or form sworn associations.

But the conflicts were by no means over. When Henry III visited Bordeaux in 1254 he convened the two parties and announced his arbitral judgement on 7 October. He banished all who had committed crimes in which blood was shed during the revolt of 1249. All leagues, conspiracies, and secret brotherhoods were dissolved and their statutes burned. Giving the call to arms (*Biafora*, "come outside") in the streets was forbidden. The new peace was sworn by the mayor and one hundred bourgeois from each party. Finally, the king expressed the fervent hope that members of the two factions would intermarry. But new bloody conflicts broke out when the Soler allied with Prince Edward and in 1260 had the Colom leaders imprisoned and their property confiscated.

These ceaseless and violent conflicts lasted for several more decades. A third powerful family, the Caillau, now joined the Colom and the Soler, but they were divided into two rival branches, and the town thus continued to be split into two hostile camps. Only from 1310 did Edward II's officials try to re-establish order by allying with all the merchants who were outside the two factions, in effect creating a third party. The mayor of Bordeaux in 1311 was a new man who was not a citizen of the town, a damoiseau named Odon de Lados. This very uncertain victory was consolidated only gradually as the royal administration increasingly took charge of the city, beginning in the 1330s.

Royal letters, trials and sentences, and peace arrangements give us a fairly exact idea of the nature of the political factions at Bordeaux at this time. Their characteristics appear conspicuously in an important document published by F. Funck-Brentano in 1879 and by Charles Bémont in 1915.[15] It is a memorandum composed in 1329 by Oliver of Ingham, seneschal of Aquitaine, about the misdeeds of Jean, the leader of the Colom party. Seventy-nine separate accusations are detailed. This is our most complete and precise text for the realities of political and social life in the town, and it can be supplemented by the information furnished by other complaints transmitted to the English king, one of them containing fifty-seven articles. All the documents were published by Charles Bémont in 1915.[16]

These documents underscore the family nature of the party and the noble social standing of its leader. Family bonds were constantly reaffirmed, and the parties assumed and kept family names. The party of the Soler, rivals of the Colom, was also called *Rosteins*, because its leader ordinarily had the Christian name of Rostan or Rostein. By a similar phonetic corruption, the Soler were called *du Cellier*.

The leaders were always called *divites* and *potentes miles*. The second term is particularly suggestive, implying membership in a seigneurial, warrior aristocracy. Indeed, Jean Colom had castles built on his domains in 1289. But their power was derived also from their wealth and commerce. Both the Colom and the Soler produced and sold wine. Amainen Colom had a boat called *la Colombe* in 1227. A century later, the Jean Colom noted above received and protected in his own house Lambert Tibalducho, a Lombard who was city mintmaster and had been accused of stealing more than 6,000 *livres*. Colom helped him to flee.

The prize for the winner in these contests was power within the town. The Colom were often mayors of Bordeaux, holding the office uninterruptedly with their allies the Doudomme or the Caillau between 1262 and 1278. Jean Colom stole the great seal of the mayor's office for six days in 1326 "and used it to seal all the documents that he wished".

The documents also clearly reveal the interference of the kings of England and France. Accused of having pillaged the mansion of a townsman at Bordeaux, Jean Colom used the right of appeal to the *parlement* of Paris to have the affair judged by French royal officials. This in itself shows the difficulties encountered by the English administration in the city. On other occasions, "the aforementioned Jean Colom obtained letters of pardon from the French king for himself and his followers . . . although the French court was not accustomed to granting such pardons unless it expected to profit from them".[17] The memorandum also accused Jean Colom of wanting to turn the region over to the king of France.

Violence and other misdeeds seem to have been quite commonplace: assassination of an English royal sergeant (Article 1), several murders of bourgeois of Bordeaux (Arts. 64–66), abductions, thefts, plundering food for one's own house, usurpations, acts of brigandage, and fiscal peculation (Jean Colom had received 300 *livres* from the men of Rue, Roan, and Saint-Julien of Bordeaux to strengthen the Porte Saint-Julien, but he had not done it). Men wearing his livery had stolen mainly fish from certain "merchants and fishmongers" of Bordeaux, in some cases to the value of over 100 *livres*. These crimes had been the work of Jean Colom, done "by his order, furtherance, and support", "frequently in broad daylight when the deeds were quite visible in the marketplace of Bordeaux". His people had also robbed butchers and bakers on another market square to obtain food for their own establishments (Arts. 46–60).

The Bordeaux party leaders were also surrounded by a substantial clientele, or by armed bands at least. The memorandum consistently uses the word *mesnie* and speaks of 'companions', "people from the mansion and retainership of Jean Colom".[18] To increase the size of his *mesnie*, Jean received in his house many exiles and felons from England. He protected criminals and murderers, such as the carpenter Ernaud Jehan, who "cut off the hand of Pierres d'Albi, merchant and citizen of Bordeaux". Ernaud took refuge first in the Dominican convent, but Jean Colom later summoned him to his palace "and threatened to have Pierres d'Albi assassinated if he brought charges against Ernaud". Justice could not be accomplished (Art. 15). Several other points of the memorandum deal with the same sort of thing (Arts. 16, 17, 19, 22–25). In another instance Jean Colom attacked the house of a citizen of Bordeaux, Raimond de Frères. He abducted the daughter of another townsman and married her to one of his menials "against the wishes of her parents and friends (Art. 6)". He armed, lodged in his house and fed all the servants of his *mesnie*, together with some apprentices, unemployed persons, and folk recently arrived from the countryside. This clientele took an oath to its leader and bore his livery:[19] "Jean Colom supported and maintained persons who robbed merchants and good people . . . so that the seneschal of Gascony and the mayor of Bordeaux could not do justice because of Jean's great following". The formula "that justice could not be done" is often found in the memorandum of 1329. As in Italy, protection of the clan and the party took precedence over civil law.

Broadly-based support could only be obtained if the party leader recruited clients among the various journeymen of the lower classes. "Jean Colom had all the dockhands, butchers, and seamen of Bordeaux take an oath to him against all other persons, including His Majesty the king." This was a bond of alliance between an aristocratic tribune and tradesmen which could threaten royal authority. Jean Colom firmly repudiated the new English royal coinage during an assembly convoked by the seneschal which was attended by "all the drapers, butchers, cobblers and all other tradesmen of the town". He told them publicly "that God would take it very ill if they did not appeal against these ordinances to the king (Art. 35)". He even incited a 'communal' movement among the guildsmen, summoning all their leaders and several other persons "so that they would act as a unit and rise against the bourgeois who controlled the city government". This set off a riot which some have called 'popular'. The journeymen of the trades, "at Jean Colom's instigation", tore down the city gates and stole the gate keys and the town seal. He had acted "so that he could become lord of Bordeaux and be free to act without constraint (Art. 41)". This is a clear example, such as we have seen in Italy, of a social revolt provoked by a real aristocrat, a man who was in no sense a renegade or traitor to his own class, but was a party and clan leader. The revolt was obviously the consequence of rivalry between factions.

On another occasion the leader of this aristocratic party even went so far as to ally with the dockworkers in their struggle to obtain better wages: "advised, supported, and maintained by Jean Colom, the dockworkers plotted secretly that they would load casks of wine only at a certain wage per cask (Art. 77)". This is a direct and important accusation. In seeking to expand his following from a merely 'domestic' to a 'popular' base, the aristocrat Jean Colom had to seek wider support and appeal to persons from several trades who could participate in street fights. The clientele was obviously the essential element, at Bordeaux as in Italy, of the party which was dominated by aristocrats and merchants. It was the principal moving force of the faction.

Economic and political conditions at Barcelona did not differ vastly from those at Bordeaux and it is hardly coincidental that similar conflicts occurred there between parties struggling to take power, although later and more sporadically than at Bordeaux.

Despite some serious economic problems, fifteenth-century Barcelona was a great centre for shipping, importing oriental spices and exporting raw wool and cloth woven in the city or elsewhere in

Catalonia. A wealthy aristocracy dominated all this activity and also owned extensive estates in the city and the surrounding countryside. Barcelona had managed to achieve a kind of administrative autonomy. Governed by its own magistrates and a council of one hundred, it even made good a certain degree of independence from the crown of Aragon, whose representatives were the lieutenant general of Catalonia and the governor of Barcelona. The king did not live in the city and spent most of his time in his distant possessions of Sicily and Naples. He was involved in difficult military and naval campaigns, such as the disaster which ended at Ponza in 1435 with the defeat of the fleet of Alfonso V the Magnanimous. Finally, dynastic conflicts and rivalries weakened the monarchy. For all of these reasons, dissensions and the absence of the king, royal power could not be exercised directly. Accordingly, the king's men sought the open assistance of a faction.

The party disputes at Barcelona are not well known and evidently only began in the 1430s. Two political groups were, however, in violent conflict by that time, the *Biga* and the *Busca*. The *Biga* were then in power, holding most seats on the Council of One Hundred. Their number included a substantial part of the aristocracy, who were called *ciudadanos honrados* (in Catalan *ciutadans honrats*),[21] terms which might be translated 'city gentlemen'. The *Busca* had a less important part in the government and tended to work behind the scenes, perhaps seeking allies outside this aristocratic milieu. This rivalry developed into an active conflict from June 1452, when the governor of Catalonia, Galceran de Requesens, and Queen Maria authorized the meeting of a *Sindicato de los Tres Estamentos y pueblo de Barcelona*: "assembly of the three estates [*ciudadanos honrados*, merchants and artisans] and the people of Barcelona". Such assemblies had often been forbidden by the Council of One Hundred, and accordingly had been held until that time in the nearby towns of Vich, Lérida and Villafranca de Penedès. This was the first official meeting at Barcelona, and it coincided with the coming to power of the *Busca*. Their victory was consolidated as a result of the troubles marking the agitated sessions of the *Cortes*, the national consultative assembly, at Barcelona between 1454 and 1458.

After the *Busca* party had assumed power, it engineered the expulsion of the *Biga* from the Council of One Hundred. It revised the lists of citizens and merchants and inaugurated a systematic repression of its adversaries: imprisonments, audits of earlier city accounts, trials of four leading councillors, and dismissals of many officials, in short an obstinate attempt to control the entire administration.[22] But the victorious party was soon rent by internal dissension. The dynastic problem and quarrels within the royal family led to a union of the *Biga* and the *Busca* dissidents. Two plots were discovered in 1462, the San Matias (24 February, St Mathias's Day) and the Pallarès (after Francesto Pallarès, in whose house it was conceived). They provoked a stern reaction but led to the fall of the *Busca*. Once again there were trials, convictions, and executions of the two most important leaders. The return of the *Biga* to power at Barcelona in 1462 inaugurated a ten-year civil war.[23]

We have given only a hasty outline of these very complex events, but the fundamental causes remain unclear. Historians have virtually ignored this two-party quarrel, contenting themselves with this superficial explanation. Only Mme Battle-Gallart, in several articles[24] and an important thesis which is a monument of erudition, has given a minute analysis of the facts, studied the men and their programs, and proposed a general interpretation.[25] We owe much to her efforts, but several of her conclusions seem to me to suffer from overly strict adherence to preconceived ideas, some even contradicting the facts and information which she has collected and examined.

Her works emphasize several essential and indisputable characteristics of the two parties at Barcelona. The vocabulary of the sources is suggestive, for the equivalents of the modern words 'faction' and *partido* are not used. The texts almost invariably say merely *Biga* or *Busca*, suggesting political entities which have become tangible realities, personalized groups. They also speak of *buscaires* and *bigaires*, or more often "the people now commonly called the men of the *Busca*" (*los homens qui hoix se appellen vulgarmente los homens de la Buscha*). Such hesitation shows clearly that contemporaries were not thinking of a solid, stable, well constituted party. Some texts even speak commonly of a *gabella de la Biga*.

Even the party names are quite revealing. They are not symbols or affirmations of a program, but rather nicknames, words implying derision, mockery, and perhaps disapprobation. There is no direct reference to an external power nor to family names, for the party was a congeries of many families who were on an equal footing. It corresponded to a more vast and complex social milieu in which no clan could make itself omnipotent.

But despite this, the internal structure of the party shows clearly the influence of the family, allies, and the neighbourhood. Mme Battle emphasizes the importance of the clientele and shows that before the *Sindicato de los Tres Estamentos* was established, the guildsmen "gravitated in the orbit of powerful gentlemen". They found this an effective protection as they furthered their businesses or functioned as officeholders. These men formed a vast clientele, called significantly *homes de casada*, who gave their votes to the party in council elections and helped it in the frequent struggles between clans or *bandos*.[26] But after 1452 and the rise of the *Sindicato*, the great families lost this following and with it much of their social prestige and political power. Some guildsmen took seats on the council. The basis for choosing councillors was changed in a development marking the end of a political system. It corresponds to the rise of the *popolo* in Italy, which likewise had sounded the death knell for the power of many great families.

The two parties were absolutely intransigent. Once battle had been joined, neither party could accept in principle an accord or a division of power. Such arrangements were realized only twice, and then briefly: in November 1451, when two merchants of the *Busca* were chosen councillors, but this encouraging development was not pursued; and in 1453, when Galceran de Requesens vainly attempted to mediate between the two factions. This intransigence seems to have been stronger among the *Busca*, whose members thought that they had a divine mission and paraded their motto "Offence to men rather than to God".

The intervention of royal authority is also apparent in Barcelona. The representatives of the Aragonese crown evidently tried to work against the local magistrates to create pretexts for reducing the city's liberty. This is why the *Busca* were protected before they came to power by Alfonso V the Magnanimous and especially by Galceran de Requesens, his governor in Catalonia. This alliance remained firm while the *Busca* were in power under Alfonso V and his brother and successor, Juan of Navarre. The parties in turn became involved in the internecine quarrels of the royal family and did not hesitate to intervene directly, even at the cost of upsetting their alliance within the city. In the winter of 1461 the *Biga* and a substantial faction of the *Busca* agreed to support prince Carlos of Viana, who was then in prison on the orders of Queen Juana Enriquez.[27]

But Mme Battle's conclusions far transcend the study of these external features, with which she was not fundamentally concerned. Her purpose was rather to determine the options and the political and social milieus of these parties. Her observations concern two principal points. She views the two parties as opposed both politically and ideologically. Her conceptual framework involves a sort of considered Manicheism, juxtaposing the forces of good and evil. The *Biga* were the oligarchical party, attached to its privileges and stamped with immobility. The party was composed of men of privilege, even oppressors who could profiteer from a favourable situation. Their only political line was terribly conservative, egotistical and blind to contemporary realities. In contrast, the *Busca* were the reform party. Mme Battle sees their origins in a movement which had drawn up a program to reform the municipal government as early as 1386.[28] The *Busca* were the direct descendents of this 'reform group'. And accordingly could represent themselves as endowed with every good intention and every virtue. They accused their adversaries of flouting the city's liberties, conducting illegal elections, displaying flagrant immorality in public administration, tolerating debasements of the coinage, imposing extraordinary taxes, particularly on food, on the people, and being responsible for commercial decline and many disorders in the city.[29] The *Busca* showed noble aspirations when they came to power:[30] they reformed local government by broadening the electoral base and refusing to base their power on a minority; they reduced taxes and secured the food supply; they upgraded the coinage;[31] and they instituted economic protectionism by forbidding the import of foreign woollens.

Certain decisive judgements and peremptory condemnations lend some credence to this analysis. But Mme Battle goes too far:

> Responsibility does not rest upon the two parties equally nor upon the monarchy, but almost entirely upon the oligarchy. Its pride kept it from admitting its *Busca* rivals to a share of power or comprehending how well suited the *Busca* program was to the new age. Its exclusive concern with defending class privileges and not those of the community at large led it to oppose the normal processes of social evolution.[32] We must understand that this intransigence was imposed upon these aristocrats by their selfish attitude. They could not comprehend the revolutionary but just claims of the popular estates.

This is a drastic oversimplification which distorts historical reality and ignores subtleties. The idea that the *Busca*'s intentions were sublimely noble is particularly absurd. They were as interested in seizing power as the others. The self-righteous accusations of the *Busca* against the party in power were standard practice and should not be taken seriously, for such diatribes from the opposition party appear everywhere and at all times. Indeed, Mme Battle herself shows that the members of the *Busca* were divided and that some allied with the *Biga*. It is doubtful if this alliance was caused to any great extent by the imprisonment of the prince of Viana; the threat posed by a new political force, the *Estamentos*, seems much more likely. Both parties were thus political opponents of a new institution, the 'people'.

Mme Battle also thinks that the opposition between the two parties was derived essentially from economic and social causes. As the very title of her thesis indicates, she emphasizes the economic milieu and the depression. The crisis was felt deeply in all areas of human endeavour, and was the most powerful historical force of the moment, causing general discontent, unemployment, and food shortages. Such problems forced the authorities, according to the author, to defend local industry by protective tariffs. But this in turn provoked the uprisings of the *remença* peasants, supported by some persons in the town and roundly condemned by others.

Mme Battle quite legitimately wants to show that the conflict between the two parties was not, as an earlier generation of historians had maintained, merely a monarchical plot to weaken an overly independent town, but was something much more complex in which social rivalries were deeply involved. But this laudable aim causes her to bind herself to a rigid scheme involving struggle between two well defined social and economic entities or 'classes'. She uses the word 'class' systematically throughout her work in reference to knights, landholders, merchants, artisans, and the lesser folk. The party struggle was a class struggle. She even considers the *Biga* a social class. The earlier 'reform' party is transformed without further ado into the 'popular' party. These expressions are her deliberate creations, for they are not used in the sources. Readers who lack her preconceived ideas obviously may find her choice of words very arbitrary. Actually, this simplistic scheme cannot even stand the test of the facts presented by Mme Battle herself in her various studies; they indicate that the social basis of party recruitment and the bonds within the aristocracy were bafflingly complex.

To be sure, the *Biga* included some rich landlords who derived considerable income from rural domains and town houses. Certain families of this party, such as the Fivaller, the Marimon, and the Llull, traced their ancestry as far back as 1200. But a more numerous group, such as the Carbo, the Sapila, the Savall, and the Seatrada, had become prominent more recently, in the fourteenth century. The social milieu was thus extremely varied. Even the party lists which Mme Battle established for 1433 show lawyers, jurists and notaries in the *Biga*, such as the Dezplà, the Vilatorta, the Fevrer and the Sesanases. The *Biga* contained eight merchant families in 1433, the *Busca* eleven. Both also contained guildsmen and artisans – fifteen in the *Biga* and twenty in the *Busca* for that year. They included a spice merchant, a carpenter, a weaver of woollens, a cobbler, and a blacksmith. The difference in social composition of the two parties was thus minimal.[34]

It seems clear that the *Busca* did not consist entirely of persons in commerce. Mme Battle notes that the 'oligarchical' *Biga* merchants were active in certain trades. They were wealthy importers of Oriental spices and of English and Italian cloth, while the *Busca* merchants were often captains of industry who controlled the local trade in Catalan wool. The *Biga* thus leaned toward international trade, while the *Busca* favoured a protectionist policy bolstered by tariffs which would keep foreign textiles out of the city. They also wanted devaluation of the coinage, which would facilitate the sale of their own cloth in other areas. In short, they acted in their own financial interest, not on behalf of the 'people'. The conflict thus involved wealthy merchant entrepreneurs whose interests clashed on one important point.[35]

The social milieu of the *Busca* was thus so composite that to view the party as comprising merchants exclusively is an oversimplification. Some *ciudanos honrados* were in this political group, for the party leaders were staunchly aristocratic: the Deztorrent, the Pallarès, the Torro, the Esquerit, and others.

This narrow circle of gentlemen was the nucleus which directed *Busca* policy. They were joined by the Gueran, Manresa, Sirvent, Oliler and others, . . . together with the barristers Boquet, Soler and similar persons, and the notaries Plana and Matella . . . and other persons holding various offices.

Yet Mme Battle dismisses these great *Busca* aristocrats as *renegados*.[36] I think that the texts which the author provides for us can lead to radically different conclusions. The participation of great aristocrats and noble or wealthy bourgeois, whose power was increased by public offices, kindred bonds and alliances, of men of considerable social prestige in an opposition party and in political or social revolt can occasion surprise only among those who remain bound to a simplistic and dualist view of social structures and struggles. Historians who are still attached to the naive idea of 'class' struggle have not been willing to admit this internal division of the aristocracy, even the oligarchy. They call leaders of insurrections or opposition parties 'renegades' or 'turncoats', such as Etienne Marcel at Paris, the Arteveldes at Ghent, and Salvestro de' Medici at Florence. But these leaders were not traitors to their 'class'. They remained firmly anchored in their family and social milieu. They were always in important positions within their clans and were often among the leaders. They did not break their family ties and might contract excellent and profitable matrimonial alliances for themselves and their children. The same is true of the *ciudadanos honrados* of the *Busca*, particularly the Deztorrent, to whom Mme Battle has devoted a precise analysis which enables us to place them very exactly in their social milieu.[37]

The elder Pere Deztorrent was on the Council of One Hundred between 1432 and 1450, with a few interruptions. This was before the victory of the *Busca*, and he thereafter held various important posts in the *Busca* regime. He married the daughter of a wealthy merchant, and his brother Francesco became a knight. Francesco bought the castellany of Mataro for 1,100 pounds and was twice King Alfonso's emissary to Castile and once to Tortosa, accompanied in this case by a squire, a page, and an opulent train with horses and ceremonial dress. But this knight continued to profit from international commerce and to invest some money from his lands in arming a ship. The two brothers remained very close, and the one paid the other's debts after the death of their father.

The younger Pere Deztorrent was also very active in politics. He was taken prisoner by the Genoese in 1435 at the battle of Ponza. He was often on the Council of One Hundred with his father between 1444 and 1460. He was one of the most active *Busca* party leaders, a career which rewarded him with the highest functions and responsibilities by 1453. He was also one of the most intransigent of his faction in the party quarrels, and refused to participate in the settlement of 1462 with the *Biga*. Persisting in his hostility, he organized the plot of San Matias and was condemned and executed.

But the wealth of the younger Pere Deztorrent made him a great aristocratic landowner with ties to the nobility. He owned annuities on land, particularly on the island of Majorca.[38] He never broke with his family, and after his execution they had him interred in the Deztorrent tomb in the chapel of San Tomas in the Dominican church of Santa

Catalina. His four brothers held very different social and professional positions, but all were undeniably aristocrats. Francesco, who belonged to the Order of Hospitallers, captained the Banyuls 'command post' of that Order in the diocese of Elna in Roussillon. Juan, a merchant, was consul of the Catalans at Palermo. Luis was a doctor of laws who became counsellor or chief administrator of the professional association of Barcelona jurists in 1460. Jaime married the daughter of a *cuidadano honrado*. His elder daughter, Clara, married a knight who was lord of Montornès in the Vallès, while the youngest, Catalina, entered a convent.

This brief discussion of the social situation of a leading Busca family undoubtedly shows that they belonged to the upper aristocracy. They had ties with the knightly world and can in no way be contrasted to the *Biga*, who as we have seen were also merchants. As in Italy, it is thus impossible here to posit an overly rigid social scheme. Such a view is conformist and outdated.

Mme Battle's social study of course extends our knowledge beyond previous analyses, which described only monarchical activity and intrigues. It enables us to emphasize the existence of clienteles and the importance of family ties and particularly of economic developments. It contributes the elements which allow us to elucidate the socio-economic and professional circumstances and levels of fortune of the various partisans. She furnishes extremely interesting information, but her approach remains bound to systems and *a priori* concepts which often contradict the information presented in her studies themselves. All in all, our investigation of the quarrel between the *Biga* and the *Busca* shows once more the extreme complexity of the origins, characteristics, and institutions of political parties in the medieval West. Certain aspects stand out particularly clearly: the domination of an aristocracy which was at once warrior and mercantile, the primary role of tightly knit prominent families and their clienteles, a dualistic political system concentrating on the acquisition and maintenance of power, a fixation which logically entailed intolerance and a refusal to share power with opponents.

Other towns of the West?

Comparative elements for the late communal period are certainly
sparse. The powers of the state and of the guilds, together with the early
appearance of political arrangements greatly resembling the Italian
popolo, either kept the party system from developing or rapidly
terminated it. We can only cite a few examples, from different parts of
Europe, which suggest that such a system may have existed elsewhere.

Political and social life at Toulouse between 1220 and 1250 was much
affected by memories of the struggle against heresy and the
Albigensian crusade. The intellectual and political climate of the city
was thus quite unique. Like many towns of Languedoc and the French
Midi, the town was divided into two topographical units which were
resolute rivals and even mutually hostile: the 'city' around the cathedral,
and the more recent 'suburb'. Political action groups were active in the
town at this time in the guise of politico-religious brotherhoods. The
White Fraternity, founded and controlled by the bishop, included
powerful patrician clans and the most prominent men of the city. The
thrust of their struggle was against heresy and usury, two sins which
contemporary minds often confused or assimilated. The Black Fraternity was strongest in the 'suburb'.[39] The Whites brought usurers to trial
and rendered the verdicts themselves. Their armed troops destroyed the
houses of those known to be moneylenders. To be sure, the texts do not
mention 'parties', but political action groups similar to the later parties in
Italy were here naming themselves after colours and placing themselves
under the protection of a patron saint.

At Louvain, all the political and administrative offices were divided
during the last two centuries of the Middle Ages between two very
powerful groups, the van den Blankarden and the van den Colveren.
These were clans or, to use the term employed here and in all lands of
Germanic Europe, races (*Geschlechten*), but they were also political
parties. They were alliances of several great families under the
hegemony of the most powerful. The word 'races' and the fact that they
bore family names suggests that the kindred bond was the determining
factor. The dwellings of the two groups were not concentrated in
compact quarters, but were dispersed in several blocs. But their rural
lands did show areas preferred for investment, for one clan was strong
northwest of the town and the other southeast. The two tracts were
separated by vast forests. This fact underscores the intimate bonds
between rural and urban life both socially and politically.[40]

The Netherlands experienced a similar party struggle which had no firmly defined economic basis. This was between the *Hoeken* (hooks) and the *Kabeljauwen* (cod), names which were used only after the parties had been in existence for nearly half a century. When William III of Holland, Zeeland, and Hainaut died in 1345, his administration was controlled by the partisans of Willem van Duvenvoorde, a bastard son of a member of the younger branch of an aristocratic family. Willem had consolidated his power by moneylending and land investment, and he was one of the greatest 'private' landlords in the Low Countries when he died, with an income higher than that of many princes. He exerted considerable influence over the young William IV, but when that prince was killed later in 1345, his power began to wane. His success had aroused envy among the older established Dutch nobility, and this helped to provoke his opponents into forming the first *Kabeljauw* union. Most of his important possessions were near Breda; family ties in this area, which he fostered, formed the basis of his *Hoek* party, and many of these families had ties with the merchants of the towns, notably Dordrecht, Middelburg, Leiden, Haarlem and Zierikzee. The *Kabeljauwen* were thus nobles excluded from the Duvenvoorde government, farmers who had been taxed severely to finance Willem's many wars, and some townsmen who did not want to be held accountable for the count's debts. The *Hoeken* were the lesser nobles, some of the townsmen, and the Duvenvoorde party in general. But the towns were divided, and party allegiances could vary with a change of magistracy.

Politics in the Netherlands became quite involved between 1345 and 1356. The count, anxious to divest himself of the Duvenvoorde party, tended to favour the *Kabeljauwen*, but after Willem died he had little to fear from the *Hoeken*, some of whom began to reappear in his entourage. There was comparative peace until the 1390s, despite the resentment of some *Kabeljauwen* to sharing power with their opponents. The party names appeared in the 1380s: *Kabeljauw* perhaps from the blue–grey livery worn by the count's partisans and in any case a name of derision, while the *Hoeken* were those who would catch the cod.

When the quarrels broke out again, changes in the towns played a role. There was a tendency for town patriciates to close themselves off from guildsmen in the late fourteenth century. The count began leaning increasingly upon urban patriciates composed of *Kabeljauwen* and nobles. Open warfare broke out in late 1392, when the strongly *Kabeljauw* mistress of Count Albrecht was murdered. Although the disorders were soon quieted, unrest was to continue in the fifteenth century over issues surrounding the four marriages of Jacqueline of Bavaria, heiress of Count William VI. Civil war raged off and on between 1417 and 1428, with Jacqueline's uncle and regent favoring the *Kabeljauwen* while the countess sided with the *Hoeken* in an effort to escape this tutelage. The dukes of Burgundy were in fact ruling the Netherlands after 1428, and Duke Philip the Good was adamant that the party names and colours be rooted out. He continued the official favoritism of the *Kabeljauwen*, although he did try to bridge the gap by appointing some *Hoeken* to office.

Thus local circumstances in the Netherlands as elsewhere determined party choices. The quarrel began as court party against outsiders, or older nobility against parvenus. Economic lines began to correspond to party ties only in the fifteenth century in the towns, when the *Kabeljauwen* were usually the wealthy exporters and the *Hoeken* the guildsmen and lesser merchants.[41]

CHAPTER TWO

Parties of nobles.   Mountain and border regions

Outside the towns proper and their rural districts, political parties were most likely to develop in areas where a nobility was able to maintain its authority over the mass of mankind and over vast clienteles of subjects and followers. This of course implies a special set of circumstances, including a certain political isolation, absence of a sovereign or at least a disinclination on his part to intervene locally, and thus implicitly the weakness of a central state which acted only sporadically from afar. There was also an economic isolation entailed by an absence of large merchant cities and important currents of trade. Great international or even regional trade routes bypassed the area or only touched its border. We have thus defined a kind of double isolation characteristic of 'marginal' regions.

The social structure of these lands often remained quite singularly marked by the considerable power of the noble clans. The 'solidarities' of the great extended noble families remained extraordinarily strong and effective. The poorest relatives, who had suffered divisions of patrimony or small inheritances, were still considered noble and did not decline into the peasant yeomanry. The class was so large that it constituted a veritable 'popular nobility',[42] which could provide a submissive, hungry clientele for the masters of the lineage, clan or party.

The Basque country of Castile is a good example. This extraordinary political unit, with a unique social structure, constituted the Vizcaya, which was part of the kingdom of Castile. Nobles were certainly more numerous here than in other parts of the West, with the possible exception of a few valleys in Navarre. Nearly all free men could claim membership at some level of a noble clan. The Vizcaya country was also characterized by the considerable power of various types of social groups and organizations, such as the peasant communities of the *anteiglesias* and noble lineages.[43] Bilbao, a port for the iron trade, was the only important town. The other communities (*villas*), the port or merchant villages, were smaller and could not expand. Thus the region remained essentially rural. Royal intervention was rare until the time of the 'Catholic Kings' Ferdinand and Isabella. Finally, the area was totally isolated politically, socially, and even ethnically. No noble from outside the region held land there, and a pretext commonly used elsewhere for external intervention was absent in the Vizcaya. The converse was also true, for no Vizcaya noble held land outside the area. These noblemen evidently did not follow the kings of Castile during the dynastic conflicts nor even during the Reconquista against the Moslems in southern Spain. They scarcely served the crown at all and received no benefits from it.

It is perhaps no coincidence that armed party conflicts among noble *bandos* in this region were even more spectacular than elsewhere and attained a virtually legendary renown. Two famous *bandos* fought each other during the fifteenth century, the *onacinos* of the *Onaz* party and the *gamboinos* of the *Gamboa* party.[44] These words are of uncertain origin. Some authors claim that they were nicknames deriving from a quarrel which had broken out at the May Day celebration between the Alava and Guipuzon brotherhoods. The issue was whether the heavy torches given in oblation should be held at the top (*gamboa*) or the base (*onaz*). Others attribute the names to two villages which once fought each other, Onate and Ulibarri Gamboa, which were held by the rival Guevara and Mendoza clans.

Actually, the conflicts and clans had undoubtedly been present earlier, and the parties had borne other, now forgotten names. The old names of two famous *bandos* of the province of Alava in the Vittoria region were sometimes still being used in the fifteenth century: that of the Ayales and the Callejas and that of the counts of Haro y Trevino. At other times the Urquitzu party, allied with the Abendano, and the Muxia, allied with the Butrones, are mentioned with reference to the entire Vizcaya. Their names were unquestionably derived from families.

In this border area an overwhelming urge to compete and dominate

swept everyone away at all times. Men and their clans fought unceasingly to decide "who was the richest" (*quién valia mas*) or "who was
the strongest" (*quién era mas fuerte*). A contemporary author claimed
that the *bandos* were held together only by jealousy, emulation,
swagger and pride. The least significant quarrel between two people in
a marketplace, in a church, or during an assembly could engender acts
of violence which by a series of affronts and reprisals which we can
easily imagine provoked interminable armed conflicts which were
ultimately inspired, as in Italy, by irreconcilable hatred. Every family
was divided between the two *bando* branches.

This situation persisted until the 'Catholic Kings' intervened decisively in the 1480s. They issued rigorous peace ordinances and
instigated numerous trials, whether by summonses to appear before
the royal court or by condemnations. There were even several police
forays. All royal acts of intervention were strongly seconded by the
merchants of Bilbao, together with the armorers and businessmen of
the other ports, who were resolutely opposed to these quarrels which
were threatening the security of trade.

Many aspects of these celebrated *bando* feuds of the Vizcaya are
still obscure. We know nothing of the *bandos'* means of recruitment,
their geographical extent nor their internal structures, let alone their
forms of government. We do, however, find that here as elsewhere,
special circumstances favoured the formation and maintenance of
these parties. The extended family constituted the essential framework
of these *bandos*, which were genuine political parties.

The *bando* régime seems to have dominated in other fringe areas of
the Iberian Peninsula. The situation is found even in the Moslem
kingdom of Granada, where the traditions of the Arab and Berber
conquerors remained very strong.[45] Chronicles and other documents
mention many conflicts of this type, but give only a recital of external
events which deprive the historian of any possibility of analysis: in
Aragon in 1402 between the Lunas and the Gurreas; at Zaragoza in
1404 between the Lanozas and the Cerdanes, a conflict which was so
violent that King Martin felt constrained to convene a special session
of the *Cortes* at Maella on 26 June 1404 to ask for special authority to
intervene; and finally at Valencia between the Centellas and the
Soler.[46] These Aragonese *bandos* bore family names, or names which
give a place of origin and which may go back to the foundation of the
party immediately after the Reconquista.

We even find the *bandos* at the very frontier of Aragon and Castile, in the city of Cuenca, where in 1427 the two lineages and family parties which had dominated the city and its environs, the Fernandez and the Rodriguez, concluded a peace by founding a new political fraternity which would transcend all the conflicts, the *Hermandad de los vecinos de Cuenca*.[47] Finally, the feuds of rival *bandos* appear in Estremadura only in the 1480s, but at that time they appear in all the towns as an unshakeable political tradition. Peace was only made feasible when the sovereigns intervened to demand and obtain an exact division of municipal offices between the rival *bandos*. Royal ordinances of 9 July 1473 instituted a new manner of nominating the *regidores* (principal officers of the town) at Caceres: the queen would nominate twenty-four *caballeros* from the 'high' lineage or party and a like number from the 'low' party. Twelve *regidores*, six from each faction, would be chosen by lot from this number. At Trujillo, a long established custom of choosing officials gave half of the twelve major positions to the Altamiranos clan and one-fourth each to the Anascos and the Bejeranos. The latter two groups had been established as the result of a schism within a clan which had earlier opposed the Altamiranos. The royal reform here meant that the officials would no longer be nominated by a party leader from among his allies. Beginning with the reform of 1491, they could be nominated by four electors who were chosen by lot.[48] This obviously gave to these two parties, which had topographical as well as family names, another form of government and perhaps suggests an internal structure which was more complex and less based on family bonds.

At any event, all of these examples, though rapidly and superficially cited, show that entire regions of the Iberian Peninsula, including the villages and towns, experienced a régime of political parties similar to the Italian model, whether permanently or only during periods of weak royal authority.

Notes to Part IV*

[1] See above, pp. 1ff.

[2] R. Cazelles, Le parti navarrais jusqu'à la mort d'Etienne Marcel, *Bulletin philologique et historique du Comité des Travaux Historiques*, 1960, 2, pp. 839–869.

* Numbers in square brackets refer to the Bibliography.

[3]R. Cazelles, *La société politique et la crise de la royauté sous Phillippe de Valois* (Paris, 1958).

[4]On the regional character and particularly on the social aspect of the recruitment of members of the two parties, see Robin [47].

[5]K.B. MacFarlane, The Wars of the Roses, *Proceedings of the British Academy* (1966), pp. 115ff. Edward IV was famous for his generosity, which drew many retainers to him. When he was living in London, his household slaughtered six cattle daily to feed his protégés and retainers. See A.H. Thomas and I.D. Thoruley (eds.), *The Great Chronicle of London* (1939), p. 207, cited by A.R. Myers, *English historical documents. 1327–1485* (London, 1969). His retainers were often bound to him for life by written contracts called indentures, which detailed all their obligations and the services which they were to render. See A.R. Myers, *The household of Edward IV* (Manchester, 1959); J.R. Lander, Attainder and forfeiture, 1453 to 1509, *The historical journal* (1961), pp. 114–151. For the family ties: J.R. Lander, Marriage and politics in the fifteenth century: the Nevilles and the Wydevilles, *Bulletin of the Institute of Historical Research* (1963), pp. 119–152; R.A. Griffiths, Local rivalries and national politics: the Percies, the Nevilles and the duke of Exeter, *Speculum* (1968).

[6]G. Busson and A. Ledru (eds.), *Actus pontificum Canomannis in urbe degentium* (Le Mans, 1901), pp. 376–378, translated by R. Latouche, *Textes d'histoire médiévale* (Paris, 1951), pp. 236–239.

[7]*Histoire du meurtre de Charles le Bon, comte de Flandre (1127–1128) par Galbert de Bruges*, ed. Henri Pirenne (Paris, 1891); English translation, with an excellent introduction, by James Bruce Ross, *The murder of Charles the Good, count of Flanders* (New York, 1967), based upon the Pirenne edition. The last six paragraphs have been added by the translator at the author's request.

[8]For the above, see H. Dubrulle, *Cambrai à la fin du Moyen Age* (Lille, 1904), particularly pp. 25ff.

[9]Lambert of Hersfeld, *Annales, M.G.H., Scriptores*, folio, V, 211; translated by O.J. Thatcher and E.H. MacNeal, *A source book for medieval history* (1905), pp. 585–586. Cited by J.H. Mundy and P. Riesenberg, *The medieval town* (Princeton, 1958).

[10]L. Musset, A-t-il existé en Normandie au XIe siècle une aristocratie de l'argent? *Annales de Normandie* (1959), pp. 286–299; S. Deck, Les marchands de Rouen sous les ducs, *Annales de Normandie* (1956), pp. 245–254.

[11]Y. Renouard, Le grand commerce des vins de Gascogne, *Revue historique* (1959), pp. 261–304; M.K. James, The fluctuations of the Anglo-Saxon wine trade during the fourteenth century, *Economic history review* (1951), pp. 170–196; and The non-sweet wine of England during the fourteenth and fifteenth centuries. Unpublished thesis (1952).

[12]J. Bernard, *Navires et gens de mer à Bordeaux* (Paris, 1968), 3 vols.

[13]C. Bémont, *Simon de Montfort comte de Leicester* (Paris, 1884); J.P. Trabut-Cussac, Le Prince Edouard et le rivalités municipales à Bordeaux, *Revue historique de Bordeaux et du département de la Gironde* (1952), pp. 9–23; P. Capra, L'administration de l'Aquitaine Anglo-Saxonne au temps du Prince Noir. Unpublished doctoral thesis (Paris, 1971).

[14]J.P. Trabut-Cussac and Y. Renouard, *Histoire de Bordeaux*, II (Bordeaux 1965), pp. 97ff., 349ff.

[15]F. Funck-Brentano, Les luttes sociales au XIVe siecle. Jean Colomb de Bordeaux,

Le Moyen Age, 1897, pp. 288–320; C. Bémont, Les troubles et les factions à Bordeaux de 1300 à 1330 environ. Documents inédits, *Bulletin philologique et historique du Comité des Travaux Historiques et Scientifiques* (1915), pp. 121–180. The numbers of the provisions given here follow the Bémont edition.

[16]*Ibid.*

[17]*Ibid.*, Articles 32–35.

[18]There are many references in the memorandum of 1329, particularly Article 15: et autres de la compaigne et maynée dudit Johan Colomb.

[19]Ernaud Johan was *de l'ostel et des robes dudit Johan Colomb*, as was William de La Molière, Articles 15, 56.

[20]C. Carrère, *Barcelone, centre économique à l'époque des difficultés. 1380–1462*, 2 vols. (Paris, 1967).

[21]J.F. Cabestany Fort, Aportacion a la nomina de los 'ciutadans honrats' de Barcelona, *Documentos y estudios* (1962), pp. 9–61.

[22]C. Battle, La ideologia de la 'Busca'. La crisis municipal en el siglo XV, *Estudios de historia moderna* (1955), pp. 187–188.

[23]J. Sobrequès i Callico, La bandera de Barcelona durant la campanya de 1462, *Estudios de historia medievales*, I (1969), pp. 85–117; and Nuevos datos sobre la guerra civil en el Ampudàn y la Selva durante el verano de 1462, *Anales del Instituto Estudios gerundeses*, XIX (1968–1969), pp. 5–64.

[24]See above, n. 22, and C. Battle, Una familia barcelonesa: los Deztorrent, *Anuario de estudios medievales*, I, (1964), pp. 471–488.

[25]C. Battle, *La crisis social y economica de Barcelona a mediados del siglo XV*, 2 vols. (Barcelona, 1973). *Resumen* published by the Instituto de Estudios medievales (Barcelona, 1975).

[26]M.T. Ferrer i Mallol, Lluites de bàndols a Barcelona en temps del rei Marti l'Humà, *Estudios F. Soldevilla* (Barcelona, 1969), pp. 75–94.

[27]Battle, Deztorrent, pp. 478–479.

[28]C. Battle-Gallart, La proyectada reforma del Gobierno municipal de Barcelona (año 1386), *Congreso de Historia de la Corona de Aragon*, III (Barcelona, 1962), 143–152.

[29]Battle, Ideologia, pp. 175, 182.

[30]*Ibid.*, pp. 189, 195.

[31]The coinage was in fact debased, not strengthened. The rate of the silver *croat* went from fifteen to eighteen pence, so that each penny was worth less. In reference to this measure, Mme Battle speaks of *devaluacion monetaria* (compare the *Resumen* noted above, n. 25). This measure must be juxtaposed to that of 1426, which in fact led to an upward revaluation, for the *croat* went from eighteen to fifteen pence. At any event, it is by no means certain that a devaluation would favour the 'people', and it certainly did not aid the journeymen of the trades.

[32]Battle, *Resumen*, p. 15.

[33]Battle, *Ideologia*, p. 174.

[34]*Ibid.*, pp. 167ff.; *Resumen*, p. 9.

[35]See also J. Sobrequès, i Callico, "Aspectos economicos de la vida en Barcelona durante la guerra civil catalana de 1462–1472 (los gastos municipales de 1462–1465), *Cuadernos de historia economica de Cataluña* (1969–1970), pp. 215–280.

[36]Battle, *Resumen*, p. 12.

[37]Battle, Deztorrent.

[38]Compare J. Sobrequès i Callico, La fortuna d'un mercader de Barcelona al segle XV: les rendes de Nicolau Bruguera, *Cuadernes de historia economica de Cataluna* (1968–1969), pp. 163–168.

[39]Mundy [44, p. 137].

[40]M. Tits, L'evolution du patriciat louvaniste, (Louvain, 1957).

[41]Convenient summary in H.P.H. Jansen, *Hoekse en Kabeljauwse twisten* (Bussum, 1966). The author thanks the translator for adding this section on the Dutch parties.

[42]On this point, see Heers [31, pp. 22–31].

[43]See exposition by J.A. Garcia de Cortozar, *Vizcaya en el siglo XV* (Bilbao, 1966), pp. 303–321. This work gives a bibliography of the Spanish literature on the *bandos*.

[44]J.C. de Guerra, *Onacinos y gamboinos. Rol de banderizos vascos con la mencion de las familias de Bilbao en los siglos XIV–XV* (San Sebastian, 1930), and Onacinos y gamboinos. Algunos documentos inéditos referentes a la epoca de los bandos en el Pais Vasco, *Revista internacional de los estudios Vascos* (San Sebastian, 1935); I. Arocena, *Onacinos y bamboinos. Introduccion a la guerra de bandos* (Pamplona, 1959); J. Caro Baroja, *Linajes y bandos* (Bilbao, 1956).

[45]J. Caro Baroja, *Los Moriscos del reino de Granada* (Madrid, 1957), especially pp. 33–53.

[46]J.E. Martinez Ferrando, Estado actual de los estudios sobre la repoblacion en los territorios de la Corona de Aragon (siglos XII a XIV). *VII Congreso de Historia de la Corona de Aragon* (Barcelona, 1964); S.I. Burns, *The crusader kingdom of Valencia. Reconstruction on a thirteenth-century frontier* (Cambridge, Mass., 1967).

[47]A. Benavadis (ed.), *Memorias de Fernando IV* (Madrid, 1860), II, pp. 75–77.

[48]This information was furnished by the kindness of Miss M.C. Gerbet, who is finishing a thesis on the social structures of Estramadura between 1450 and 1520.

PART V

COLLECTIVE PSYCHOLOGY AND POLITICAL SOCIETIES

We have seen that the social structure of the party had two essential bases: a rather narrow circle of close relatives, persons bound by blood or marriage, and a larger group which included protégés, friends, and clients in alliances of varying extent, complexity, and stability. These two groups can be identified with comparative ease. But superimposed upon them, the political action groups or societies which we have been calling parties relied for support on a much broader population base, on temporary alliances, and on masses of people who were in sympathy or at worst on mobs supporting their activity who were brought into often violent battles. Mob participation was obviously sporadic, uncertain, and capricious, but it was nonetheless an essential element of political power. Any study of how the parties functioned thus necessarily involves a better understanding of the psychological framework and of the manipulation of the mobs of 'lesser people', particularly in the towns. We must also understand their feelings and spontaneous, immediate reactions, the incentives which provoked and moved them, throwing them into the street against an adversary often called only by its leaders' names. Our study can only be a tentative approach, limited to a few specific points, particularly to that essential, even primordial collective sentiment: the competitive spirit.

CHAPTER ONE

Competition. Moral support of the political group

Allies, whether permanent or temporary, were distinguished by their consciousness of belonging to a separate group which was clearly distinct from others, opposed and even hostile to all. The importance attached to the party name, which was often a personal surname, shows this collective consciousness very well. It was a summons amounting to a war cry. The magic of the name, which families, quarters, and parishes also felt, appears strikingly in the parties. The pride and haughtiness of the group, its intolerance and contempt for outsiders and enemies, was similarly demonstrated.

Literary evidence

Party competition, dramas and civil wars, together with the exaltation of the group's virtues, appeals to courage or unity among allies, insults and accusations hurled at adversaries and traitors, appeals for assistance, despair, long controversies over the merits of particular persons – each of these inspired an essentially political literature which was quite original but remains little known. It was extremely important in the civilization of its time and was part of everyone's common cultural heritage.[1] This literature might be serious or satirical, even to the point of burlesque, illustrated by numerous storytellers, moralists and poets whom we consider minor figures, who were themselves often caught up in the party struggle and political activity.

To limit ourselves to several of the more original examples, A. Masséna's study of the sonnets emphasizes several principal themes from the poetry of the political wars.[2] It shows the often virulent invective and the accusations of cowardice launched at one's adversaries. Rustico Filippo, who died between 1291 and 1300, mocked the Guelfs who were returning to Florence after the defeat of Manfred by Charles of Anjou at Benevento in 1266 had assured their safety:

> You fled in fear
> But you may return in absolute security.[3]

Accusations of weakness and cowardice were also hurled at one's own party comrades to stir them to greater valour. Folgore di San Gimignano, who died around 1330, addressed his Guelf allies in this vein:

> You Guelfs have made a shield out of your backsides,
> You are just lions transformed into hares.
> The only time you really spur your horses on
> Is when your faces and the reins are turned toward home.[4]

This literature also shows hatred for traitors, persons who had abandoned their own cause and that of their party. The treason of Castruccio Castracani, tyrant of Lucca, forced Pietro de' Faitinelli into exile in 1337 and inspired these bitter verses:

> Yes, Castruccio, you castrated me when you betrayed Lucca,
> Although I was no sheep,
> And I shall have no more pleasure from my loins.
> I shall always live chastely because of you.[5]

Treason is often the poet's explanation of defeat. Whether true or false, this idea enabled the defeated party to keep its pride. The case of Niccolo de Rosso of Treviso shows this. He studied at Bologna, was entrusted with a diplomatic mission to the pope at Avignon in 1339, and died just after 1348. He was an extremely prolific writer of sonnets, nearly all of them with political overtones.[6]

Political literature also shows the noble's contempt and hatred for the guilds and their master artisans, whose governments were ruled not by prestigious leaders of men, family or party chieftains, but by simple, obscure tradesmen. Pietro de' Faitinelli scornfully castigated the 'popular' government of Lucca. In a long poem of harsh and choppy metre, he mentions thirty-seven masters of the manual trades, each more obscure than his predecessors. They are mentioned only by their proper names, without even a modest family name. They were unknowns, whose professions were subject to ridicule and insults in a real cry of disdain:

> And Truglio and Puglio and Mastino, Farinato,
> Fabin, Britto, and Casato,
> Migliaio and Argomento were the masters.
> Mastrello was a basketmaker and Puccia a dyer,
> And Caper was a carder...
> And Bontar and Pecchio were streetsweeps
> And Nello a man of the lesser people....[7]

The group, whether a party or a town dominated by a party, proclaimed from the rooftops its own superiority over all the rest. The exiles, although often well received in neighbouring, allied towns, emphasized in their sonnets the differences of customs and clothing. The poet then mocked the peculiar outfits, the attachment to certain sartorial fashions which he found ridiculous. Folgore di San Gimignano wrote from his exile at Pisa:

> You are rather squirrels than ermines
> You other counts, knights and squires of Pisa,
> And by the care with which you choose your hair styles
> You think that you will gain superiority over the Florentines.[8]

Political literature was a specialized but also diverse literary genre which was not limited to appeals to hatred. The poets sang of inspired combats and tried to unite and maintain the solidarity of their party faithful and settle their internecine quarrels. Such discords, as they often said, were the source of all weaknesses and misfortunes:

> Thus, whether in war or peace,
> You Guelfs are always divided,
> And reason never reigns among you...
> Do you not remember Montecatini,
> And the grieving wives and mothers
> Made widows by the Ghibellines,
> And your fathers, brothers, children and kinsmen....[9]

Or this appeal for internal peace among the Guelfs:

> I cry everywhere 'Courtesy! Courtesy! Courtesy!
> But no one answers me anywhere...
> For we are all descendants of Adam and Eve.[10]

This appeal for concord was obviously directed only to the members of one party, to enable them to fight their adversaries more efficaciously and to put the odds in their favour.

Other sonnets justify the political choice and the action undertaken and express the hope of ultimate triumph. They also affirm the good faith of the partisans and the superiority of the suzerains who protected them and fought beside them. Merely citing some of the titles which A. F. Masséna gives to various sonnets in his collection conveys an excellent idea of the political involvements of this time:

> As long as Charles was ruling, no prince could come to Italy to assume the imperial crown.
> No, the Angevin will not dare oppose Alfonso of Castile!
> Woe unto him who dares oppose Charles of Anjou.
> The pros and cons of a new imperial candidate.
> Oh, that a lord would come from Germany to put Charles to flight.

The controversies, justifications and discussions, whether reasonable or passionate, between the spokesmen of the political factions moreover gave rise to a very special poetic genre in the form of sonnets which were undoubtedly heirs of certain classical rhetorical exercises. These were the *tenzioni*, the Italian version of the French literary *combats* of the same period. The word *tenzioni* was used by the poets themselves from that time (*ma i' non voglio con voistare a tenzione*),[11] and A.F. Masséna devotes several parts of his collection to the *Tenzioni politiche fiorentine* (*tenzione tra Orlanduccio Orafo e Pallamidesse di Bellindote del Perfetto*; *tenzione tra Monte Andreà e Schiatta di Messer Albizzo Pallavillani*; *tenzione tra Monte Andreà e un ignoto*; *tenzione tra ser Cione Baglioni e Monte Andreà*; and especially the famous *tenzione tra Dante Alighieri e Forese Donati*).[13] These poems were in the form of debates and exchanges of arguments. Each contestant spoke in turn, either in two or three verses or in an entire sonnet. All these poems reflect a passionate interest in contemporary affairs. The authors garnished their verses with many allusions, direct or veiled, to the great personalities of the day, to competitors for the imperial throne or for the right to rule Italy: Manfred, Conradin, Charles of Anjou, Richard of Cornwall, and finally Rudolf of Habsburg, who was recognized by Pope Gregory X in 1274 and who was expected as a result to come to Italy.

Another literary genre which is invaluable for the study of political mores is the portrait of the partisan: an often strongly biased description of the manners of the passionately involved party man, *arrabiato*. A good example is Fastel, the enraged Guelf described by Rustico Filippi, a sworn enemy of the Ghibellines who "harangued people on the square day in and day out".[14] Such literary exercises, whether affected and artificial or spontaneous outbursts, show a strong party feeling and a collective sense of belonging to a political group which was engaged in a continual struggle. This collective consciousness frequently provoked fierce hatreds which extended to entire groups.

Religious feeling: the case of the Pataria of Milan

The spirit of competition was also fed by another collective conscious-ness, that of belonging to the same spiritual community, the seamless web of Christendom whose honour and truth had to be defended. Some of the political sonnets which we have already discussed were veritable professions of faith which sometimes contained a sort of ideological statement, almost invariably in favour of the Church. The Guelf poets proclaimed their fidelity to Christ and the pope. Niccolo del Rosso said that his stance was dictated neither by a bellicose temperament nor partisan hatred, but rather by a desire to fight the enemies of the pope and Christ:

> I am not such an extreme Guelf
> That I want others to suffer disgrace or damage
> In the name of the party...
> But I nonetheless see that the Ghibellines,
> Enemies of the pope, who is vicar of Christ,
> Tyrannize their enemies by force.

Another sonnet, whose astrological allusions are quite unusual, recal-led how Italy had been joyous (*tutta d'oro*) under Jupiter's shadow, far from Saturn's influence. Then the misdeeds of the emperor Henry VI were vigorously condemned (*allor sfreno del labirinto il toro*). He had spilled Guelf blood unjustly and had dared provoke a confrontation with the Church (*che la Cronce non cura né Deo teme*). Niccolo del Rosso then emphasized the service of God:

> My realm is not of this world,
> Christ could say. It is also a sacrilege
> To offend his vicar.[15]

The concept of total collective responsibility also led partisans to drive out the foreigner or the heretic. Such people had to be excluded from the neighbourhood if not the community. This idea also nourished a strident religious and political intolerance, exacerbating the hatred between adversaries, which was bad enough anyway. Religious quarrels greatly influenced the political destinies of Italy at various times, particularly during the Investiture Contest and its sometimes dramatic ramifications. It was often hard to distinguish religious from political factions.

The best example of this is undoubtedly the terrible and interminable Pataria affair, a complex conflict with manifold complications. It arose from the confused situation created at Milan by the death of the famous Archbishop Aribert in 1045. Against the new primate, Guido da Velate, an imperial nominee, a strong party was constituted of religious 'reformers', principally laity and secular clergy, together with several young noblemen educated at the abbey of Saint-Bénigne of Dijon, an affiliate of Cluny. There was also a strongly Catharist element in the thought of this party, for that heresy had spread considerably in rural Lombardy. These people had themselves called *Patarini* (a corruption of the word *pannosi*, meaning beggars). They praised moral purity and castigated married priests. The Pataria leaders were the wealthy Nazario, who leased the right to coin money, and three clerics who thenceforth would be very famous: Anselmo de Baggio and Arialdo and Landolfo Cotta. The conflict broke out violently when on 10 May 1057 a religious procession of the archbishop's followers encountered a cortege of men going to the Roman theatre, where Arialdo and Landolfo were scheduled to preach. The town immediately divided into two hostile factions, a condition that would persist for years. The Pataria and the pope were on one side; in 1061 Anselmo de Baggio was elected pope and took the name Alexander II. The other side was the imperial faction, which included the nobles and priests of the cathedral church: "the clerics of the aforementioned church, whose numbers are as infinite as the sand of the sea, incited the captains and the vavasours, who had commercial dealings with the churches and were related to the clerics' concubines".[16] Archbishop Guido da Velate led this party. Excommunicated in 1066, he recruited numerous partisans and placed an interdict on the town in order to prevent the Patarines from preaching. One party was thus based on the archiepiscopal palace and the cathedral, the other on the house of Erlambardo Cotta, the brother of the since deceased Landolfo, the personal envoy of the pope, and on the *canonica*, the private church where Arialdo lived with a little community of reformist priests. From this place there issued innumerable sermons inspired by the Patarines which enflamed the multitudes:

One fine day, commending themselves to God and to the blessed chief of the apostles, they addressed a sermon to the people which was full of divine grace.... Before numbers which were increasing daily, these worthy virtuosos of God vigorously outdid themselves in preaching.... They remained several days to fortify the resolve of the faithful by powerful sermons.[17]

As a result of this preaching, terrible accusations of simony or heresy filled the town. Guido's opponents claimed that he was an illiterate simoniac who kept a concubine, while the cathedral clergy were "bound in the knot of simoniacal heresy". Endless controversies, bloody conflicts, flights, exiles, and even assassinations were the result. In 1067 the body of Arialdo, who was generally assumed to have been murdered on the archbishop's orders, was brought in triumph to the cathedral of Sant' Ambrogio by an enormous crowd. Guido da Velate had to flee, then abdicate. His death in 1072 opened a new period of harsh confrontations. This time, however, they reflected not merely the struggle between pope and emperor, but also a strident particularism which ranged Milan and some of its clergy against Rome. These events are of course well known: thirty years of civil warfare and bloody party conflict sustained by hostile political forces animated by fanatical religious conflict, in the case of one faction at least.

The second phase of this long quarrel is equally interesting for the study of collective psychology and tensions within the various interested groups, but it is less well known and deserves closer attention.[18] In 1102, against the wishes of the Milanese, the pope engineered the election of a new archbishop, Grossolano, who at the time was bishop of Savona. A *parte ambrogiana* then arose which was resolutely hostile to Rome and to the new prelate. The battle between the parties of Rome and Sant' Ambrogio was joined immediately with excommunications, interdicts, and accusations of simony. One leader of the *Ambrogiani* was the priest Liprando, an aged Patarine who had long been involved in Milanese party warfare. While celebrating mass, he dared wear the *subcinculum*, a sacerdotal ornament granted by Rome. Since Liprando's deed symbolically proclaimed the illegitimacy of Grossolano's election, a strange conflict arose to seize this symbol. To confound his adversaries, Liprando agreed to undergo judgement by fire. His followers erected a stake, but the other side tore it down. The trial by ordeal finally was held on the square of Sant' Ambrogio. The chronicler's narrative emphasizes the ceremonial character of the proceeding: two days of feasting in the presence of an immense crowd inaugurated the ceremony. Liprando won the trial, and his enemy the archbishop had to flee. The quarrel then died down for a time. When precious relics were discovered in the church of Santa Maria alla Porta, a truce was concluded with a great festival; a parade commemorated this event every year thereafter.

The Milanese parties continued, of course, to squabble until at least about 1110. But during these extremely troubled times, the parties, their alliances and fortunes constantly changed with fluctuations in the pope's attitude, the emperor's intentions, and particularly the imperatives of the ambitious, expansionist policy of Milan, especially during the conflict with neighbouring Lodi. The complexities and infinite vicissitudes of these clashes and the impossibility of discerning a relatively simple and solid line of development are disconcerting. But it seems that at Milan, as in other Italian towns of this period, the bitter Investiture Contest led to the formation of politico-religious parties which were consolidated in their fury against the adversary by their perception of a community of faith. The party leaders and their followers were enthusiastic contestants in this struggle, heroes and champions of their faith. Some became martyrs. Religious sentiment thus established intimate bonds which incited the enthusiast to action and determined collective psychoses of hatred.

Similar situations and conflicts are of course found in other cities of the West in times of religious reform movements and rivalries between clergy of differing persuasion. The troubles at Laon, particularly between 1107 and 1112, offer a good example which can only be explained by the hostility between two strong politico-religious parties. They were not the result of a simple 'communal movement', as has often been claimed, but were rather the products of conflicts between the party of the nobles, led by the house of Coucy, the bishop, and the 'conservative' clergy against the 'reform' party, which was particularly strong among the archdeacons and which included several knights who had just returned from the crusade. The clergy and cathedral chapter were divided between these two factions, one of which was strongly supported by the king of England.[19]

Religious feeling: sermons, processions and excommunications

To change our focus to a somewhat later period, the Dominicans did not invariably pray and speak for peace and party reconciliation. Many were

deeply involved in supporting the pope's friends, particularly in
Tuscany and at Florence. In the 1230s, Piero da Verona, who has already
been noted for his appeals for concord between factions, founded a new
Order in the convent of Santa Maria Novella at Florence, the *Servites* or
Servi di Maria, who followed the Augustinian rule and fought for the
papal cause. It also incorporated lay partisans of Rome into a tertiary
Order of Dominicans and into a company called the *Laudesi di Santa
Maria Novella.* They met each night to sing the *laudi*, religious chants
for the glory of the Church. Similarly and at the same time, the
Cistercians and *Umiliati*, who favoured the pope, established
themselves at San Frediano to preach Rome's cause.[20]

It thus seems evident that at the height of the struggle between the
imperial and papal parties, papal partisans throughout Italy could count
not only on the intervention of His Holiness' armies, but also on spiritual
weapons which could move hearts and minds and set into motion vast
currents of public opinion, collective reactions of passion. The
interminable sermons, processions, threats of proclamations of the
interdict against opposing towns, and excommunication, were all papal
weapons.

These often spectacular actions were intended to abase the enemy,
exclude him from the Christian commonwealth, and isolate him from his
partisans and sometime allies. They are found quite commonly outside
Italy as well. Most struggles between political factions assumed
religious overtones. Much later and under radically different circumstances, we find such interventions designed to strike the collective
imagination of the masses occurring during the famous quarrel between
the Burgundians and the Armagnacs in France. These involved not the
pope, but the clergy of Paris, which was deeply involved in party
warfare. The author of the famous *Journal d'un Bourgeois de Paris sous
Charles VI*, who was undoubtedly a Burgundian churchman, evokes in a
few lines an invaluable portrayal of the political activity of the Parisian
clergy in 1411. The Armagnac and Burgundian parties were then
strengthening their position and extending their activity into the
religious sphere. Both depended for support not on political groups and
institutions, which seem singularly vague and weak to us and in any case
unstable, but rather on religious brotherhoods, which were more
effective because they provided their members with a consciousness of
belonging to a genuine religious party, a community of faith. The
Burgundians founded a confraternity dedicated to Saint Andrew, their
patron, in the parish of St Eustace, the members of which wore garlands

of roses on their heads, of which sixty dozen were distributed.[21] The Armagnacs in turn established the brotherhood of St Lawrence, called the *Blanc Manteau* (White Coat) or "Brotherhood of the Good and True Catholics".[22] The latter designation is very significant, indicating a clear intention of claiming that this party was the only one worthy of belief. Others, who did not belong to the true Christian party, were to be excluded, condemned as heretics or deviates. We recognize the members of the Armagnac party among the "closely knit bands who wore linen on their shoulders, borne across the left arm just as a deacon would wear his vestment in performing the divine services".[23] The allusion to the mass is obvious here, particularly if we remember that the motto of this party, which was always inscribed on a cross, was "the straight way". The conflict was undoubtedly as much religious as political.

The Bourgeois of Paris also describes a public politico-religious ceremony whose purpose was to place the Armagnacs under a curse and exclude them from the Catholic community. His tone is enthusiastic, with no sign of reticence or a feeling of constraint or shame. On the eve of the winter festival of St Martin,

a general procession was made to Notre Dame of Paris. There, before all the people, the entire Armagnac company was anathematized and excommunicated, together with all who gave them aid and comfort. The lords who led this accursed band were mentioned by name: the dukes of Berry and Bourbon . . ..[24]

Excommunicating princes and leaders was nothing new, but the collective and anonymous excommunication of an entire group was much more significant, for spiritual excommunication was thus striking all members of the opposing faction indiscriminately. The sin was no longer a personal action, but simple membership in a party, which now ceases to be a purely political choice and assumes the character of a religious and moral act. The concept of moral responsibility was forcefully asserted: the individual became part of the pressure group in which he was active, sharing its risks and rewards. The involvement was spiritual as well as political: all forms of collective solidarity were united here.

The clergy used every kind of theatrical trick to play on the spirit and the imagination. The procession of 1411 which we have mentioned above took place on the day of a solemn religious ceremony, the festival day of a venerated patron saint. The shameless use of such a weapon undoubtedly occurred frequently, for our Bourgeois showed no trace of self consciousness in adding that "similar processions and excommunications had been tried against this false band two or three times previously".

The sanction also included various ecclesiastics, such as "the archbishop of Sens, the brother of the aforementioned Montaigu". Several monks were preaching quite actively on the Armagnac side, for among the anathematized was one "Augustinian friar named Jacques le Grant, who was the most misguided of all." The spiritual milieu and the support of the clergy was thus involved too.

These manifold religious developments appear clearly in these few lines of the *Journal d'un Bourgeois de Paris*. The party was no longer simply a tactical alliance for political purposes, whose sphere of competence was limited to overt acts. The entire person was subsumed in the party, down to the most private beliefs. The partisans were constantly sustained by religious or para-religious assistance ("all those giving them aid and comfort"). The Bourgeois of Paris has a virtually spontaneous intellectual reaction which was perhaps subconscious but the more revealing for that very fact: the enemies were an 'accursed' band. God and religious beliefs were involved.

CHAPTER TWO

The competitive spirit. Festivals and war games

The competitive spirit and the solidarity among members of the political group were also reinforced more materially by various events which established or strengthened social bonds: festivals and quasi-military games, which might with equal accuracy be called sports, which heightened opposition between teams, clans, and factions.

The central position of the festival in medieval culture and its role in social, political and religious life must not be overlooked. It was a very sure means of demonstrating power over the governed, of showing spiritual authority over the faithful, social standing, economic superiority and prestige among the clienteles.[25] It easily evoked a collective consciousness. The festival could incite rivalries which might range from peaceful competition to bloody brawls. It generated collective psychoses and exasperations which led to hysterical outbursts of religious feeling and thus to various spontaneous reactions which were uncontrollable and could be dangerous. It afforded anonymity to foreign or fringe elements of society and as such furthered them.

Festivals and the apotheosis of political power

The affiliation of a community to its leader or prince was often marked by general merrymaking. During royal or princely 'entries', the towns showed their submission by arranging processions of notables and guild masters. Devices manned by people, various allegories, living tableaux and theatrical performances extolled the generosity and good deeds of the sovereign at the town gates, at fountains on the town squares, and at crossroads. The circumstances varied, but throughout the West pretexts for such diversions, with their displays of riches and fine clothing, were created when a conqueror returned in triumph,[26] when newly annexed territories rendered homage, when princely nuptials were celebrated,[27] or when foreign visitors or emissaries were received.[28]

At Venice, brilliant 'political' festivals throughout the year punctuated the ordinary humdrum routine of life and recalled the victories and glorious days of the past. Every 1 February the town commemorated the deliverance of some Venetian girls who had been enslaved in the tenth century by Slav pirates from Istria as they were being married in the cathedral of San Pietro in Castello. The ceremony was called the *Marie*, and was only ended in 1379. Twelve girls laden with jewels from the treasury of St Mark began by hearing a solemn mass in the basilica. Then, accompanied by the doge, they traversed the grand canal as far as Santa Maria Formosa, whose parishoners were said to have been instrumental in avenging the original wrong. On Ascension Day the doge celebrated his symbolic marriage with the sea to commemorate the departure of Pietro II Orseolo for Dalmatia in 1000 and the victory of the Venetian galleys over Frederick Barbarossa's fleet in 1173. During this ceremony the doge, mounted on the ship of state, threw his gold ring into the sea. On Maundy Thursday the Venetians celebrated their victory over the patriarch of Aquileia in 1162, when the latter had opposed the Venetian patriarch of Grado. On that day the patriarch of Aquileia sent to Venice a tribute of a bull and twelve fat pigs, recalling his capture and that of twelve of his canons by the doge Michael II Vitale. The pigs were slaughtered in the Piazzetta di San Marco by the smiths and the butchers. Finally, Venice celebrated with pomp the anniversary of the conquest of Constantinople, which had created its eastern empire in 1204. This ceremony was a triple anniversary, for it also commemorated the failure of the uprising led by Baiamonte Tiepolo on St Vitus' Day 1310 and the condemnation of Marino Falieri on St Isidore's Day, 1355.[29]

Even religious festivals, particularly those of the patron saint, assumed strong political overtones in the great conquering cities. St Mark's Day and Palm Sunday at Venice were highlighted by magnificent processions, sumptuous corteges which were both religious and political in design:

eight standardbearers with silk flags embroidered in gold, white, green, blue and red; then came heralds with their silver trumpets and fife players covered from head to toe in red; magistrates, ambassadors, and finally the doge under a gilt parasol, with the emblems of sovereignty borne on a cushion before him.[30]

The festival of St John the Baptist was celebrated similarly at Florence. Oblations given in homage to the town by allied or subject lords and cities were ostentatiously and haughtily borne in solemn procession: the great ornamental wax tapers and the banners.[31] Giovanni Villani reports that this festival of the Florentine *signoria* was particularly spectacular under the tyranny of the duke of Athens, who in 1343 "had it done by the guilds in the ancient manner". The twenty tapers from the castles under the commune's jurisdiction were paraded solemnly through the streets, then "twenty-five textiles or rather standards of gold brocade, and bracelets, hawks offered in homage by Arezzo, Pistoia, Volterra . . . and all the lesser barons and counts of the vicinity". This was a "noble affair and a gorgeous festival". The tapers, banners, and tributes were put on display on the public square of Santa Croce before being brought to the duke's palace and finally offered to St John.[32]

All political power was based on festivals and spectacles. This was true throughout the West, but particularly in the towns of northern and central Italy, which had a stronger Roman heritage in all aspects of social life. As Machiavelli said, "The prince must provide his people with festivals and games at certain times of the year".[33] Princes, tyrants, podestàs and often party leaders deliberately used the festivities and great public spectacles to gain mob approval, just as the Roman emperors had done. The virtues of the celebrated *panem et circenses* had by no means been forgotten. The duke of Athens tried to bolster his sagging prestige and popularity by organizing great festivals at the Easter celebrations in 1343 for the citizens as well as his barons, constables, and men at arms. He arranged several games, lasting for some days, on the square of Santa Croce. But Villani, who was quite smug about the failure of the duke's efforts, says that "few citizens played there, for the duke's demeanour had already begun to displease both the great and the *popolani*".[34] The duke made a renewed effort to get popular sympathy and support by Mayday games. This time he appealed to the lesser folk, whom he called upon to forget their cares and to form *brigate* of dancers. But once again he failed to draw large crowds.[35]

The presence of sizeable gatherings at these festivals and games was obviously a reflection of a lord's prestige. Public festivals at Verona also demonstrated the leaders' intentions and reinforced their authority over the citizens and even the inhabitants of the surrounding countryside. In 1242 the podestà Enrico de Egna, trying his best to curry popular favour, "held a great *corte* and festival with certain horsemen and the ladies of Verona, together with other persons from all walks of life at the town hall . . . and the ladies danced on the wooden platforms erected outside the palace".[36] Princely marriages also gave rise to festivals at Verona, particularly on two occasions. In late May 1238, Frederick II simultaneously celebrated the nuptials of his natural daughter Salvaggia with Ezzelino da Romano and those of his natural son with Adelasia de Torres. The chroniclers say that 1,800 persons were invited to these great Ghibelline' festivals, which continued for more than three days in the presence of the emperor himself.[37] Even more splendid ceremonies, if collective memories are any indication, attended the wedding of Cangrande II della Scala with Agnese de Durazzo on 5 June 1343. The celebrations lasted more than five days in the presence of numerous groups of notables who had been invited, accompanied by trains of nobles and retainers. The marquis of Ferrara and Reina della Scala, wife of Bernabò Visconti, came "with a noble and magnificent company of beautiful Milanese ladies", while Francesco da Gonzaga, lord of Mantua, was accompanied "by many other gentlemen and ambassadors of Lombardy".[38]

There was an old tradition at Verona and the other towns of Lombardy of proclaiming or holding a *corte bandita* during the great public festivals. This meant sending a notice, a public *bando*, to neighbouring princes, nobles, lords, and knights.[39] Hence for the military and political festival of 1328, a succession of tournaments, games, banquets, and balls was given in the town by Cangrande della Scala to celebrate his recent victory and acquisition of Padua, which he had so ardently desired. This festival of course provided what most celebrations did, an occasion for wearing finery and reaffirming the leader's prestige, but it also had a clear socio-political significance: it was to culminate in the elevation of thirty-eight followers of the della Scala party to knighthood.[40]

The triumph of the victorious party

Emotional solidarity and *esprit de corps* as well as the competitive spirit were reinforced by the great festivals and spectacular ceremonies which were permeated by a strong aura of religiosity. They celebrated party triumphs with ostentation and insolence. At least in Italy, every victory of a faction was solemnized by great processions or cavalcades in the traditional manner, similar to the strictly religious processions of penitents.

These triumphs exalted the virtues of the victorious clan, a theme which also inspired literary works.[41] They were among the most noteworthy collective spectacles which the town produced. The awe-struck descriptions of the chroniclers and the artists, particularly of the Tuscan school, show us their magnificence and their place in contemporary culture and social life. They were ostentatious displays put on before the entire population. They are better known at Florence from the later Medici period and at Rome from the age of the Borgias, when the festivals, freighted with allusions to the ancient past, sang the praises of contemporary heroes in the manner of Roman emperors.[42] But long before this, victorious party leaders in the Italian towns, particularly the imperialists, held magnificent ceremonies of public rejoicing and triumphal processions. When Frederick II defeated the Milanese and their allies of the Lombard League and the pontifical party, the men of Padua, Treviso, Ferrara, and others, at Cortenuova on 26 November 1237, he organized a magnificent triumphal entry at Cremona, the town nearest the site of his victory. "Frederick, heady with pride from such a remarkably complete triumph, wanted to enter as a conqueror."[43] The *carrocio* or war chariot of Milan, which had been captured on the battlefield, was the central attraction and was placed at the center of the procession. Preceded by many trumpeters, the chariot was drawn by an elephant. In a subsequent imperial triumph it was displayed on the capitol at Rome. The victory cortege also contained a train of prisoners: Pietro Tiepolo, who was later to be hanged, was put on exhibit attached to the Milanese *carrocio* by a rope around his neck, and was followed by a large group of other prisoners.

The victorious parties deliberately instituted annual festivals which were simultaneously public celebrations and thanksgiving services to commemorate their own success or the failure of their adversaries' efforts, which were naturally called treasons. To give only the best example of such victory celebrations in Italy, the masters of the Florentine guilds and the city magistrates decided, after the fall of the duke of Athens on St Anne's Day, 26 July 1343, "that the festival of St Anne should always be considered a second Easter at Florence, to be celebrated by a solemn service and thanksgiving by the commune and all the guilds".[44] With a civic religious cult, public oblations in the form of sacrifices, the triumphal festival symbolized, as did Easter, a resurrection, and we can see clearly the spiritual and religious level on which the city fathers placed their conflicts and their involvements.

Riot at the festival

The festival interrupted the ordinary course of affairs and obviously introduced a disturbing element of varying degrees of seriousness into the town. It was not part of everyday life and was on the peripheries of recognized institutions, accepted hierarchies, and tacitly admitted taboos. It was thus necessarily an occasion of disorders and sometimes even of riots or at least of political activity which could mobilize the mob.

This assumed various forms. Internal and foreign enemies could profit from an element of surprise on the festival day and attack from within or outside the city, which was off its guard, for the inhabitants were assembled and often disarmed, either in their churches, dining rooms, or in street processions, or in the squares viewing the spectacles. All the authorities understood how difficult it was to maintain rigorous discipline to guard against enemies on a festival day. In the little city of Fermo, in the march of Ancona, "the townsmen arranged a celebration " on 23 March 1326 to celebrate the recent agreement with the Church. "Ladies and gentlemen were dancing throughout the town." Their opponents, the Orsini clan, and other "exiled Ghibelline leaders", took advantage of the situation to breach the town walls and set fire to the city hall, where the council was meeting. "And many men of good repute died there from burns or wounds."[45]

Great political figures and party leaders came from Pavia, Lodi, Mantua, Ferrara, the Romagna, and even Tuscany for the imperial coronation of Ludwig of Bavaria in the church of San Ambrogio in Milan in 1327, before the marquis of Montferrat and many nobles and lords. Cangrande of Verona appeared at the head of a redoubtable company of two thousand armed cavalry and five hundred infantry. They were undoubtedly intended to swell his cortege in the parade and to participate in various tournaments and war games. But some authors also say that the knights of the della Scala leader took advantage of the celebration to get into Milan unhindered so that they could attempt a quick coup d'état while the city was being weakened by the internal dissension of the Visconti leaders. At any event, Cangrande was appointed imperial vicar for the entire Verona-Vicenza region during the coronation ceremony.[46] Later that year, Ludwig was recrowned at Rome with great pomp and evidently in a spontaneous and very 'popular' manner, which his partisans had already sponsored in several other places *en route*. When the news reached Pisa, "there was great joy. Certain exiles from Florence and other towns and some of the lesser folk of Pisa were celebrating by running through the streets crying 'Long live the emperor! Death to the pope, King Robert and the Florentines!'". But the town fathers soon regained control of the situation[47] and expelled all the Ghibellines.[48] In so doing, they undoubtedly suppressed an attempt to use the occasion of a festival celebrating the victory of a party leader to seize the city.

The exacerbation of religious sentiment, spiritual solidarities, and intolerance during the festivals was another source of trouble and violent outbursts. The 'outsider' became even more detestable to the group on that day; he was an enemy to be fought. The persecutions of the Jews, during which mobs attacked and massacred these 'outsiders', may of course have been furthered by an unfavourable economic situation, by wartime anguish and particularly by the terrible scourge of the epidemics and devastating plagues. But these persecutions also seem to have resulted directly from the mendicants' sermons and the great religious festivals, particularly when these were accompanied by long processions which mobilized and assembled men and prepared them for action. The Christians attacked the *moreria*, the Moslem quarter and party of Valencia, on the evening of 1 June 1455, the day of the Holy Trinity, while the citizens were celebrating the elevation of a native son to the papacy as Calixtus III. A score of youths (*minyons*) carrying banners, crosses, and tiaras split off from the procession and appeared at the gates of the *moreria*, demanding that the infidels accept baptism. After waiting several days, they resumed the assault on the evening of 5 June, Corpus Christi Day, and this time were victorious.

The mobs were led on by their religious fervor and a veritable panic provoked by the groundless rumour that the Moors were about to make an amphibious landing. Cries of alarm (*Moros vienan*! 'The Moors are coming!') sustained the level of hysteria.[49]

The religious act became a purely political symbol. The general mentality attached special importance to solemn festival days and dated past events in relation to them. A political and military society of San Faustino was established at Brescia in 1200, undoubtedly on that saint's day. It was a 'popular' society which nonetheless had a noble podestà, Count Narisino. When these men expelled their opponents in 1210 after a brutal but fruitless intervention by the emperor, the chroniclers noted, perhaps in a slight distortion of reality, that the victory occurred "about the time of the festival of San Faustino".[50] The saint was playing his role of protector and even party leader. It is in any case very significant that the great victories of the political parties were often won on the day of a religious festival. It was on Christmas night, 1266, that the Florentine Guelfs re-entered their city as conquerors after an unhappy exile of seven years. The symbol of the resurrection was obviously the expression of a considered collective will.

The presence of unaccustomed persons who were difficult to keep under surveillance circulating freely in the city streets also contributed to making the festival an occasion of political activity or unrest. These were interlopers who were normally excluded from political life. From the standpoint of human relations, the festival offered an opportunity to express oneself in what sometimes became a violent deed of vengeance. Most of these people were outsiders drawn to the town by the spectacles: peasants of the environs, but also persons not easily classified who were not part of any well defined social group. They were often beggars or dangerous vagabonds. At the gates of the *moreria* of Valencia in 1455 the small group of youthful leaders were immediately seconded by a band of beggars, ruffians, and adventurers.

On the other hand, it seems clear that the disorders and the social and political activity during the public festivals, when crowds thronged the squares and streets, were often provoked by a very active and aggressive social group whom the chroniclers call the 'youth'. This word did not have its modern connotation of a certain age group in either Latin or the vernacular languages. The *juvenes, damoiseaux* and 'children' of our sources were celibates, persons not yet established in society and were thus suffering from this deprivation, whatever their age may have been. At a time long past, when some families tried to hinder subdivision of the patrimony by exercising stringent control over the number of marriages, younger sons remained single or married late. Marriage was thus a symbolic social triumph. The idea of youth "is thus bound to a situation of social immaturity".[51] Hence bitterness, jealousy and discontent arose, together with a profound social and demographic instability and an enforced leisure which gave rise to mass movements, troubles, and vagrancy. The most spectacular example, which unfortunately has been misunderstood for generations, was the famous Children's Crusade of 1212.

David Herlihy has divided the Florentine population of 1427 into age groups and has appropriately called our attention to the close inter-relationship between social disorders and the great number of young persons, both in a physiological and a social sense, in the city. The mean age of the population was twenty-six in 1427. Half were twenty-two or under, and over half the males were between fifteen and thirty. The age gap between fathers and sons was extraordinarily great, a trait especially marked in the wealthy families where the sons were particularly aggressive and turbulent because they were still subject at a comparatively advanced age to paternal authority. Another obvious trouble spot was the lack of women. There were 116 men to every hundred women in the entire population, and 132 to one hundred in the age group between eighteen and thirty-two. The difference becomes even more important if we consider only the unmarried, for the girls were often married very early to much older men.[52]

Hence there was plenty of opportunity, particularly during public balls and street dancing, for chance conflicts over young ladies which often were bloody and violent and had serious consequences. The ball which led to a party confrontation was a constant theme of the chroniclers and historians of political life in Italy. The most famous example was the bloody ball of the evening of 1 May 1300 at Florence, when the division between Blacks and Whites was beginning to harden. The young people, collateral relatives and lesser clients of the two parties circulated armed and on horseback through the city. That evening, "seeing ladies dancing on the square of Santa Trinità, the parties began hurling abuse and pushing against one another with their horses. This gave the signal for a terrible riot in which many were hurt".[53]

The *Castello d'Amore* was often another occasion of serious conflict provoked by women. This was a somewhat 'courtly' but often brutal game consisting of a simulated assault on a wooden model of a castle by a group of young persons. Girls were imprisoned in the castle. This was a common theme of all medieval courtly literature and became yet another game or test of which the lady was the prize. Troubadour poetry and the great verse epics obligingly describe these castles and assaults in which many allegorical personages might intervene. The actual assaults during the festivals seem to have been peaceful, and the men contented themselves with throwing flowers, perfume, spices or confetti. But group rivalries, the sense of honour, wounded egos and the spirit of competition were often the prelude to very serious conflicts. During a *Castello d'Amore* at Treviso in 1214, a violent quarrel broke out when a Venetian insulted a Paduan youth. The Paduans tore down the pavilion of San Marco, and this began a long war between the two cities.[54]

Festivals and competitions.   War games

Over and above exciting religious feeling, the festival nourished and accentuated the competitive spirit among many social groups and thus by extension between the two parties. For ordinary marches, parades, and secular or religious processions, teams of a sort were formed in the town, squadrons called *brigate* in contemporary documents. They were made up of young people dressed in uniform who claimed that they were the champions or heroes of a political or social group. This occurred particularly often at Florence, where the *brigate* seem to have been a firmly established tradition: "*brigate* and companies of men and women were organized throughout the city to celebrate the entertainments and balls of the calends of May each year".[55] A month before the festival of St John the Baptist in 1331, "two artisan *brigate* were formed at Florence. One was centred on the *Via Ghibellina*, with some three hundred men all dressed in yellow".[56] This *brigata* was thus firmly based on one section of the city and was generally coterminous with the Ghibelline party; as a solidly based and numerous group, was a very real threat both during and after the festival. Another example comes somewhat later from Florence. Six *brigate* were formed in May

1343 during the time of the duke of Athens. "To celebrate the festival among the *popolo minuto*, they danced through the streets" with all members of each *brigata* clothed alike. These *brigate* of dancers were quite an original feature, but they had a firm structure. They too were based on quarters of the city and followed their own leaders. They had names or nicknames, or one might say battle sobriquets, behind which they could reconnoitre and rally their 'fighters'. The strongest *brigata* was in the *città rossa*;[57] it was led by a man called 'emperor'. And as we can easily imagine, Villani notes that "a quarrel broke out between two of these brigate".[58] Under such circumstances, conflicts between rival *brigate* were probably inevitable.

Rivalries and the danger of armed conflict seemed much more serious during genuine war games, when the troops were no longer armed with flowers, as for the *Castello d'Amore*, but with wooden or blunted lances and swords. These games were quite common and occurred frequently. Highly valued by the mobs as some of the choicest spectacles of the city, they were actually confrontations between squadrons of firmly constituted hostile parties. These combats exacerbated hostilities, exalted the collective ego of the group and the desire to conquer and humiliate the adversary, and fed the hatred of the faction which began as a mere rival but soon became an enemy. Such public confrontations occurred frequently throughout the year, and were anything but simple sporting or military exercises, let alone friendly diversions. Followed by the mob, they involved the valour of all. Their social dimension and their repercussions were considerable. The most trifling incident might lead to unforeseen consequences, although totally predictable results were usually bad enough. The game became a street fight in which all partisans, who had been mere spectators at first, intervened to defend their champion. The entire city was carried away on a wave of emotion. The first serious party conflict between the knights and the *popolo* at Piacenza broke out in 1090 under such circumstances: "during a fight ... on a vacant lot between the church of Santa Maria del Tempio and the Arcina road, a certain knight happened to be fighting disgracefully with a footsoldier". When the *populares* saw their man losing, they threw mud and stones at the knights, then began to fight them more seriously with clubs. "When the knights who were present saw this, they injured the footsoldier." A riot broke out, and suddenly "a clamour was heard everywhere". The parties assembled their allies at various points throughout the city, and a general war broke out in towns and countryside which was to last several months.[59]

War games were traditional throughout northern Italy. They occurred regularly in every city on Sundays or at the celebration of great public festivals. The author of the *Annales Cremonenses* speaks of "battles and military engagements" in which the men of the "new town" vied with those of the "upper town" on the main square of Cremona, called the *Bosalurium*.[60] Rolandino of Padua notes that "war games, jousts, tournaments, and other simulated battles were customarily held, with knights clad in the same livery holding horse races and similiar public entertainments".[61] A war game called *bagordare e armeggiare* was often featured on the public squares of Verona. "It consisted principally of noble youths, magnificently attired in the same liveries, weapons and coats of arms riding on horseback, showing their valour by feigning battles with lances and swords."[62] Every Sunday at Pavia armed *societates* or *cohortes* wore cloth-lined wooden helmets, with the insignia of their societies carved or painted on an iron plaque placed in front of the face, and fought with wooden lances.[63] This tradition was still being continued much later, for Villani, writing around 1340, describes such a combat at Modena in 1263. The two factions or squadrons, whom he called Guelfs and Ghibellines, "came to fight an internecine battle on the town square, as is customary in Lombardy".[64] The same word, *battaglia*, is used here to mean both a war game and a real fight.

These games could even become pure spectacles on certain occasions. Bands of armed youths traditionally went to meet princes who had been invited to their city. "They met them along the road ... by feigning a combat among themselves with lance and sword."[65] Such war games were cavalcades in the form of fantasias, tournaments, and jousts. They reinforced, sometimes violently and sometimes dramatically, the hostility between quarters, clans, or parties. Quite often they were the pretexts or occasions of real conflicts in which blood was spilled.

CHAPTER THREE

The competitive spirit.   Insignia. Rallying the forces

In difficult times and even in many aspects of daily life, emotional and spiritual bonds were also exacerbated by emblems which permitted the members of the politico-social group to identify one another, rally support, and especially to fight their rivals and enemies. These insignia varied greatly. Speaking of the party clashes in the cities of Lombardy, Della Corte, whose *Istoria di Verona* was published between 1592 and 1594, justly observed that "not only the diversity of standards and armorial bearings, but also that of clothing, manners and more surprisingly of language and even of ways of walking and eating distinguished the factions from one another".[66] He was carried away by a flair for literary hyperbole and rhetorical bombast which would strike his readers' imaginations, but he still reflects nicely a factional consciousness and a desire to distinguish the party groups by a number of visible signs in all aspects of public life.

War cries

We are well aware of the decisive importance of war and rallying cries in all past civilizations. They permitted members of the same war party to assemble and recognize one another and gave them a strong feeling of solidarity. They afforded a kind of consolation when the fighting began, that of the presence of relatives and allies. The names of some political parties were even derived from these cries. Other forms of the same phenomenon were the slogan, the call to arms or rebellion, and the cry of admiration for the person whom one desired to proclaim leader and on whom the fate of the group would depend. Such calls and cries were veritable commands which could mobilize instantly not only all the partisans but also neighbours, the curious, the unemployed and those on the fringes of society. In the cities of the French Midi they could rival the town bell as a primary summons to action during political or social conflicts. The factions of Bordeaux summoned their adherents by having *Biafora* ('Come outside!') cried in the streets.

The tyranny of the duke of Athens was established at Florence in 1342 by acclamations of this sort, imposed artificially in the beginning by the hard core of faithful or hired agitators: "and when the duke paraded through the streets, they cried 'Long live the lord!'". Villani then noted and analysed the means of group political action taken: the duke's power had been established "by having certain carders and men of the *popolo minuto*, together with the retinues of a few prominent men, begin to shout 'Long live the signoria of the duke!'"[67]. The same duke of Athens was to be driven out the following year by enemies crying out against him in the streets.[68]

Banners and coats of arms

If we may again use the tyranny of the duke of Athens as an example, we see plainly that during his rise to power the citizens' loyalty was demonstrated by the fact that "his escutcheon had been painted on nearly every square and palace of Florence by the citizens, in some cases to curry favour and in others out of fear".[69] The coats of arms were a clan symbol for all noble races, while for the families and parties they were the most striking, indispensable and omnipresent signs to rally the faithful. Bearing a man's standard signified beyond question one's submission to his political leadership, adhesion to his party or to a well-defined group.

Certain coats of arms suggest virtually indefinable and very complicated beliefs which have scarcely been examined. They show that the family, clan, or even party could claim that it was a symbolic group. Animals were used everywhere, on escutcheons and even in family names or surnames of the leader, in a sort of veneration or cult. The Bolognese noble house of the Cazzanemici was divided into two branches, the *piccoli* and the *grandi* or *dell'Orso* [*orso*: bear], who had a bear on their escutcheons.[70] Were these Bolognese coats of arms perhaps the same as those of the Orsini of Rome? We find them also in France, where from 1383 the Jouvenel had the Orsini bear on their standards and were called Jouvenel des Ursins from 1410. In 1432, Jean Jouvenel des Ursins was consecrated bishop of Beauvais at Rome by Cardinal Giordano Orsini, who received him in his palace,[71] thus acknowledging implicitly the alliance of two very distantly related families. The same Jouvenel des Ursins spoke at length in his chronicle of the emperor Sigmund's visit to Paris in 1416 and of how the Ursins received and entertained in their house Count Berthold der Bär, a German in the imperial entourage, "for they were of one name and coat of arms".[72]

The most striking example of this comes from Verona, where the entire della Scala party and clan was under the totemic sign of the dog (*cane*). Its leaders were named Càn, Cangrande, Cagnetto and Mastino (mastiff). The dogs were also present on the escutcheons, where they carried the ladder (*scala*), on the seal and on their helmets. The tomb of Cangrande, sculpted in 1329 and now housed at the Castelvecchio museum, shows the tyrant as leader of his party, wearing, flung back behind his head, a helmet in the form of an enormous dog. Two cringing dogs bear the ladder on the coat of arms, and four kneeling dogs support the arch at the base. The two old and traditional parties at Orvieto, the Monaldeschi and the Filippeschi, changed their names around 1330, after the death of one of their leaders. Thenceforth they were called the della Vipera and the della Cervara (viper and stag) factions. This too is a reminder of the totemic representations which we find in several other towns of Tuscany and central Italy for the quarters and some politico-social organizations such as the *contrade*. Salimbene recounts that at Parma in 1233, when the adherents of the Great Alleluia were preaching, each *vicinia*, the political organization of the quarter, wanted its banner with the portrait of its own patron saint embroidered above (*suo genus martyrii sancti sui*). Thus St Bartholomew graced the banner of his *vicinia*, which was kept in his church.[73] During the conflict of 1250 at Piacenza, the *populares* formed behind their insignia at the sign of the bells (*armati cum signis eorum*), while the party of the knights, led by the marquis of Andito, stood under his family standard.[74] The considerable role of the banner and escutcheon in all groups appears clearly from the fact that the principal officers of these political societies, professional guilds, quarter organizations and Tuscan *popoli* always had the name *gonfalonier*, standard bearer.

Quarters and political groups also frequently bore simpler, sometimes geometric designs on their standards. Villani lists all the *gonfalonieri* of Florence when the first *popolo* was established in 1250. With four *gonfalonieri* per sixth, this meant a total of twenty-four standards, each identified by its own colours, figures and many animals. But the emblems of war belonging to the infantry and cavalry companies were simply in different colours without much ornamentation.[75] A century later, when the fall of the duke of Athens in 1343 provoked an administrative reorganization of the city, the sixths were replaced by four quarters, which were given precise topographical boundaries and new coats of arms: a white dove on an azure background for Santo Spirito, a golden cross on azure for Santa Croce (which included part of the *Via Ghibellina*), a golden sun on azure for Santa Maria Novella, and finally the chapel of San Giovanni embroidered with gold thread on azure for San Giovanni.[76] But while the authorities obviously wanted to give an easily distinguishable standard to each quarter, they also did not want the contrast to be too spectacular: each of the four banners had an azure background and three were of gold embroidery. Interestingly, the single slight divergence from this pattern, the inclusion of the white dove, was for the quarter of Santo Spirito, which constituted the old sixth of Oltrarno, renowned for its particularism.

Similarly, other designs represented and symbolized the communes, which were political societies on a much larger scale. At Florence the civic device was a red lily on a white background. The obvious rallying sign of the *popolo* in this new form of political life was stressed by carrying new standards. In 1322 at Colle di Val d'Elsa, the citizens, who had decided to organize a *popolo*, wanted to do it "with the insignia of the Florentine *popolo*".[77] Even at Florence the duke of Athens tried to assure his political success and proclaim his domination over the city more strongly by giving a new standard to the priors chosen in 1343. It grouped three insignia symbolically: the communal escutcheon (the red lily on a white background) on the upper part that of the *popolo* (the red cross on a white background) below, and that of the duke himself (a golden lion on an azure background, bearing a coat of arms with the symbols of the *popolo*) in the centre.[78] But the old insignia had not been forgotten, and during the rising against the duke several months later "everyone carried banners in his *contrada* and *vicinanza* with the escutcheons of the *popolo* and the commune".[79] Giovanni Sercambi describes a conflict at Lucca in 1371 between citizens favouring the party régime and those who wished the city to establish a *popolo* to rule: "the escutcheons of the *popolo* were painted wherever it was deemed necessary".[80]

Every political society from the simple *popolo* of the quarter to the great *popolo* of the entire city had its coat of arms. Group solidarity was thus symbolized and stimulated. The same was true of the parties, which might adopt the name and escutcheon of some powerful clan or the leader of the faction, the podestà, the imperial vicar, or even the pope. But the parties might also have their own coats of arms, each element of which had an exact meaning. The exiled Florentine Guelfs received their party escutcheon in 1266 from Pope Clement IV: a red eagle holding a green serpent in his claws against a white background. Shortly afterward, after their victorious return to their fatherland, they added a small red lily on the eagle's head.[81] These symbolic armorial crests were thus also totemic reminiscences.

When the *usciti* of Lucca were defeated in a vain attempt to besiege their city in 1396, they abandoned six hundred horses and "many trunks" to their opponents. One of these, belonging to Lando Moriconi, contained many "banners and escutcheons" which the partisans had "wished to deploy as soon as they got into the town". The spirit of the times demanded that victory and seizure of the town be accompanied by a display of new coats of arms. The banners, standards and escutcheons in this trunk were enumerated. Some belonged to the *popolo* and others to the commune of Lucca, but there were also two banners which seemed directly tied to the exiles' party and its political activity: a large azure flag was adorned only with "golden letters which spelled 'liberty'", while several others had an eagle and a lily on an azure background.[82] Another trunk belonging to the rebel Giovanni da Castilliani contained a standard with an eagle painted on a yellow background.[83] These various armorial bearings were symbols and rallying signs. At Lucca "it was decided that cloths for the altars of San Martino would be made from these banners".[84] The painted coats of arms of the defeated adversary, the standards captured during battle, had to be exhibited as trophies marking the triumph on the altars of the victors' church.

Parties and colours

Uniforms and colours also were used symbolically in these party struggles. Members of the same faction could be recognized by various distinct sartorial signs, especially ribbons, armbands, and entire liveries which often had a special colour. To the contemporary collective mentality, this was not a mere convenience to facilitate mutual recognition by members of the group, but rather was the mark of a genuine community. The leader's cloak had a virtually magical, protective quality. The emissaries whom the exiled Florentine Guelfs sent to Conradin in 1261 to ask him to come to help them against Manfred could only announce on their return that his intentions were honourable and that he would come soon. But "as a sign and token of Conrad's coming, they had him give them his squirrel's fur jacket. When it arrived at Lucca a great festival was arranged, and it was exhibited like a relic".[85]

The colour of the clothing seems to have played a decisive role in the factional struggles. The Italian chroniclers tell us this when describing the *brigate* formed during festivals for ceremonial processions, dances, and war games, for the men of the *brigate* were all clad in the same colour. At a somewhat later time in France, parties as loosely structured as the Armagnacs and the Burgundians recognized one another by articles of clothing in different colours. The Burgundian partisans always hung or sewed the cross of St Andrew, which was the symbol of Burgundy, on their clothes.[86] The cross was often adorned with a little armorial with a fleur-de-lys or a J (the initial of John the Fearless). The Armagnacs also wore a cross, but in the form of a Latin cross sewn on a white scarf worn across the body. Each party distributed pieces of clothing with its colours to its followers to assure their security. In 1401 and 1411 all the men, women and children of the Burgundian faction wore a light blue cap with a long cornet hanging to the right.[87] Only persons wearing these blue caps were allowed to leave Paris by the guards stationed at the city gates. But in 1413 their allies, the Cabochiens, enforced the wearing of white caps to distinguish themselves even from their Burgundian allies. Some three or four thousand persons are said to have thought it advisable to wear them.[88] The white caps were undoubtedly chosen as a gesture of respect for the Flemish towns, to recall the revolt of the men of Ghent, who in 1379 wore caps of this colour in the streets at the height of the revolt.

But the Parisians reverted to the blue or bluegreen colour for the triumphal entry of the duke of Burgundy into their city in 1418.[89] The Armagnac leaders in turn entered Paris in 1413 in large, sleeveless cloaks which were open on two sides, hoods of purple cloth and caps which were half red and half black, with the bill to the left.[90] Thus the costume seemed essential in such dramatic moments: "the hood became a kind of safe-conduct which only those who had proved their fidelity might possess".[91]

In England too, wearing the livery or uniform of a particular colour demonstrated fidelity to a landlord, a clan, or a princely party. It was also a sign which could rally forces, bring mutual recognition to partisans and reinforce solidarity. The great princely houses kept exact records of the men to whom these liveries had been issued. The livery roll of the earl of Devon, Edward Courtenay, for 1384 and 1385, lists all men wearing his colours and livery: seven men named Courtenay apart from the earl himself, seven knights of good families, forty squires (including a rich and famous merchant of Dartmouth), fifty-two yeomen, fourteen barristers, four minstrels, eight priests, six pages, and three damoiselles.[92] This constituted a clientele of 130 persons of widely divergent social outlooks. The famous statute of 12 May 1390 limiting the bearing of liveries could only affect the lesser nobles, and indeed contributed to preserving this practice among the princes. When Margaret, duchess of Clarence, returned to Normandy in 1419, her livery roll mentioned 143 persons, including eighteen knights, twenty-five squires, and forty-five yeomen.[93] Later, during the great wars between the dynastic parties, the princes extended the bearing of their colours, signs, and symbols not only to their household retainers, but to all their partisans, sometimes quite distant, who in their turn were involved in the factional struggles and wanted to be able to recognize one another. Then England experienced "an age which loved outward signs of institutions [and] saw the widespread wearing of liveries and badges, granted by the lord, as a token of connexion. It was therefore an act of political significance".[94]

The king intervened on several occasions to forbid the use of these tokens of recognition. An example of this was Edward IV's regulation of 1472 against the "tokens, liveries, signs, making of retainers" in the town of Coventry.[95] But the signs were used anyway and triumphed everywhere as the badge of party membership. In 1459, Queen Margaret had her badges with the white swan distributed to all her partisans in Cheshire and elsewhere.[96] In 1458 the earl of Warwick entered London with several hundred men, all wearing "red jackets with white ragged staves upon them",[97] while in 1470 the garrison of Calais proclaimed its change of allegiance by abandoning the badge of the white rose of York for the ragged staff of Warwick.[98] For these other external signs of political affiliation obviously gained currency in the English dynastic quarrels along with the white and red roses of the Yorkist and Lancastrian parties.

Uniform colours on the liveries of men at arms became usual at about the same time. Of course, we can cite other precedents in British military costume, such as the tartans worn by the Scottish clansmen for war, hunting, and ceremonies. We are also reminded of the influence and example of the knightly Order of St George, whose members wore red uniforms in combat. It seems quite possible that party colours profoundly influenced military customs of the time and thus led to the wearing of real combat uniforms.

The study of party names shows that the colours were also becoming important in Italy. We have noted that for many years in northern and central Italy the names of political factions seemed extremely varied and fluctuating: clan or family names, sobriquets, statements of a program, references to the protector-ally, particularly for the Church and imperial parties and for Guelfs and Ghibellines. This lasted for some time. But the names of colours gradually became common, first at Pistoia, where Whites and Blacks appeared just as the Guelfs and the great Cancellieri clan split into two hostile factions around 1300. We do not know why these colours were chosen, but they were evidently linked to rallying signs or articles of clothing. The same development is found at Arezzo in 1308, but in a different form: a citizen party expelled the Tarlati, who were lords of Pietramola, from the city and recalled the Guelfs, who had been exiled twenty years earlier. "Those who governed the town thenceforth, including both Guelfs and Ghibelline., were called the Green party."[99] The desire to find new names which lacked the old associations is obvious. The choice of a colour represented a new need.

Eventually, the White and Black parties came to dominate throughout Italy. But this may not have been an innovation. At Toulouse, two rival politico-religious brotherhoods were confronting each other around 1220: Whites and Blacks. The final conflicts or divisions between the parties which we have noted in Italy had reference only to the Whites and the Blacks. At Genoa in the 1480s and even later, political life was always permeated by the arbitrary division of all great families and political offices between the Whites and the Blacks. Scholars and chroniclers remembered the names of Guelfs and Ghibellines, but they were never used in daily life or in official papers. The transactions of the Council of the Ancients show clearly that magistracies were divided equally between Blacks and Whites. Within this division, an equal number of seats went to nobles, merchants, and guild masters. White and Black factions similarly divided Milan at the time of the assassination of Galeazzo Maria Sforza in 1476.[100]

Party nomenclature and the external signs denoting membership thus show clearly the evolution of a collective outlook, of profound psychological reactions within political societies. Political factions of varying origins and with complex, sometimes even indefinable institutions for a long time reflected chiefly the fundamental conflicts between families or clans. These factions sought alliances with rulers, and accordingly served the interests of pope or emperor. At this time the parties naturally had family names or were called parties of Church or Empire, Guelf or Ghibelline. Coats of arms were very important and assumed a symbolic psychological significance, at times even evoking the memory of the totem animal, a cult peculiar to the great clans.

But the parties subsequently assumed a very different social and intellectual importance. They relied on wider bases of support or in any case on more highly developed collective reactions. The spirit of competition between groups became essential and took precedence over family rivalries. The mobs of partisans were no longer drawn into the fray because they were the clienteles of the powerful clans, but also because of this competitive spirit, of what began as a 'game' or sport, but which ended as bloodshed and warfare. From this we derive the considerable importance accorded to emblems which glorified this very spirit of broadly based competition, and hence the colours.

The victory of Charles of Valois, who supported the Blacks, at Florence in 1302 was followed immediately by a wave of popular enthusiasm in favour of this colour and led to reactions which seem infantile to us. The city magistrates decided after a solemn deliberation that black would thenceforth be the colour of joy and favourable auspices. Fortunate or particularly favourable occurrences would thenceforward be celebrated by black, rather than white. Such occasions were the birth of a son, public meetings or councils, or favourable votes. Voting approval of a proposition would be shown by a black rather than a white bean. It is also very significant that at Genoa between 1440 and 1460 the sources, reflecting common parlance, speak of 'colours', rather than parties, to denote political factions.

The chronological stages of this evolution were certainly disparate and cannot be discerned precisely. They can perhaps be compared with the best known factions of medieval Byzantium.[101] At the start, there were four popular parties in the capital city of Constantinople, and they corresponded to topographical districts of the town. These parties played a certain role in governing the city and in raising the militia. But later, from about the twelfth century, there were only two, Blues and Greens, who competed against one another from that time on. But this competition was limited almost exclusively to the chariot races in the Hippodrome, where teams wore the two colours, so that the parties were merely athletic teams supported by a ferocious competitive spirit.

From the standpoint of collective social and mob psychology, the real significance of these 'political' party quarrels rests there: the spontaneous struggle which was sustained within each group by the desire to measure up to the opponent, by the competitive spirit, some of whose aspects we have been able to analyse. It was in the last analysis the primal urge to fight. In this sense, the comparison between the circus games and politics cannot help inspiring some interesting reflections.

Notes to Part V*

[1]A. A. Castellan, Venecia como modelo de ordinamento politico en el pensamiento italiano de los siglos XV y XVI, *Anales de historia antigua y medieval*, XII (Buenos Aires, 1967), pp. 7–42.

[2]Masséna[41, I, pp. 250–251]. On one specific point compare C. Cipolla and F. Pellegrini, *Poesi minori riguardanti gli Scaligieri.*

[3]Masséna[41, I, p. 1].

[4]Masséna [41, I, p. 172]. On the same theme, see also the exhortations of Ser Pietro de' Faitinelli, Masséna [41, I, pp. 187–189].

[5]Masséna[41, I, p. 189].

[6]Masséna[41, I, p. 227].

[7]Masséna[41, I, p. 191].

* Numbers in square brackets refer to the Bibliography.

[8]Masséna[41, I, p. 171].

[9]Folgore di San Gimignano, Masséna[41, I, p. 172].

[10]Folgore di San Gimignano, Masséna[41, I, p. 173].

[11]Masséna[41, I, p. 1].

[12]Masséna[41, I, pp. 39, 56].

[13]Masséna[41, I, pp. 59–62].

[14]Masséna[41, I, p. 2].

[15]Masséna[41, I, pp. 227–228].

[16]Bonizo of Sutri, *Liber ad amicum*, VI, *M.G.H.*, *Libelli de Lite*, I (Hanover, 1891), 592. Text called to my attention and translated by Mme. P. Leclercq.

[17]Bonizo of Sutri, pp. 591–592.

[18]On this point, see especially Rossini[48]; G. Zerbi, La chiese ambrogiana di fronte alla chiesa romana dal 1120 al 1135, *Studi medievali*, VI (1943), pp. 136–216.

[19]R. Kaiser, Laon aux XIIe et XIIIe siècles, *Revue du Nord* (1974), pp. 421–426, a review of S. Martinet, *Montloon, reflet fidèle de la montagne et des environs de Laon de 1100 à 1300* (Laon, 1972).

[20]Renouard[46, pp. 319–320].

[21]Michaud (ed.)[6, *anno* 1418, p. 652]: mais avant qu'il fust douze heures, les chappeaulz furent failliz; mais le moustier de Saint-Hustasse estoit tout plein de monde, mais peu y avoit homme prestre ne autre, qui n'eust en sa teste chappeau de roses vermeilles, et sentant tant bon au moustier, comme si'il fust levé lavé d'eau rose. Cited by Robin[47, p. 103]. See English translation[6, p. 116].

[22]Jean Juvenal des Ursins, *Chronique*, ed. M. Michaut. Nouvelle Collection des Memoires relatifs a l'Histoire de France, II (Paris, 1854), 490, cited by Robin[47, p. 105].

[23]Enguerrand de Monstrelet, *Chroniques*, ed. L. Douet d'Arcq (Paris, 1857), II, 89, cited by Robin[47, p. 103].

[24]Michaud (ed.)[6, *anno* 1411, p. 588, English translation p. 59].

[25]See in general J. Heers, *Fêtes, jeux et joutes dans les sociétés d'Occident à la fin du Moyen Age* (Montreal and Paris, 1971), pp. 13–44.

[26]B. Guenée and F. Lehoux, *Les Entrées royales françaises de 1328 à 1515* (Paris, 1968).

[27]For two Italian examples, see below, p. 272.

[28]On the visit of Emperor Charles IV of Luxembourg to Paris in 1377 and his reception by King Charles V of France, see *Les Grandes Chroniques de France. Chroniques des règnes de Jean II et de Charles V*, ed. R. Delachenal, II (Paris, 1916), pp. 210–211. Several miniatures of Jean Fouquet recall certain events of this visit. See: Paris, Bibliothèque Nationale, MS. fr. 6465, fos. 419, 442, 443, 444. For Venetian receptions of foreign princes, see D. Malipiero, Annali veneti dall'anno 1457 a 1500 ordinati e abbreviati dal senatore Francesco Longo, *Archivio storico italiano*, VII (1843), p. 227, M.M. Newett, The sumptuary laws of Venice in the fourteenth and fifteenth centuries, *Historical essays of the Owen College* (Manchester, 1907), p. 250, cited by E. Pavan, Maisons, urbanisme et structures sociales à Venise à la fin du Moyen Age, unpublished Mémoire (University of Paris – Sorbonne, 1975), p. 96.

[29]Pavan, Maisons, p. 95, with bibliography.

[30]Pavan, Maisons, pp. 97–98.

[31]C. Guasti, *La feste di San Giovanni Batista in Firenze descritta in prosa e in rima da*

contamporanei (Florence, 1884); G. Mancini, Il bel San Giovanni e le feste patronali di Firenze descritte nel 1475 da Piero Cennini, *l'Arte* (1909).

[32]Villani[15, XII, ch. 15, p. 21].

[33]Pavan, Maisons, p. 100.

[34]Villani[15, XII, ch. 15, p. 20].

[35]Villani[15, XII, ch. 15, pp. 20–21].

[36]Cited by Gaspar (ed.)[8, p. 164].

[37]Gaspar (ed.)[8, p. 158].

[38]Gaspar (ed.)[8, p. 233].

[39]Gaspar (ed.)[8, pp. 77–78].

[40]Gaspar (ed.)[8, p. 78].

[41]A. Pezzana, *Storia della città di Parma* (Parma, 1852), IV, appendix 9, pp. 18–23: Tre Canti triomphali intorno all'impresa della città di Vittoria fatta dai Parmigiani nell'anno 1248.

[42]Heers, *Fêtes*, p. 82.

[43]Della Corte[10], cited by Gaspar (ed.)[8, p. 157, n. 6].

[44]Villani[15, XII, ch. 17, p. 37].

[45]Villani[15, X, ch. 205, pp. 182–183]. We could note other similar occasions, for example, on 3 May 1382, when the militia of Ghent surprised the Brugeois as they were celebrating the procession of the Holy Blood, defeating them outside the walls of Bruges at the Beverhoutsveld (event called to my attention by D. Nicholas).

[46]Gaspar[8, pp. 204–205].

[47]Villani[15, X, ch. 24, p. 24].

[48]Villani[15, X, ch. 24, p. 25].

[49]M. Gual Camerena, Los mudejares valencianos en la época del Magnanimo, *IV Congreso de la Historia de la Corona de Aragon. Mallorca 1955. Actas y Communicaciones*, I (Mallorca, 1959), pp. 467–494.

[50]*Annales Brixienses*, cited by Judic[37, pp. 154–155].

[51]On all the above, see Toubert[55, pp. 729ff].

[52]Herlihy[34, pp. 143–148].

[53]Villani[15, VIII, ch. 39, p. 44].

[54]Rolandino[13], cited by M. Boni, Poesia e vita cortesa nella Marca, in[54, pp. 163–188].

[55]Villani[15, X, ch. 216, p. 196].

[56]Villani[15, VIII, ch. 39, p. 42].

[57]Villani mentions on several occasions a bloc of houses set apart and with peculiar features. The *città rossa* was in the heart of the commercial quarter on the right bank of the Arno.

[58]Villani[15, XII, ch. 15, pp. 20–21].

[59]*A.P.Gu.*, anno 1090, p. 411 line 7 to p. 412 line 2, cited by Judic[37, pp. 216–217].

[60]*Annales Cremonenses*, p. 805, cited by Judic[37, p. 67].

[61]Rolandino[13, II, 10], cited by Gaspar (ed.)[8, p. 77].

[62]A. Viscardi and G. L. Barni, L'Italia nell'età Comunale, in *Società e Costume*, IV, cited by Gaspar[8, p. 229].

[63]*Anonymi Ticinensis* [5], p. 25.

[64]Villani[15, VI, ch. 87, p. 310].

[65]On this point see Gaspar (ed.)[8, p. 229].
[66]Della Corte[10], cited by Gaspar (ed.)[8, p. 269].
[67]Villani[15, XII, ch. 3, p. 8].
[68]Villani[15, XII, ch. 16, p. 31].
[69]Villani[15, XII, ch. 3, p. 8].
[70]Gozzadini[27], for the Cazzanemici family.
[71]C. de la Roncière, P. Contamine and R. Delort, *L'Europe au Moyen Age*, (Paris, 1971), 11–12.
[72]*Ibid.*, p. 9.
[73]Salimbene de Adam[16, p. 99].
[74]*A.P.Gib.*, *anno* 1250, pp. 499–502, cited by Judic[37, pp. 225–227].
[75]Villani[15, I, 262].
[76]Villani[15, XII, ch. 18, p. 38].
[77]Villani[15, IX, ch. 148, p. 242].
[78]Villani[15, XII, ch. 15, p. 16].
[79]Villani[15, XII, ch. 17, p. 31].
[80]Sercambi[14, II, CCXXXVIII, p. 204].
[81]Renouard[46, p. 335].
[82]Sercambi[14, II, CCCCI, pp. 332ff].
[83]Sercambi[14, II, CCCCV, p. 350].
[84]Sercambi[14, II, CCCCIV, p. 348].
[85]Villani[15, VI, ch. 84, p. 308].
[86]Jean Juvenal des Ursins, *Chronique* (see above, n. 22), p. 466, cited, together with all which follows, by Robin[47, pp. 102–105].
[87]Jean Juvenal des Ursins, *Chronique*, p. 466.
[88]Michaud (ed.)[6, p. 637, Eng. trans. p. 72].
[89]Jean Le Fevre, seigneur de Saint-Rémy, *Chronique*, ed. Morand (Paris, 1876), I, 333.
[90]Jean Juvenal des Ursins, *Chronique*, p. 490.
[91]Robin[47, p. 102].
[92]K.B. MacFarlane, *The nobility of later medieval England* (Oxford, 1973), p. 111.
[93]*Ibid.*, p. 112.
[94]Myers, *English historical documents* (see above, n. 5), p. 953.
[95]Cited *Ibid.*, doc. 666, p. 1132.
[96]*Ibid.*, p. 953.
[97]*Ibid.*, p. 955.
[98]*Ibid.*, p. 953.
[99]Villani[15, VIII, ch. 99, pp. 132–133].
[100]V. Ilardi, The Assassination of Galeazzo Maria Sforza and the reaction of Italian diplomacy, in Martines (ed.)[57, p. 83].
[101]A. Maricq, La durée du régime des partis populaires à Constantinople, *Bulletin de l'Académie Royale de Belgique, Classe des Lettres*, 1949, pp. 63–74.

Bibliography

A. Sources

[1] *Annales Brixienses. Monumenta Germaniae Historica* [hereafter *M.G.H.*], *Scriptores*, XVIII (Hannover, 1863), pp. 812–820.

[2] *Annales Cremonenses. M.G.H., SS.*, XVIII, pp. 800–807.

[3] *Annales Placentini Gibellini. M.G.H., SS.*, XVIII, pp. 457–581.

[4] *Annales Placentini Guelfi. M.G.H., SS.*, XVIII, pp. 411–457.

[5] *Anonymus Ticinensis*, ed. L.A. Muratori. *Rerum italicorum scriptores...*, XI, pt. 1. Milan, 1727.

[6] *Journal d'un Bourgeois de Paris sous le règne de Charles VI. 1409–1422*, ed. M. Michaud. Nouvelle collection de mémoires relatifs à l'histoire de France... II (Paris, 1854), 631–639. English translation by J. Shirley, *A Parisian Journal, 1405–1449*. Oxford, 1968.

[7] *Annali Genovesi di Caffaro e de' suoi continuatori*, ed. L.T. Belgrano. *Fonti per la storia d'Italia*, XI, 1, anni 1099–1293. Rome, 1890.

[8] Une chronique de Vérone inédite. 1115–1405, ed. M.H. Gaspar. Unpublished thesis, University of Paris X. 1972.

[9] Compagni, Dino. *Cronaca delle cose occorenti nei tempi suoi. 1208–1312*, ed. L.A. Muratori. *Rerum italicarum scriptores...* IX. Rome, 1726. New edition by J. Del Lungo in *Rerum italicarum scriptores*, 2nd ser. IX, 2. 1907–1915.

[10] Dalla Corte, G.C. *L'Istoria di Verona del Signore Girolamo d. C. gentilhuomo veronese divisa in due parti et in Libri XXII.* 2 vols. Verona, 1584–1592.

[11] Dominici, Ser Luca. *Cronacha. I. Cronaca della venuta dei Bianchi e della Moria*, ed. G.C. Gigliotti. II. *Cronaca seconda*, ed. Q. Santoli. *Rerum Pistoriensium scriptores...* I–II. Pistoia, 1933.

[12] Rolandino. *Chronicon Parmense ab a. 1038 usque ad a. 1338*, ed. G. Bonazzi. *Rerum italicarum scriptores*, new edn., IX, 9. Citta di Castello, 1902.

[13] Rolandino. *Rolandini Patavini Cronica in factis et circa facta Marchie Trivixane. 1200cc–1262*, ed. A. Bonardi. Rerum italicarum scriptores, VIII, 1. Citta di Castello, 1905.

[14] Sercambi, Giovanni. *Le Croniche di Giovanni Sercambi lucchese*, ed. S. Bongi. 3 vols. Rome, 1892.

[15] Villani, Giovanni. *Cronica di Giovanni Villani*, ed. F.G. Dragomanni. 3 vols. Florence, 1849.
[16] Salimbene de Adam. *Cronica*, ed. F. Bernini. 2 vols. Bari, 1942.

B. Literature

[17] Bowsky, W.M. The anatomy of rebellion in fourteenth-century Siena: from Commune to Signory? in *Violence and civil disorder in Italian cities. 1200–1500*, ed. L. Martines. Berkeley and London, 1972. See [57].
[18] Brucker, G.A. *Florentine politics and society. 1343–1378*. Princeton, 1962.
[19] Brucker, G.A. The Ciompi revolution, in *Florentine studies. Politics and society in Renaissance Florence*, ed. N. Rubinstein. London, 1968.
[20] Brucker, G.A. The Florentine *popolo minuto* and its political role. 1340–1450, in *Violence and civil disorder* [57].
[21] Cristiani, E. *Nobiltà e popolo nel comune di Pisa. Dalle origini del podestariato alla signoria del donoratico*. Naples, 1962.
[22] Doneaud, G. *Sulle origini del Comune di Genova e degli antichi partiti di Genova e della Liguria*. Genoa, 1878.
[23] Enriques, A.M. La vendetta nella vita e nella legislazione fiorentina, *Archivio storico italiano*, 1933.
[24] Fasoli, G. Signoria feudale et autonomia locale, in *Studi ezzeliani* [54].
[25] Fedou, R. Le cycle médiéval des révoltes lyonnaises. *Cahiers d'histoire*, 1973.
[26] Fonseca, C.D. Ricerche sulla famiglia Bicchieri e la società vercellese dei secoli XI et XIII, *Raccolta di studi in memoria di Giovanni Soranzo*. Milan, 1968.
[27] Gozzadini, G. *Delle Torri gentilizie di Bologna e delle famiglie alle quali appartenero*. Bologna, 1875, 2nd edn. 1965.
[28] Gutkind, C. *Cosimo de' Medici il Vecchio*. Florence, 1940.
[29] Heers, J. *Gênes au XVème siècle. Activités économiques et problèmes sociaux*. Paris, 1961. 2nd edn. abridged, 1973.
[30] Heers, J. Urbanisme et structures sociales a Gênes au Moyen Age, *Studi in onore di Amintore Fanfani*, I. Milan, 1962.
[31] Heers, J. *Le clan familial au Moyen Age. Etude sur les structures politiques et sociales des milieux urbains*. Paris, 1974. English translation: *Family clans in the Middle Ages. A study of political and social structures in urban areas*, Amsterdam, 1976.
[32] Herlihy, D. *Pisa in the Early Renaissance. A study of urban growth*. New Haven, 1958.
[33] Herlihy, D. *Medieval and Renaissance Pistoia. The social history of an Italian town. 1200–1430*. New Haven, 1967.
[34] Herlihy, D. Some psychological and social roots of violence in the Tuscan cities, in *Violence and civil disorder* [57].
[35] Hyde, J.K. *Padua in the age of Dante*. Manchester, 1966.
[36] Hyde, J.K. Contemporary views of faction and civil strife in thirteenth and fourteenth-century Italy, in *Violence and civil disorder* [57].

[37] Judic, B. *Les partis politiques en Lombardie d'apres quelques chroniqueurs du XIIIe siècle*. Unpublished Mémoire, University of Paris–Sorbonne, 1974.

[38] Larner, J. Order and disorder in Romagna. 1450–1500, in *Violence and civil disorder* [57].

[39] Lupo Gentile, M. Sulla consorteria feudale dei nobili di Ripafratta, *Giornale storico e letterario della Liguria*, 1905.

[40] Masi, G. La struttura sociale delle fazioni politiche ai tempi di Dante, *Il Giornale dantesco*, 1928.

[41] Masséna, A.F. *Sonetti burleschi e realistici dei primi duei secoli*. 2 vols. Bari, 1920.

[42] Mélis, F. *Aspetti della vita economica medievale. Studi nell' Archivio Datini di Prato*. Siena, 1962.

[43] Mor, C.G. 'Dominus Eccerinus'. Aspetti di una forma presignorile, in *Studi ezzeliani* [54].

[44] Mundy, J.H. *Liberty and political power in Toulouse. 1050–1230*. New York, 1954.

[45] Poleggi, E. Le contrade delle consorterie nobiliari a Genova tra il XII ed il XIII secolo, *Urbanistica; revista dell' Instituto Nazionale di Urbanistica*, nos. 42–43.

[46] Renouard, Y. *Les villes d'Italie de la fin du Xème au début du XIVème siècle*. 2 vols. Paris, 1969.

[47] Robin, F. Armagnacs et Bourguignons; étude sociale. Unpublished Mémoire, University of Paris X, 1969.

[48] Rossini, R. Note alla 'Historia Mediolanensis' di Landolfo Juniore, in *Raccolta di studi in memoria di Giovanni Soranzo*. Milan, 1968.

[49] Salvemini, G. *Magnati e popolani in Firenze dal 1280 al 1295*. Florence, 1899. 2nd edn. Milan, 1966.

[50] Santini, G. *I Comuni di Valle del medioevo. La costituzione federale del 'Frignano'*. Milan, 1960.

[51] Santini, P. La Società delle torri in Firenze, *Archivio storico italiano*, 1887.

[52] Sismondi, J.C.L. Simonde de. *Histoire des républiques italiennes au Moyen Age*. 2 vols. Paris, 1818.

[53] Soranzo, G. Collegati, raccomendati, aderenti negli stati italiani dei secoli XIV e XV, *Archivio storico italiano*, 1941.

[54] *Studi ezzeliani*, ed. Istituto Storico Italiano per il Medioevo. *Studi Storici*. Rome, 1963.

[55] Toubert, P. *Les structures du Latium médiéval. Le Latium méridional et la Sabine du IXe a la fin du XIIe siècle*. 2 vols. Rome, 1973.

[56] Ventura, A. *Nobiltà e popolo nella società veneta del' 400 e' 500*. Bari, 1964.

[57] *Violence and civil disorder in Italian cities. 1200–1500*, ed. L. Martines. Berkeley and London, 1972.

[58] Vitale, V. Guelfi e Ghibellini a Genova nel duecento, *Revista storica italiana*, 1948.

[59] Waley, D. *Medieval Orvieto: the political history of an Italian city-state: 1157–1334*. Cambridge, 1952.

[60] Waley, D. *The Papal State in the thirteenth century*. London, 1961.

Index

Deztorrent, Barcelona, 241–243
Dijon, 262
Dini, Giovanni, 167
Dominican order, 200–201, 264–265
Dominici, Luca, 74, 131, 204
Donati
  family, Florence, 34, 69, 70, 105, 113,
    159–160, 164, 170, 195
  Amerigo, 164
  Corso, 160, 184
Dordrecht, 245
Doria family, Genoa, 52, 112, 114, 212
Doudomme, 233
Dovara, Buoso de, 48
Dovaria, Gerardo di, 47, 135
Dueria, Pietra, 128
Durazzo, Agnese de, 272
Duvenvoorde party, Netherlands, 245

Edward I, king of England, 232
Edward II, king of England, 232
Edward IV, king of England, 251 n. 5, 287
Enrico de Egligen, 'della Scala', 148
Egna, Enrico de, podestà of Verona, 272
Egypt, 109
Elba, 19
Elna, 243
Embriaci family, Genoa, 17
Emilia, 44
Empoli, 146, 182
Engels, Friedrich, 16
England, 9, 11, 22, 68, 151 n. 64, 191, 204,
    221, 223–224, 226, 228, 231, 233–234,
    264, 287
Erembald clan, Bruges, 226–228
Esquerit, Barcelona, 241
Estamentos, 240
Este
  family and party, Ferrara, 52, 54, 63, 76,
    103, 121, 123, 144
  Azzo VIII d', 52
  Obizzo d', 104
Estremadura, 223, 250

Fabro quarter, Orvieto, 184
Fabruzzo, L., 74
Faenza, 124, 131, 145, 189, 195
Faitinelli, Pietro de', 258

Falconieri, 75
Falieri, Marino, 270
Fallabrini, 109
Fano, 131, 186
Fastel, 260
Fei, Ser Arrigo, 175
Feltre, 48, 58, 200
Ferdinand II, king of Aragon, 248
Fermo, 136, 148, 174, 212, 274
Fernandez (Cuenca), 250
Ferrara, 44, 63, 76, 123, 144, 147, 181, 200,
    203, 272–274
Fevrer, Barcelona, 241
Fieschi, Orvieto family, 52, 119, 131, 149
Fifanti family, 104–105
Filippeschi, party and family of Orvieto,
    38, 158, 183, 184, 206, 283
Filippi, 131
Filippo, Rustico, 258, 260
Filippo, archbishop of Ravenna, 46
Fiorentino Castiglione, 148
Fivaller, Barcelona, 240
Flagellants, 203
Flanders, 191, 226–229
Flodoard, 25
Florence, 9, 20, 21, 24, 31, 34–36, 43–44,
    46–47, 57, 59, 61, 64–65, 68–72, 75–77,
    80–88, 90 n. 11, 102–105, 110, 112–
    113, 115, 120, 125–126, 129–131, 136,
    140, 143, 146, 148–149, 151 n. 64,
    158–160, 162–171, 174, 176, 178–182,
    184, 186–188, 190–193, 195, 197, 201,
    204, 207–209, 211–213, 216 n. 83, 242,
    258, 265, 271, 273–279, 282, 284, 289
Fogiano, family and party, 37
fondachi, 119
Fondo di Porta San Gervasio quarter,
    Lucca, 180
Fontana
  clan, 125, 128
  Alberto da, 37, 105–106, 113
  Antonio Leccafarina da, 105
  Cagno da, 106
  Guido da, 106
  Pleneame da, 112
Forlì, 131
Foscarini, Egidio, 201
Fouquet, Jean, 291 n. 28